CULTURE CLASH

Law and Science in America

Steven Goldberg

New York University Press
New York and London

NEW YORK UNIVERSITY PRESS
New York and London

Library of Congress Cataloging-in-Publication Data
Goldberg, Steven, 1947–
Culture clash : law and science in America / Steven Goldberg.
p.   cm.
Includes bibliographical references and index.
ISBN 0-8147-3057-4 (acid-free paper)
1. Science and law.   2. Research—Law and legislation —United
States.   I. Title.
KF4270.G65   1994
344.73'095—dc20
[347.30495]   94-12247
CIP

New York University Press books are printed on acid-free paper,
and their binding materials are chosen for strength and durability.

Manufactured in the United States of America

10   9   8   7   6   5   4   3   2   1

To Benjamin Goldberg

Contents

Acknowledgments

I am grateful to numerous faculty members, students, and staff at the Georgetown University Law Center for their help with this book. In faculty workshops and in seminars in law and science and law and religion I invariably learned a great deal. Contributions of particular importance were made by my colleagues Thomas Krattenmaker, Louis Michael Seidman, and Girardeau Spann, as well as by my research assistant Janice Marchiafava. The Law Center provided financial support in the form of writer's grants, and I benefited as well from workshops at the Indiana University School of Law at Bloomington and Yale Law School.

I am grateful to several law reviews for permission to draw on the following articles of mine that originally appeared in their pages: *The Central Dogmas of Law and Science*, 36 Journal of Legal Education 371 (1986), © 1986 by the Association of American Law Schools; *The Changing Face of Death: Computers, Consciousness, and Nancy Cruzan*, 43 Stanford Law Review 659 (1991), © 1991 by the Board of Trustees of the Leland Stanford Junior University; *The Constitutional Status of American Science*, 1979 Illinois Law Forum 1 (1979), © 1979 by the Board of Trustees of the University of Illinois, *Controlling Basic Science: The Case of Nuclear Fusion*, 68 Georgetown Law Journal 683 (1980), and *The Reluctant Embrace: Law and Science in America*, 75 Georgetown Law Journal 1341 (1987), © 1980 and 1987 by The Georgetown Law Journal Association and Georgetown University.

Finally, I would like to thank Missy, Joe, and Becky, who know that the most valuable seminars are the ones we hold at the dinner table.

Culture Clash

Introduction

America's relationship with science is paradoxical. On the one hand, we proudly support basic research that yields stunning breakthroughs and Nobel Prizes. We then relish the ensuing debate about the implications of scientific advances. Will genetic engineering change our basic nature? Will artificial intelligence challenge our sense of human uniqueness? On the other hand, the actual implementation of new technology is often slow and sporadic. The technologies that were supposed to provide abundant energy, inexpensive medical care, and a new sense of humanity always seem a few years away. The result is grumbling about a wasteful and uncompetitive American economy.

The cause of this paradox is the subject of this book. The slippage between the promise of American science and the reality of commercial technology has triggered national debate. Some blame government regulation for the burdens on technology; others call for government support of new products in an effort to mimic Japan.

But the roots of the paradox lie deeper in the soil of American society. Government "regulation" and "support" do not appear by magic or disappear by fiat. Understanding our situation requires a detailed look at the intersection of two cultures—law and science—rarely considered in tandem. Their relationship encompasses far more than a court injunction against a power plant; it shapes the entire process from basic research to public debate about values to the implementation of new technology. Our analysis will show the fundamental strengths and weaknesses of our research-and-development system as well as explain what measures could alleviate the current gap between promise and performance in American science.

The book begins, in this chapter and the next, by looking at the dominant position of law and science in American culture and at the characteristic ways of thought of lawyers and scientists. The process orientation of lawyers is contrasted with the progress orientation of scientists.

We turn next, in chapters 3 and 4, to the legal status of America's basic research effort. We demonstrate how the Constitution and the relevant statutes provide extraordinary support for basic science and for the central role of the scientific community in controlling the direction of research. The legal community, including the courts, is seen to be remarkably weak in this area.

Chapter 5 looks at the legal status of religion, a possible counterweight to the scientific perspective. In the American legal system, however, religion fares poorly when it conflicts with science; consequently, not only scientific research but scientific perspectives on moral issues permeate our culture.

Chapter 6 turns to the commercialization of technology and demonstrates that here the constitutional and statutory system puts the lawyers firmly in charge. The scientific world view, far from being dominant, is a marginal factor. The result is what I call the *regulatory gap,* the cause of the screeching halt that often greets new ideas that fared well in the scientific world but not so well in the world of the lawyers. The paradigmatic case of nuclear energy is among those considered. The emergence of what I term the *science counselor* is also described, as scientists attempt to bridge the regulatory gap by bringing social concerns into play earlier in the research process.

Chapters 7, 8, and 9 present case studies of the human genome initiative, nuclear fusion, and artificial intelligence. In each situation, dramatic research is shaping our hopes and our values. But in each case, the regulatory gap looms dead ahead as the controversial social consequences of new technology, processed through the lawyers' adversary model, make restrictions and delays inevitable in our pluralistic society. We see as well that science counselors are at work in all three areas limiting our expectations and boosting public approval for socially acceptable technology. Chapter 10 concludes with a summary of the relationship between law and science in America and a set of suggestions for strengthening the role of science counselors without imperiling pure research.

Underlying our entire treatment is the reality that science and law are central features of the American social and cultural landscape. With science, the evidence is clear—from the Enlightenment goals of the framers of our Constitution to the latest proposals to "fix" our social problems, the scientific world view has long influenced American ways of thought and policy-making.[1] The scientific stress on progress and on the new has matched the American ethos at many points.[2] As a result, pure scientists enjoy a more favored role in the United States than in any other society. References to the "scientific establishment" in America are routine; indeed Ralph Lapp took the next step and called scientists "the new priesthood."[3]

At this point it is customary to note that scientific perspectives face a humanistic rival in shaping our society. The "two cultures" idea, popularized decades ago by C. P. Snow, has come to stand for the notion that two ways of thought—scientific and artistic—compete for authority in modern life. They should, according to Snow, learn more about each other, but they are the two dominant points of view.[4]

It is customary to invoke Snow's two cultures, but it is wrong. The notion that literary values operate as some kind of equal counterweight to scientific values in modern American attitudes and policy-making is simply untenable. It should be noted from the outset that the two cultures idea has always had a distinctly British, as opposed to American, provenance. In 1959, when C. P. Snow delivered "The Two Cultures, and the Scientific Revolution" as the Rede Lecture at Cambridge University, he did discuss America as well as Great Britain as suffering from a "gulf of mutual incomprehension" between scientists and humanists.[5] But just five years later, in his "Second Look," Snow noted that in America the gulf was nowhere near as large as in Great Britain:

In the United States, for example, the divide is nothing like so unbridgeable. There are pockets of the literary culture, influenced by the similar culture in England, which are as extreme in resisting communication and in ceasing to communicate; but that isn't generally true over the literary culture as a whole, much less over the entire intellectual society.[6]

But even to talk about "the literary culture as a whole" in America today is to take a leap of faith. There is concern that students receive humanistic values in their education, but the fragmentation of the American literary intelligentsia makes even this concern virtually impossible to satisfy. Poll any ten recent graduates from ten American colleges. If there are two serious literary works that have been read by a majority, your poll will make history.

It is impossible here to assess all of the factors, ranging from the mass media to the nature of American universities, that have weakened coherent humanistic values in American life. One key reason may well be the very interchange between science and literature called for by Snow. Beginning in the 1930s and accelerating in recent years, literary intellectuals have read and talked a great deal about the philosophical issues raised by modern physics. The notion of relativity and the probabilistic nature of quantum physics have given rise to considerable musing about cause, effect, and reality. Scientists, of course, although aware of the philosophical issues, have plowed on with their work, explaining ever more of the world in terms of their empirical approach. Many literary intellectuals, however, have been happy to leave the field of reality by saying that literature and science are united in being fundamentally fictitious ways of describing the universe. The impact of this on education has been substantial. As Gerald Graff has written, "students are quick to perceive that their [literature] teachers no longer hold the naive view that literature can explain anything."[7]

Whatever the reasons, the progressive, empirical values of science utterly overwhelm literary values in American culture today. As Peter Schuck put it in his perceptive commentary on Snow's work, "misunderstandings between science and literature today are rather a sideshow, peripheral to the main event."[8]

Even the social sciences—such as economics, political science, and psychology—are enormously influenced today by the scientific approach, with its emphasis on quantifiable, testable results. Indeed, this may be yet another reason why literary values do not counterbalance scientific values. According to Gertrude Himmelfarb, humanists have "chosen to capitulate" to science, and thus we have seen "the attempt of political philosophy to transform itself into political science, history into social science, literary criticism into semiotics, and most recently, theology into semantics."[9]

But there is a limit to the influence of the scientific world view in America, and that limit opens the door to the legal culture. Science alone cannot produce consensus on public policy issues, even though those issues often involve technical factors. When a new power plant is proposed, citizens with different incomes, backgrounds, and places of residence can all adduce sophisticated arguments as to why their position, for or against the plant, is more persuasive. After all, environmental groups, no less than industry groups, rely on scientific expertise. The ultimate questions that must be resolved in public policy involve diverse interests and values, not scientific calculations. In our culture, these ultimate questions must be resolved peacefully, if not rationally, and divergent interest groups must be heard, even if they are not all equally expert.

In the resulting culture of dispute resolution, the lawyers are king. It is a commonplace observation (and a correct one) that lawyers dominate modern American legislatures, state houses, and government agencies, and most public issues end up, in whole or in part, in court. It is also an old observation, going back not only to de Tocqueville in 1835,[10] but to Edmund Burke, who told the House of Commons in 1775 that in the American colonies the legal profession "is numerous and powerful; and in most provinces it takes the lead."[11] As to why law is so vital in America there are as many theories as there are for the lack of vitality in the literary culture. Law may have benefited, for example, from the nature of American democracy, from the heterogeneity of American society, and from the absence of an American aristocracy.[12] In any event, a mature and powerful legal system is in place as the primary social testing ground for scientific developments with policy implications. There are, to be sure, rival arts. In recent decades, business schools and public policy schools have begun to produce policy analysts of various stripes seeking a major say in science policy decisions. It is too early to say whether these disciplines or some combination of them will someday provide a coherent alternative framework to the legal system for resolving important social disputes. At present they do not. Their insights today are often important only to the extent to which they can be brought to bear in a legal proceeding. A government official may be upset when a memo runs into problems with a policy analyst. This official's situation is much worse, however, when the memo runs into problems with the general counsel.

Thus it is law and science today that provide the central frame of reference for the policy disputes brought on by advances in research. Under the circumstances, we begin by looking at the ways of thought of lawyers and scientists.

· T W O ·

Lawyers and Scientists

For many years I have begun my law and science seminar by asking the students to write down the name of the most brilliant person who ever lived. I instruct them to write the first name that comes to mind using whatever definition of brilliance they like. I then collect their responses and read them aloud. They always fall into the same categories. Scientists predominate, led by Einstein and Newton, but Shakespeare and Mozart do rather well too. There is often a smattering of support for da Vinci, and I have seen occasional votes for Plato, Freud, and many others. There is one thing, however, of which I can be absolutely sure: No one ever names a lawyer—no Brandeis, no Mansfield, no Holmes, no Cardozo. My students are all in law school, so it cannot be from a lack of familiarity with great lawyers and jurists. Nor is this result limited to law students. I have asked the same question of scientists, musicians, and others, and the result is always the same. No one ever names a lawyer.

Having read aloud their responses, I ask the students why scientists are often thought to be brilliant but lawyers rarely are considered so. A few possibilities are quickly eliminated. It cannot be that there is one continuum of intelligence on which scientists rank higher. If that were so, a great scientist would inevitably make a great lawyer or judge—a proposition few are ready to support.[1] Indeed, the occasional forays of scientists into other disciplines make it clear that for some, scientific ability implies very little about ability in other fields. Isaac Newton's historical writings, for example, are something of an embarrassment to his admirers. Thus the biographer Edward Andrade, who regards New-

6

ton as "one of the greatest names in the history of human thought," says of Newton's *Chronology of the Ancient Kingdoms Amended*, "I am afraid no one reads it nowadays or would take it very seriously if they did. Newton thought that he could not be more than twenty years wrong with any of his dates: modern opinion is that he was often wrong by centuries." [2]

Nor can it be that a scientist's contributions are more individualistic or unique than a lawyer's. On the contrary, an important feature of the history of science is the prevalence of simultaneous independent discovery. If one scientist had not made a breakthrough, often another would have, if not right away then perhaps within a decade or two. Einstein agreed with historians of science that the special theory of relativity was very much in the air among scientists at the beginning of the twentieth century; on the other hand, the role of the U.S Supreme Court was arguably shaped in a fundamental way by Chief Justice John Marshall in the early nineteenth century. [3]

Progress in Science

To explain the results I encounter when I take my survey, we look not at the intelligence quotient of scientists and lawyers, but rather at the nature of science and law. Scientists are most often thought of as brilliant because science appears unambiguously to make progress. It may be a truism to say that scientists today know more than scientists in the past, but it is a truism with important implications. An assistant professor of biology today may know more about evolution than Darwin. That does not mean the professor is brighter than Darwin, but only that the professor stands on Darwin's shoulders and on the shoulders of many other scientists. Because science is in this sense cumulative, it is possible to say that a particular scientist has made an important contribution. Scientists achieve this consensus on progress largely by adhering to a standard of testability for evaluating theories. A scientist can come up with a hypothesis about the natural world through any process at all—systematic study, inspired speculation, or fevered dreams. But that hypothesis must ultimately be subject to controlled tests, reproducible by others. A new hypothesis that stands up to testing and explains important matters not previously understood will eventually be accepted by other scientists. Thus, a side effect of this emphasis on progress is an emphasis on priority—the one who first makes a discovery is the one to be rewarded. The result is a community in which outstanding achievement—brilliance—can be agreed upon and honored.[4] Brilliance is manifested by doing something no one has done before.

Traditional notions in the philosophy of science demonstrate that the idea of "testability" needs to be clarified. No matter how many times a hypothesis is "verified" by a test, it remains possible that a later test will prove it false. The fact that your car has started everyday does not prove it will start tomorrow. In this sense, science presents us only with theories that fit the available data as best as possible under the circumstances. Those theories may well change as scientists learn more.

What then distinguishes a scientific theory from any other kind? To the philosopher of science Karl Popper it is "not the *verifiability* but the *falsifiability* of a system" that is a key criterion of its being scientific.[5] Scientific statements are those that can, in principle, be disproved by an experimental result. This is why the vast majority of scientists do not, for example, regard astrology as science:

Astrologers can so hedge their predictions that they are devoid of genuine content. We may be told that a person will "tend to be creative" or "tend to be outgoing," where the evasiveness of a verb and the fuzziness of adjectives serve to insulate the claim from repudiation. But even if a prediction should be regarded as a failure, astrological devotees can go on believing that the stars rule our destinies; for there is always some item of information, perhaps as to a planet's location at a long gone time, that may be alleged to have been overlooked.[6]

Given this approach, it is not surprising that we use the word *science* primarily when we speak of the natural sciences. The framing of falsifiable hypotheses and the running of controlled experiments is far more difficult, perhaps even impossible, when the subjects are people rather than chemicals or protons. In any event, for purposes of this book, scientists are those seeking cumulative, testable knowledge about natural phenomena. These are people who, when things go right, make progress in their chosen field.

There are important modern scholars who challenge this formulation. To some, all knowledge is contingent and dependent on cultural assumptions—not just the interpretation of a literary text, not just the conclusions of an economist, but even the laboratory results of a scientist.[7] But even from this perspective, science ends up appearing a good deal more progress oriented than other fields of human endeavor.

The Kuhn Critique

The starting point for modern critiques of the idealistic view of science is Thomas Kuhn's enormously influential *The Structure of Scientific Revolutions*.[8] Kuhn introduced the idea of a paradigm—a model, such as Newtonian physics, that is powerful and successful in explaining phenomena and attracting adherents, while sufficiently open-ended to leave problems that researchers can work on.[9] Those who work within an established paradigm do not challenge its basic nature. They labor instead to solve the scientific puzzles that come up within the paradigm's assumptions. Kuhn refers to this "puzzle-solving" activity as "normal science."[10] But over time, research results may challenge a paradigm itself. There then may be a revolutionary change—a paradigm shift—to a new paradigm, such as Einsteinian physics.

It is vital to remain clear where this account does and does not challenge the classic view of science. "Normal science" presents no such challenge; indeed, Kuhn himself describes normal science as "a highly cumulative enterprise, eminently successful in its aim, the steady extension of the scope and precision of scientific knowledge. In all these respects it fits with great precision the most usual image of scientific work."[11] It is with the paradigm shift that Kuhn sees something new, because "[t]he transition from a paradigm in crisis to a new one from which a new tradition of normal science can emerge is far from a cumulative process, one achieved by an articulation or extension of the old paradigm. Rather it is a reconstruction of the field from new fundamentals, a reconstruction that changes some of the field's most elementary theoretical generalizations as well as many of its paradigm methods and applications."[12]

Under the circumstances, according to Kuhn, choices between an old and a new paradigm "can never be unequivocally settled by logic and experiment alone."[13] The data will often largely fit either paradigm, at least in the early stages of the revolution, and choices must be informed by other factors. Some suggest, for example, that a theory's "simplicity" will attract scientists to it, a possibility that introduces a "nagging subjectivity" into the decision as to what counts in favor of a hypothesis.[14]

Kuhn has argued that a theory will be judged in part by whether it is fruitful in the sense of setting forth a new research agenda,[15] another factor that departs from a strict emphasis on laboratory results.

Kuhn's notion of paradigm shifts has not gone unchallenged by historians of science, some of whom still maintain that science proceeds in increments rather than through revolutionary shifts.[16] But even within Kuhn's approach it is remarkable how much of the traditional model of science is preserved. This is sometimes obscured when people toss around the notion of "paradigm shift" outside of the natural sciences, and find such shifts on a monthly basis with little to choose between the old and the new paradigm. This is not the sort of thing Kuhn was writing about, and those who read *The Structure of Scientific Revolutions* in its entirety find that Kuhn marveled at the coherence of the scientific community, a community that ultimately reaches consensus on which paradigm should be followed. Thus, to Kuhn, the vital questions at the end are, "Why should progress also be the apparently universal concomitant of scientific revolutions? . . . Why should scientific communities be able to reach a firm consensus unattainable in other fields?"[17] Kuhn speculates that the key is precisely that choices in science are made not "by heads of state" or "the populace at large," but rather by a "well-defined community of the scientist's professional compeers."[18]

After Kuhn, and to some extent independent of his work, other scholars have applied deconstructionist techniques in an effort to show that scientific knowledge is as culturally contingent as any other kind.[19] In this literature also, however, there is recognition that the scientific community is remarkably adept at defining itself and at adjudicating what is and is not good science from its own professional perspective.[20] Indeed, the argument that scientific knowledge is "constructed" and thus not objectively true in some ultimate philosophical sense strengthens rather than weakens the role of the scientific community in self-definition. The critique does open the door to alternate accounts of what ought to be considered good science, but those accounts have had remarkably little impact in the mainstream scientific community or in public perceptions of that community.

In any event, it is not necessary to resolve the ultimate philosophical status of science to proceed with our inquiry. The scientific community will never persuade everyone that its approach is a sure route to any ultimate reality. Skeptics, from the ancient Greeks to the present, have asked whether science tells us more about the outside world or about ourselves. Scientists may put great emphasis on testable propositions, but whether one should do that is not itself testable. What we can say is that in our society today science is a remarkably well-defined activity with a vigorous band of practitioners who do experiments (not philosophy) and who appear to accumulate vast knowledge about the natural world. It also appears beyond reasonable doubt that this scientific community is of great importance to American society at large.

Thus the central reality from our perspective is that the scientific community in America today is a self-governing republic. Scientists, not governments or voters, decide what is good and what is bad science. Entrance into this scientific community depends on rigorous professional training, whereas high standing in that community is evidenced by membership in groups such as the National Academy of Sciences and the science faculties at major universities. The scientific community is not equally united on all issues. There are cutting-edge issues on which scientists are deeply divided or at least concede that science has not as yet reached a clear conclusion. In other areas, however, scientists are, if not unanimous, then nearly so. The scientific community retains its internal authority by agreeing that if individuals disagree on too many of these basic points, they are expelled from the community. It is barely possible to be a member in good standing of the American scientific community today if you disbelieve in evolution or believe in laetrile. It is impossible to be a member if you hold both views.[21]

The Limited Role of Practical Applications

Viewing scientists as members of a professional community who love progress may appear to leave out a central feature of the scientific endeavor: the emphasis on utility, on the technology that grows out of science and benefits the public at large. Many scientists do care greatly about the ultimate practical impact of their work, but that concern is often secondary to the fundamental search for knowledge. Practical utility is an uncertain basis for performing basic research because, as many scientists are aware, the link between science and technology is much more complex than the public usually supposes. The link between basic science and technology is often uncertain and indirect, and the technology that results is sometimes, from the scientists' point of view, undesirable.

The uncertainty in the science-technology connection has three distinct aspects. First, many areas of scientific research turn out to be unproductive in scientific terms, let alone in terms of practical impact. There are no certainties in exploring the unknown and some research simply does not succeed. Second, even when research does result in a scientific advance, that is no guarantee of a practical payoff. Few discoveries have been more historic in intellectual terms than Einstein's general theory of relativity, which concerns the fundamental structure of the universe. The general theory, however—unlike Einstein's special theory of relativity, which led to nuclear energy—has had no practical technological applications in everyday life. Finally, even when a scientific theory does lead to important applications, they may be distant applications never imagined by the theorist. When Einstein published his initial work on the special theory of relativity, he had no idea it would ultimately lead to nuclear power. His first paper concerned fundamental properties of matter, space, and time; even he did not see the related energy-mass equivalence and its implications for several years.[22]

Finally, the science-technology link is not direct. It is rare for a scientific discovery to immediately lead to a new device. More often it takes a chain of scientific discoveries and engineering advances to bring a product to fruition. Indeed, although in theory inventions may always rely on some underlying scientific principle, many inventors have little or no knowledge of scientific theory and rely instead on their own intuitive ideas about improving previous inventions. Numerous studies, including those related to sophisticated post-World War II military inventions, show that many inventions are based primarily on earlier technology rather than on science.[23] Of course, scientific theories may ultimately provide a full explanation of why a device works, but that is hardly an argument for the direct utility of science. Cooks have known for centuries that chicken soup makes you feel better; a modern scientific explanation of why that is so does not improve the world's cuisine.

Moreover, even in those areas where the practical implications of science are enormous, scientists may be reluctant to boast about them if those implications are undesirable. Scientists cannot control how society uses newly discovered powers and many scientists would oppose some of those uses, such as new weaponry, that society chooses. Thus, although scientists might defend their work on the ground that new discoveries are inevitable and there is no telling where they will lead, that is very different from doing the research primarily because of its social impact.

In sum, whereas science can directly aid society, traditional scientists cannot rely on that as a sole or even fundamental motivation for their work. References to the unbreakable link between science and technology are useful at budget time, but not as useful as a central value for the working scientist.

The image of the scientist's values that emerges here—the love of progress, the caution about utility—was well illustrated in J. Robert Oppenheimer's speech to the Association of Los Alamos Scientists on November 2, 1945, a few months after the atomic bombing of Hiroshima and Nagasaki:

> But when you come right down to it the reason that we did this job [building the bomb] is because it was an organic necessity. If you are a scientist you cannot stop such a thing. If you are a scientist you believe that it is good to find out how the world works; that it is good to find out what the realities are; that it is good to turn over to mankind at large the greatest possible power to control the world and to deal with it according to its lights and its values.[24]

Doing the scientific work that led to the atomic bomb is not a routine experience for scientists, but Oppenheimer's speech isolates values that are typical. Doing research is "an organic necessity" because to be a scientist means "finding out how the world works" and "finding out what the realities are." Last, chronologically and often in importance, is the "turning over to mankind at large" the fruits of your labors.

Process in Law

Does the law, with its focus on the affairs of mankind at large, share anything with the norms of science? Surely the fundamental thrust is in a different direction. The scientists' emphasis on progress is replaced by the lawyers' emphasis on process. Rather than seeking greater knowledge of the natural world, the law seeks the peaceful resolution of human disputes.

Saying the law emphasizes process is not to deny that individual laws have substantive content. A law punishing murder creates a substantive rule. But society has other rules and goals as well. The legal system and the legal profession are primarily concerned with accommodating the numerous social goals applicable to a particular dispute in a socially acceptable way.

The evolution of legal rules in our society is largely the work of appellate judges who write opinions interpreting judicial precedents and the often vague language of statutes and the Constitution. These opinions cannot be tested in a strictly scientific way. Human history does not lend itself to the running of controlled experiments. Thus if a court in 1973 issues an opinion broadening the definition of obscenity so that a wider variety of books can be banned, it is difficult to test whether that decision is right. Suppose the decision was based in part on the belief that reading obscene books leads some people to commit sexual assaults. How can the belief be tested? Even if in the ten-year period following the decision there is a decrease in the number of rapes, the matter remains uncertain. Any number of factors might have caused that decrease. There might, for example, have been an increase in police patrols during the period. It is not possible to go back to 1973, issue a different decision, hold everything else constant, and see what happens to the crime rate. Moreover, even if we did have a sense of the effect of the 1973 decision on crime rates and on the equally uncertain question of what books were not written because of the new obscenity standard, we would still not be sure if the decision was right. Suppose we somehow knew that the 1973 decision led to a one percent reduction in crime, but also to the nonwriting of three great novels. There is no scientific way to balance these outcomes to decide which outweighs the other. Indeed there may not be a social consensus on how much crime reduction is worth how much literature.

This contrast can be overstated. Social judgments, however imprecise, can sometimes be reached on legal outcomes. If a court's decision appears to lead to a sudden surge in the crime rate, it may be judged wrong. If it appears to lead to new opportunities for millions of citizens, it may be judged right. The law does gradually change to reflect this kind of social testing. But the process is slow, uncertain, and controversial; there is nothing in the legal community like the consensus in the scientific community on whether a particular result constitutes progress.

An additional pressure on the legal system is that whereas ultimate judgments of right or wrong may take decades, particular disputes must be resolved more quickly. The law does not have the luxury of waiting for all the relevant evidence to come in, because with public policy delay is a decision. While we wait, an individual is or is not in jail; a power plant is or is not constructed. Law must stress process in part because it is not in a position to ascertain ultimate truth. As Peter Schuck has argued:

The law is usually in much more of a hurry to decide than science is. Ironically, however, law's findings, although less reliable and tested than those of science, are treated as more final and authoritative. Law operates under pressure to resolve particular disputes speedily and conclusively. . . . [Scientific] consensus often takes a long time to assemble, yet even then it is conditional, always open to revision on the basis of new data or theories.[25]

If an appellate judge's opinion cannot be tested in a scientific way, how is it to be assessed? On its face, an opinion often appears to be, in part, an effort at a logical demonstration. General principles are stated and deductions are made. Yet a judge's opinion obviously is not a mathematical proof. At any given moment in the history of mathematics there is, in a particular field, reasonable agreement on the definition of terms and on the postulates to be used.[26] There is no such consensus in our society about legal principles. Two judges can use impeccable logic and yet reach different results because their assumptions vary. One might postulate that free speech is of value only to the extent that it furthers other goals, such as an informed electorate, while another believes speech is a good in its own right. Or the judges' disagreement may manifest itself in a dispute over definitions: for one judge "speech" includes musical performances, for the other it does not. Thus, any notion of assessing judicial opinions in purely formal terms is unlikely to succeed.

That judicial opinions are neither scientific nor mathematical does not mean they are irrelevant. The opinions themselves are part of the process by which socially acceptable decisions are reached. After all, why write an opinion if it does not irrefutably "prove" anything? In a society in which the rule of law meant nothing more than brute force, courts could simply issue judgments without explanation and police could enforce them. In our society, however, judicial opinions themselves become part of the governing process as people judge their strengths and weaknesses and, if unpersuaded, work to change the law. Judicial opinions then, although they are not right or wrong in scientific terms, are successful or unsuccessful depending on the extent to which they effectively draw on commonly held values to persuade the interested segments of the population. Judges, in other words, engage in the practice of rhetoric—not rhetoric in the modern, pejorative sense of ornate or empty linguistic flourishes, but rhetoric in the older sense of persuasive communication designed to win support for views on questions of values.[27]

It might be argued that whereas fundamental legal questions are not susceptible to scientific proof, the factual questions often involved in legal proceedings are. It is true that most legal disputes involve factual issues. For example, a jury must decide where a person was on a given date, and an agency must decide how much radiation escaped from a reactor. Surely, one might argue that these matters could be resolved in a scientific manner. The courts could then apply the legal tests—what is a crime or what is an unsafe level of radiation—to the scientifically established facts.

Of course, some factual issues do not lend themselves to a strict application of the scientific method; there is often no certain way to test conflicting stories about the whereabouts of the accused. But there is, nonetheless, cause for believing that some legal facts can be derived scientifically. Our legal system does separate, to some extent, factual from legal questions by having a jury or an expert agency make factual decisions while leaving the ultimate resolution of legal questions to judges. But even here it would be a mistake to think that the scientific approach plays a dominant role.

The law is rarely concerned solely with factual truth in the scientific sense because that is rarely society's sole concern. Consider, for example, the trial of a criminal case. John Smith is accused of murdering Mark Evans at 6 p.m. on August 1. If the only question were a narrow factual one—that is, did Smith kill Evans at the time stated?—one would expect our society to resolve that question in at least a quasi-scientific way. Although it may not be technically possible to verify assertions about the past scientifically, we could at least attempt to limit the judicial system to an objective, expert inquiry into what happened last August 1.

Under this approach, the inquiry would presumably be conducted by people with expertise in such matters. We might expect to see, for example, the growth of a profession of "fact finders" wise in the ways of fingerprint analysis, eyewitness testimony, and the like. We would not expect to see what we presently have—a lay jury utterly inexperienced in the narrow task of factfinding. But that is because the narrow factual question—whether Smith killed Evans at the time stated—is only one of many questions of interest to society. Suppose Evans was a terminally ill, elderly patient in intractable pain, and Smith, his doctor and best friend, halted his treatment? Or suppose Evans was a healthy athlete running down the sidewalk, whereas Smith was a mentally ill or drunk driver who swerved onto the sidewalk for no good reason, accidentally killing Evans? Or suppose that Evans had threatened Smith at 5:30 p.m., and when Smith saw Evans at 6 p.m. he killed him, wrongly believing Evans was about to pull a gun? The legal doctrines that have grown up around cases like these make clear that society wants juries to make moral and practical judgments as well as purely factual ones.

Technically, the judge tells the jury the relevant law—whether it be on euthanasia, the insanity defense, self-defense, or some other doctrine—and the jury finds the facts. In practice, however, the law and the facts are so closely intertwined that the jury will do more than simply find the facts. It will, within the broad outlines of the relevant legal doctrine, decide whether applying a doctrine such as self-defense is sensible in the case before it. Society does not want jurors to be automatons; it wants them to make the unavoidable moral judgments involved in applying disputed facts to necessarily imprecise legal doctrines. As Holmes wrote in 1899:

I confess that in my experience I have not found juries specially inspired for the discovery of truth. I have not noticed that they could see further into things or form a saner judgment than a sensible and well trained judge. I have not found them freer from prejudice than an ordinary judge would be. Indeed one reason why I believe in our practice of leaving questions of negligence to them is what is precisely one of their gravest defects from the point of view of their theoretical function: that they will introduce into their verdict a certain amount—a very large amount, so far as I have observed—of popular prejudice, and thus keep the administration of the law in accord with the wishes and feelings of the community.[28]

Much the same is true with the heads of administrative agencies. In regulatory decisions we want agency members who can make clear-eyed factual judgments. But, we also want them to be able to make the sound policy decisions inevitably involved when legal principles are coupled with disputed facts. Under many statutes, for example, judgments on an appropriate level of environmental safety involve a variety of factors, including cost, emission levels, compliance levels, and the like. Courts have generally held that agencies must consider the numerous private interests affected by their decisions as an "essential predicate" to balancing all of the elements necessary for a just determination of the public interest.[29]

Thus, on both legal and factual matters, our legal system stresses the process by which a decision is reached in an attempt to ensure that the decision will be, at the very least, something society can accept. The most dramatic manifestation of this concern for process is the adversary system, under which lawyers for each side present the best arguments they can to support their client's case. The individual lawyer, of course, is not seeking the truth; it is the process itself that is supposed to foster accuracy by presenting the judge or jury with the best arguments on both sides. But if accuracy were the only concern, it is not obvious that the adversary system would be used. A vigorous investigation by an impartial expert might do as well. Scientists, after all, rely heavily on peer review. The adversary system, however, serves process goals. It provides both sides with a highly visible day in court—a public presentation of views, ensuring that all sides are heard. Part of the value of such a day in court may be cathartic, but that too contributes to the peaceful resolution of disputes.

Consider in this light the observations of David L. Bazelon, when he was Chief Judge of the U.S. Court of Appeals for the District of Columbia, a federal court with a heavy volume of cases involving scientific and technical issues. Concerning such cases, Bazelon advocated open decisionmaking after a full airing of opposing views:

This kind of openness is in everyone's best interests, including the decisionmakers'. . . . When the issues are controversial, any decision may fail to satisfy large portions of the community. But those who are dissatisfied with a particular decision will be more likely to acquiesce in it if they perceive that their views and interests were given a fair hearing.[30]

There is quite a contrast between Oppenheimer's assertion that it is "an organic necessity" for scientists "to find out what the realities are"[31] and Bazelon's observation that legal process, at best, "may fail to satisfy large portions of the community," but at least it can earn "acquiescence" if the contending parties are given "a fair hearing."

Under the circumstances it is not surprising that a lawyer's work rarely shows outward signs of brilliance. Attorneys present views they know are one-sided as part of an overall process designed to ensure fairness. A judge disguises new ideas as old in order to enhance their social acceptability. At best, resolving human conflicts is an imperfect, unending task in which progress is difficult to define, let alone measure.

Thus the fundamental difference in values between science and law is subtle, but important. Science is not a compendium of timelessly true statements. It is, in a sense, a process for formulating and testing hypotheses about the natural world, hypotheses that are always open to revision. But in science this process is a means to an end, and that end is progress in our knowledge of the world. In law, process is not simply or primarily a means to an end. In an important sense, process is the end. A fair, publicly accepted mechanism for peacefully resolving disputes is often the most one can reasonably ask for in human society. As Justice Felix Frankfurter wrote in an opinion for the U.S. Supreme Court, "the history of liberty has largely been the history of observance of procedural safeguards."[32]

The fundamental difference between the scientist's love of progress and the lawyer's adherence to process has secondary implications for the value systems of scientists and lawyers. Scientists looking for empirically verifiable truth have to believe there is some kind of order in their universe, whether it is expressible in traditional cause-and-effect terms or in probabilistic equations. And the search for order is closely allied to the search for beauty—scientists often testify to the aesthetic motivations for their theories. From a scientist's perspective, beauty and simplicity are not sought, as some non-scientists contend, because there is no other way to choose between theories. Rather, beauty serves to confirm a theory's accuracy because of a scientist's underlying faith about the very nature of the universe. Werner Heisenberg, for example, wrote, "I frankly admit that I am strongly attracted by the simplicity and beauty of the mathematical schemes with which nature presents us."[33] Judges, by contrast, confronted with the pressing need to resolve a social dispute peacefully, will often trade order and beauty for a patchwork solution that works for the problem before them. As Jerome Frank wrote, "[M]ost judges are too common-sensible to allow, for long, a passion for aesthetic elegance, or for the appearance of an abstract consistency, to bring about obviously unjust results."[34]

Now, of course, this depiction of scientists and lawyers as champions of progress and process is the depiction of ideals, not of living, breathing human beings. Like everyone else, scientists and lawyers may be motivated by greed, lust, or an insatiable desire to be famous. Moreover, the problems they work on do not grow out of abstract conceptions of progress or process, but rather out of the social and cultural environments in which they live. But the fact remains that these professional norms of progress and process shape the professional lives of scientists and lawyers, and shape them in very different ways.

The Daubert Case

The contrast between progress and process was on display when the U.S. Supreme Court discussed the admissibility of scientific evidence in 1993.

The case of *Daubert v. Merrell Dow Pharmaceuticals* [35] arose when Jason and Eric Daubert were born with serious birth defects. During pregnancy, their mother had taken Bendectin, a prescription antinausea drug marketed by Merrell Dow. Believing that Bendectin had caused the defects, the Dauberts brought suit.

At trial, Merrell Dow was able to show that numerous published epidemiological studies concerning Bendectin failed to establish any link with birth defects. The Dauberts responded by proffering expert witnesses, who challenged the conventional wisdom that Bendectin was safe on several grounds. In particular, the Dauberts wanted to introduce experts who reanalyzed the published studies and obtained different results, although this reanalysis had not itself been published.

The trial court ruled, among other things, that the Dauberts could not present the jury with experts who relied on unpublished reanalysis. The court applied precedent holding that only techniques "generally accepted" as reliable in the relevant scientific community could be presented by expert witnesses to juries. The trial court, following the lead of other federal courts, concluded by ruling in favor of Merrell Dow. After a federal appellate court affirmed, the case reached the U.S. Supreme Court.

In the Supreme Court, the technical issue was whether the Federal Rules of Evidence displaced the "generally accepted in the scientific community" test that the lower courts had used, and, if so, what the new test should be for the admission of expert scientific testimony.[36] But the case attracted considerable attention in the scientific community because of its broader implications. Numerous scientists banded together in groups and filed thoughtful briefs.[37] From our point of view, they are of particular interest because of the insight they provide into the scientist's world view.

The scientific community was not united on the proper approach to the question of the admissibility of expert testimony. This was, after all, not a matter that fell within some consensus concerning what is good science; indeed, it was not a scientific question at all.

The scientists who addressed the Court largely fell into two groups. The first supported the proposition that judges needed considerable power to prevent juries from hearing testimony from witnesses who were far outside the mainstream of the scientific community. These scientists were concerned with "pseudoscience" or "junk science" that does not contribute to the search for truth. As one brief put it, "The impact and influence of scientific rhetoric can easily sway and mislead a jury."[38] Particularly when potential witnesses have not published their conclusions, there is the danger that these witnesses are biased in favor of one side in the case; in other words, there is the danger that legal rather than scientific norms drove the research:

Quite often, the experiments will have been conducted with a pending case or at least potential litigation in mind. On the other hand, scientific journals are typically concerned with progress in a particular field, and in making progress with sound methodology.[39]

On the other side were scientists equally devoted to the cause of scientific progress, but they focused on the more dramatic kind of progress that often is resisted initially in the scientific community. These scientists were inclined to let the jury hear and evaluate any expert's ideas; any screening role for the judge was suspect:

Science progresses as much or more by the replacement of old views as by the gradual accumulation of incremental knowledge. Automatically rejecting dissenting views that challenge the conventional wisdom is a dangerous fallacy, for almost every generally accepted view was once deemed eccentric or heretical. Perpetuating the reign of a supposed scientific orthodoxy in this way, whether in a research laboratory or in a courtroom, is profoundly inimical to the search for truth.[40]

The Supreme Court ultimately ruled that the old "generally accepted in the scientific community" test had indeed been superseded by the Federal Rules of Evidence. But, beyond that, it did not endorse either of the approaches presented by the briefs for the scientists. The Court declined to say that judges should screen out all expert scientists who deviate from accepted approaches, but is also declined to say that judges should play no gatekeeper function at all. It crafted a traditional legal compromise, setting forth a variety of factors, such as whether the testimony proffered had been tested or published or widely accepted in the scientific community.[41] These factors, none of which are dispositive, are to be applied on a flexible, case-by-case basis by trial judges.[42] Clearly the question of what sort of expert evidence gets to the jury will emerge, indeed will be indistinguishable from, a continuing process of individual dispute resolution. In certain cases, juries will hear controversial experts; in other subtly different cases, they will not.

In the course of reaching this rather traditional legal result, the Court gently responded to the all-or-nothing rhetoric contained in some of the scientists' briefs. As to the first group—the scientists who maintained that pseudoscience would mislead the jury—the Court replied by noting the numerous procedural devices that protect against this eventuality when an expert with unconventional views testifies. The Court found that the scientists were "overly pessimistic" about the capabilities of the adversary system, given the availability of "[v]igorous cross-examination, presentation of contrary evidence," and the like.[43] The Court also noted that a judge can even direct a verdict after testimony has been given if the evidence presented is extremely weak.[44]

On the other hand, the Court criticized those scientists who, in the name of Galileo, maintained that judges should perform no gatekeeper function at all. The Court recognized that even a flexible gatekeeper will at time prevent the jury from learning of "authentic insights and innovations."[45] But, the Court stressed, that cannot determine the issue:

[T]here are important differences between the quest for truth in the courtroom and the quest for truth in the laboratory. Scientific conclusions are subject to perpetual revision. Law, on the other hand, must resolve disputes finally and quickly. . . . [The] Rules of Evidence [are] designed not for the exhaustive search for cosmic understanding but for the particularized resolution of legal disputes.[46]

In the end, all of the scientists in the Daubert case were preaching on behalf of scientific progress. Some stressed the careful progress of "normal science" where professional competence weeds out pretenders. Others emphasized the paradigm shifts of "revolutionary science," where progress threatens the old establishment. The Court gave weight to both concerns, but within a framework of process values in which final resolutions on imperfect data are often necessary.

It would be a mistake to believe that these differences between law and science prevent members of these professions from understanding each other. There is no reason why lawyers and scientists cannot comprehend the different nature of the other's work and appreciate when it is being done well. A lawyer can admire a scientist who frames and tests a beautiful hypothesis about the structure of the stars. It would be a misguided lawyer indeed who complained that due process protections were not provided when the hypothesis was created. A scientist can admire a legal system that crafts a workable solution to a nasty problem of self-defense in homicide cases. Only a remarkably narrow-minded scientist would complain that the solution was insufficiently scientific.

The real conflicts arise when law and science begin to infringe on each other's turf. The most important area for such problems today is the social dispute in which a high level of technical information is involved. In such cases the differing value systems of lawyers and scientists can indeed lead to problems, for example, in disputes over the safety of nuclear reactors, the risks of genetic engineering, and the efficacy of new drugs. In the pages that follow, I argue that these problems arise largely from vastly different legal attitudes toward basic research as opposed to the application of that research.

Defining Terms

Obviously this approach requires that I explain how I am using terms such as *basic* and *applied research*. It is notoriously difficult to draw sharp distinctions in this field because there are no bright lines on the continuum that stretches from pure science through applied technology.[47] Let me begin by discussing the pure science end of the continuum.

The values of the scientists discussed previously are based on the institution of pure science. Pure scientists pursue knowledge wherever it leads and for its own sake. Their work may, as we have seen, lead to practical applications, but those applications are often years away and come in areas the scientists themselves never would have predicted. Under the circumstances, it is not surprising that relatively few American scientists actually do absolutely pure science. Most of what is usually called scientific research, including most of the research funded by the government, is a step or two over on the continuum from pure science. Although it might be called basic research, it is part of a program designed to accomplish a particular mission. Unlike pure scientists, the government and others funding research are primarily interested in utility, that is, in practical results. Thus, a university scientist receives a grant to do cancer research. This scientist's work may involve gaining a fundamental understanding of cellular processes and it may lead to surprising findings with unexpected implications. But the work is being funded because it may lead to a cure for cancer. Or, consider a scientist in a national laboratory doing research on materials for solar collectors. This persons's work may involve learning basic facts about the properties of certain elements, but it is mission-oriented work, aimed toward the ultimate development of a solar energy device.

When I discuss legal attitudes toward basic research, I will typically be referring to mission-oriented research, not absolutely pure research. But it is important to realize that scientists doing mission-oriented research draw their value system largely from pure science. As Victor Weisskopf wrote, "The style, the scale, and the level of scientific and technical work are determined in pure research; that is what attracts productive people and what brings productive scientists to those countries where science is at its highest level."[48] Most of our examples of basic research will concern university scientists working under research grants from federal agencies like the National Institutes of Health or the National Science Foundation. Although they are working as part of an overall mission, these scientists want to make scientific progress, add to the cumulative store of scientific knowledge, and publish in reputable scientific journals. Thus, in achieving the government's goals, they look, to the extent possible, for the most scientifically attractive solution, which means the one that establishes progress and priority in scientific terms.

When I discuss legal attitudes toward applications of science, I will be moving away from pure science and mission-oriented research and toward the production of new products for the marketplace. Here the emphasis will be on such developments as energy systems that are ready to be tested, drugs that are ready to be marketed, and computer systems that are starting to go on-line.

Let us begin then with legal attitudes toward basic research. As with much of American law the starting place is our fundamental charter—the U.S. Constitution.

THREE

The Constitutional Status
of Basic Research

Because the U.S. Constitution says little about science explicitly, analysis of the role of science in American society is rarely perceived as having an important constitutional dimension.[1] Yet numerous provisions of the Constitution have the intent and effect of shaping the relationship between government and science. The result is a framework that is extremely supportive of basic research.

The Enlightenment Background

This result is hardly surprising, given the background of the framers of the Constitution. Veneration of science was a central tenet of eighteenth-century Enlightenment thinking[2] for science was believed to illuminate not merely natural phenomena but political and theological matters as well.[3] Isaac Newton was not simply revered; he was nearly deified. Alexander Pope's tribute to Newton is illustrative: "Nature and Nature's Laws laid hid in night; God said, Let Newton be! and all was light."[4] Leading Americans of the Revolutionary era shared this Enlightenment view.[5] Science and public affairs were so closely related that any distinction between scientific and political leaders was difficult to maintain. David Rittenhouse and Benjamin Rush were important officeholders and political figures. Rittenhouse was a self-taught astronomer whose famous mechanical orrery demonstrated the motions of the heavenly bodies. Regarded by his fellow Americans as a scientist of the first rank, he was a member of Pennsylvania's general assembly and of that state's constitutional convention. He also provided scientific advice in the Revolutionary War, aided in defining U.S. weights and measures, and served as first director of the U.S. Mint.[6] Rush was a physician who contributed to medical theory and chemistry. He inspired Thomas Paine to write *Common Sense,* attended the Continental Congress, and signed the Declaration of Independence.[7]

Both Rittenhouse and Rush were close friends of Thomas Jefferson, whose scientific interests are well known. Jefferson's observations on natural history in *Notes on the State of Virginia* constitute his most extensive scientific work, but he commented as well on a variety of other fields, including paleontology and geography.[8] James Madison was also intrigued with natural history,[9] whereas Alexander Hamilton studied medicine, enjoyed mathematics, and urged friends to learn chemistry to improve their thinking.[10] With Ben Franklin, the boundary between scientist and political leader dissolves altogether. One of the world's leading physicists and America's foremost ambassador, Franklin was, to many European philosophers, the Enlightenment incarnate.[11]

The science that so appealed to America's founders, and that continues to be valued today, was an outgrowth of the revolutionary advances in astronomy and physics associated with Galileo and Newton. It was characterized by reliance on empirical data as opposed to sacred texts or royal pronouncements, and by an effort to use man's knowledge of nature to improve the human condition.[12] In the eighteenth century, when Newtonian principles were applied to virtually all human endeavors, the very word *science* referred to knowledge generally.[13] Jefferson listed "the sciences which seem useful and practicable" as "Botany, Chemistry, Zoology, Anatomy, Surgery, Medicine, Nat'l Philosophy, Agriculture, Mathematics, Astronomy, Geology, Geography, Politics, Commerce, History, Ethics, Law, Arts, Fine arts."[14] Thus when the framers used the word *science,* they meant to include (among other things) what today would be referred to as basic research in the natural sciences.

Scholars have devoted considerable attention to the way in which infatuation with this type of science affected the building of political institutions. In opposing unicameral legislatures, for example, John Adams invoked "one of Sir Isaac Newton's laws of motion, namely—'that reaction must always be equal and contrary to action' or there can never be any rest."[15] But the building of a clockwork constitution accounts for only half of the science-government relationship. The Constitution that resulted had an impact on the further development of science.

Free Speech for Scientists

The most dramatic example of that impact came in the First Amendment's requirement that "Congress shall make no law . . . abridging the freedom of speech, or of the press," a restriction on government designed in part to assure freedom for scientists. America's founders believed that the protection of civil liberties in a free state was essential to the growth of science, a growth they strongly favored. This idea found expression in the poems of the Jeffersonian journalist Philip Freneau, who wrote in "The Rising Glory of America" that without "sweet liberty . . . science irretrievably must die."[16] The Enlightenment union of political and scientific progress was also reflected in Freneau's "On the Death of Dr. Benjamin Franklin": "Who seized from Kings their sceptred pride, and turned the lightning's darts aside!"[17]

Rittenhouse and Rush were among the numerous other writers and orators who explicitly linked scientific progress with civil liberty.[18] Jefferson, in a 1789 letter to the president of Harvard College, concluded a call for research in botany, mineralogy, and natural history with the same message: "It is the work to which the young men, whom you are forming, should lay their hands. We have spent the prime of our lives in procuring them the precious blessing of liberty. Let them spend theirs in showing that it is the great parent of science and of virtue; and that a nation will be great in both always in proportion as it is free."[19]

The notion that free speech applied to science was an inevitable result of the idea that proper political decisions came not from monarchical pronouncements but from the application of scientific thinking to social problems. Thus Jefferson, in opposing tariffs on learned treaties, observed that "[s]cience is more important in a republican than in any other government."[20] Indeed, Jefferson's devotion to the free exchange of scientific ideas may have exceeded his devotion to the free exchange of political views that differed from his own.[21]

The intimate relation between science and civil liberty is illustrated in a 1774 letter from the Continental Congress to the inhabitants of Quebec that described freedom of the press as important in part because it advanced "truth, science, morality, and arts in general."[22] Limiting free speech and press to narrowly political concerns would have been unthinkable; freedom that did not reach the work of Galileo, Newton, and Franklin did not reach far enough.

Judicial interpretations of the speech and press clauses accord science the protected status envisioned by the framers of the Constitution. We are concerned here with the application of those clauses to scientific publications. Chapter 6 discusses the very different constitutional status of technological applications.

The case law makes clear that First Amendment protection from government regulation applies when scientific results or theories are published. Obscenity decisions furnished the earliest demonstration. The first major obscenity precedent relied on in the United States was articulated in 1868 in the British case of *Regina v. Hicklin*.[23] Although *Hicklin* did not concern a scientific publication, Chief Justice Cockburn noted during oral argument that "[a] medical treatise, with illustrations necessary for the information of those for whose education or information the work is intended, may, in a certain sense, be obscene, and yet not the subject for indictment."[24] This straightforward recognition that a ban on sexual matters per se would hinder science and is therefore unacceptable became one of the few consistent threads in the development of obscenity law in the United States. Early decisions limited circulation of medically oriented sexual materials to doctors and students, but by 1940 it was reasonably clear that anyone could have in their homes medical encyclopedias or sex manuals.[25]

Thus, by 1957, when the Supreme Court decided *Roth v. United States*,[26] which set forth a general test for obscenity, science was safely outside the category of the obscene. The government conceded as much in its brief in *Roth*.[27] The Court, while holding that obscenity lies outside the realm of the First Amendment, squarely held that the portrayal of sex in "scientific works is not itself sufficient reason to deny material the constitutional protection of freedom of speech and press."[28] This principle was applied shortly after *Roth* to protect the importation of material for a university's sex research institute, and the principle has not been challenged successfully since.[29] When the Court, in the 1977 case of *Miller v. California*,[30] changed the test for obscenity, the status of science was retained. The Court held in *Miller* that the "First Amendment protects works, which taken as whole, have serious . . . scientific value."[31] Indeed, in his opinion for the Court in *Miller*, Chief Justice Burger's sole illustration of protected material resembled Chief Justice Cockburn's observation 105 years earlier: "Medical books for the education for physicians and related personnel necessarily use graphic illustrations and descriptions of human anatomy."[32]

In a variety of other contexts, the courts have given scientific material the same high level of protection given to political and social commentary. Prior restraints are extremely difficult to justify;[33] thus a state, through its dental society, cannot require prior approval of a radio broadcast on "scientific dental matters."[34] Legal redress for inaccurate reporting must allow leeway for unavoidable mistakes to avoid chilling the dissemination of knowledge;[35] thus, the First Amendment protects a publisher from a suit based on lost profits stemming from a mistake in its chemical encyclopedia.[36] Accurate advertising is also entitled to First Amendment protection;[37] thus a scientific laboratory can advertise that it will test cholesterol levels for a fee.[38]

First Amendment protection is no more absolute for scientific speech than for any other variety.[39] National security considerations have at times led the government to restrict the dissemination of certain scientific information, usually by classifying such information pursuant to executive order.[40] The classification of scientific work was most widespread during and after World War II when basic advances in nuclear physics were tied intimately to the construction of nuclear weapons.[41] In the postwar period, when First Amendment rights generally fared poorly, scientific work was hampered by severe security restrictions on research and even on teaching, particularly in the area of nuclear physics.[42]

The courts have had little occasion to define precisely the limits of the government's power to classify scientific material. Courts and scholars generally agree that technological plans for advanced weapon systems can be subject to restrictions and even prior restraints. After all, the classic case for a valid use of prior censorship is to prevent publication of "the number and location of troops";[43] revelation of the design of a secret weapon would have at least as great an impact on national security. Thus it is not surprising that in 1979 a federal district court enjoined publication of an article that purported to give details on how to build a hydrogen bomb.[44]

At the other extreme, basic and widely known scientific truths cannot be suppressed merely on the ground that they can be used to build weapons. As the Supreme Court has stated, a state may not "prohibit possession of chemistry books on the ground that they may lead to the manufacture of homemade spirits."[45] Only a significant imminent threat to national security can justify the removal of scientific material from public view.[46]

The view that science is fully protected by the speech and press clauses is not undercut by occasional academic and judicial statements that "political" speech of one type or another lies "at the core" of First Amendment values.[47] As leading First Amendment scholars have long recognized, suppression of scientific information is inconsistent with the democratic political process.[48] When a scientist publishes a theory on the consequences of power plant emissions, for example, that theory has at least as much relevance to a political controversy on power plant location as does a local politician's speeches. Even when scientific work is not immediately applicable to political controversies, it plays an important role in maintaining a free and informed society. Such was the view of the framers, and it has been the consistent view of the courts. Thus, the observation that political speech lies at the core of the First Amendment does not mean that scientific speech lies elsewhere.

Government Support for Science

In sum, scientific speech receives the full protection of the speech and press clauses of the First Amendment. Yet if science were free but ineligible for direct government support, American science would be a shadow of its present self. Fortunately, government funding for science is built into the constitutional system and is based primarily on firm historical and institutional precedents rather than on short-term political developments.

The Constitution does not state explicitly that the federal government shall fund scientific research. Certain clauses, however, virtually require government support of science, whereas others permit such support for a broad range of activities.

In the early years of the republic, the power conferred in the Constitution to establish a seat of government led to important surveying efforts in Washington, D.C.[49] Madison contended that congressional power over the district also included the power to create a federal university, although such a university was never created.[50] The power to regulate commerce helped justify activities such as research on the causes of steamboat boiler explosions,[51] and the power to take the census made the government a major source of social science data.[52]

But from the framers' point of view, three areas of congressional authority—the military, coinage weights and measures, and patents— were the most important in bringing about government support for science. And in our times a fourth power—to spend for the general welfare—has outstripped all of the others in this respect.

Let us look first at the military. At least since the time of Leonardo da Vinci, scientists have contributed directly to the development of sophisticated weaponry.[53] At times, the needs of the military have inspired science; at other times, science has inspired the military.[54] During the Revolutionary War, the colonies' leading scientists participated fully in the war effort. David Rittenhouse performed general science advisory work and, in addition, substituted iron for the lead clockworks in Philadelphia to obtain lead for bullets.[55] Benjamin Rush devised a gunpowder production method used at the Philadelphia saltpeter works.[56] One colonial scientist, David Bushnell, even invented a submarine—the American Turtle—which, although unsuccessful militarily, was an important advance in its field.[57]

The constitutional clauses concerning national defense were not written to aid science, but they were written with an understanding born of the Revolutionary War experience that science was an important part of the military effort.[58] After enactment of the Constitution, the military power became the source of some of the federal government's earliest expenditures for science. Wartime experience had convinced George Washington, for example, that the country needed a military academy to train engineers.[59] Thus West Point, established in 1794, became America's first national scientific institution—from the beginning, West Point taught physics and mathematics as well as engineering, and graduates played a major role in government surveys and related activities.[60] In 1802, military needs furnished part of the justification for congressional funding of the Lewis and Clark expedition, which made valuable findings in fields such as botany and zoology.[61] From those early years until the present, military expenditures have included scientific research in a variety of areas, ranging from astronomy to health to nuclear physics.[62]

The only constitutional provision that arguably poses a barrier to the military-science relationship relates to the congressional power over military appropriations. As a concession to those who opposed a standing army, the Constitution provides that Congress shall have the power "to raise and support armies, but no appropriation of money to that use shall be for a longer term than two years."[63] The debates at the constitutional convention[64] and in the *Federalist Papers*[65] indicate that this clause was designed to provide close congressional oversight of military expenditures. If read broadly to include, for example, prohibition of funding for long-term research programs, the clause could hamper the military's relationship with science: it is difficult to require short and specific time limits for research and development contracts as distinguished for ordinary military procurement because such time limits can hinder the scientific endeavor.[66] Opinions of the attorney general, however, have concluded that the two-year appropriation clause does not limit the military's power to make long-term contracts.[67] Thus the military portion of the constitutional connection between government and science is secure.

Congressional authority over coinage, weights, and measures provides another constitutional link between government and science.[68] Effective implementation of the coinage power was thought at the outset to require the highest order of scientific talent. President Jefferson appointed the ubiquitous Rittenhouse to be the first director of the Mint,[69] and for half a century the Mint was headed by scientists.[70] The appointment of scientists to this directorship was only partially successful. Coinage requires skill, but not that of a scientist.[71] Today, the Mint occupies only a modest place in the government's scientific activities.

The federal power over weights and measures had the opposite development. Although presidents from Washington through John Quincy Adams urged development of exact standards, a task requiring considerable research on fundamental physical constants, Congress was reluctant to spend much money.[72] The study of weights and measures was limited to a minor effort in the Treasury Department's Coast Survey, and even that effort was not formalized until establishment of the Office of Weights and Measures in 1836.[73] In 1901, however, Congress created the National Bureau of Standards and combined its power over the preparation of standards with power to solve "problems which arise in connection with standards; the determination of physical constants and the properties of material, when such data are of great importance to scientific or manufacturing interests."[74] Creation of the bureau was a major event for America's physicists and chemists.[75] Although bureau funding vacillated over the years, it made important contributions to scientific research since its inception.[76] Today, the bureau, now known as the National Institute of Standards and Technology, carries out basic research in a variety of fields, including physics, mathematics, chemistry, and computer science.[77]

The final direct constitutional link between science and government stems from the patent clause in the Constitution, which provides that "Congress shall have the power . . . to promote the progress of science and useful arts, by securing for limited times to authors and inventors the exclusive right to their respective writings and discoveries."[78] Because both the patent and copyright powers stem from this clause, some contend that the clause should be analyzed as a "balanced sentence," giving Congress two separate powers: "to promote the progress of science . . . by securing . . . to authors . . . the exclusive right to their writings" and "to promote the progress of . . . useful arts . . . by securing . . . to inventors . . . the exclusive right to their . . . discoveries."[79] This reading limits the word *science* to the copyright power, a possible result in light of the broad eighteenth-century usage of the word. The "balanced sentence" approach has been challenged vigorously on the ground, inter alia, that early patent laws referred to the "art" and "science" of invention, and thus the patent power properly extends to both "science and useful arts."[80]

In practice, patent law includes what is termed science and technology, subject to limitations such as the nonpatentability of laws of nature. The origins of the patent clause, with emphasis on the key goal of spurring progress, have been exhaustively studied.[81] From our perspective, it is important to note that awarding patents does not involve the government directly in funding[82] or in choosing precise areas of research. Nevertheless, the patent monopoly is an incentive for scientific progress, and the range of patentable items defines the broad areas in which that incentive will operate. Prior to the American Revolution, European patents were granted at times to protect old as well as new products.[83] The American aversion to monopolies and the Enlightenment goal of furthering knowledge combined to limit the patent clause to those inventions that promote progress.[84] Congress and the courts have been reasonably consistent in adhering to this limitation. Thus patents are not available for obvious developments, however valuable.[85] Nor are they available for nonobvious discoveries such as Newton's laws, because permitting monopolies on laws of nature or mathematics would take essential building blocks away from other scientists and retard the development of science.[86] As a result, the patent power is limited to those discoveries that fall somewhere between the mundane and the magnificent. From the point of view of intellectual property, an obvious discovery or a newly discovered law of nature might be just as valuable as a patentable device, but progress, not value, sets the constitutional standard.

Science Spending for the General Welfare

If government spending for science had been limited to direct further-ance of the constitutional provisions just discussed, that spending would not have risen to its current heights. But from the time President Wash-ington told the first Congress that "there is nothing which can better deserve your patronage than the promotion of science,"[87] American leaders have favored spending for science in areas quite remote from Congress' enumerated powers.

It was Alexander Hamilton who provided the constitutional theory. In his *Report on the Subject of Manufacturers,* Hamilton supported monetary rewards to spur "new inventions and discoveries . . . particu-larly those which relate to machinery."[88] In the midst of discussing this proposal, Hamilton states that "[a] question has been made concerning the constitutional right of the government of the United States to apply this species of encouragement," but he argues that the constitutional basis is found in Congress' power to "lay and collect taxes . . . to provide for the . . . general welfare . . . ," that is, in what we now term the spending power.[89]

Hamilton was advancing what we now think of as the broad view of the spending power: the constitutional power to spend "for the general welfare" extends beyond the ability to spend for Congress' enumerated powers. The narrow view, that spending for the general welfare must be linked to a specific power (such as support for the military), is in the early years of the Republic identified with Madison.[90] But spending for science has been seductive throughout American history: there is evidence that even Madison took a broad view of congressional power when science was involved.

When John Churchman of Maryland came to Congress in 1789 seeking funds for an expedition to Baffin Bay to test his ideas on determining longitude by the magnetic variation of the compass, Madison, a member of Congress at the time, supported the request.[91] In an argument that foreshadows modern political support for science, Madison maintained that "[i]f there is any considerable probability that the projected voyage would be successful, or throw any valuable light on the discovery of longitude, it certainly comports with the honor and dignity of Government to give it their countenance and support. Gentlemen will recollect, that some of the most important discoveries, both in arts and sciences, have come forward under very unpromising and suspicious appearances."[92]

Brant, Madison's biographer, argues persuasively that support of Churchman "could be justified only under Hamilton's interpretation of the Constitution . . . [that is] only by a sweeping interpretation of the power to spend for the general welfare."[93] In any event, Congress rejected Churchman's petition because of the young nation's troubled financial state.[94]

In general, such proposals had difficulty securing congressional support in the first half of the nineteenth century because of constitutional objections, limited money, the fear of centralized federal power, and attacks on the "speculative" of "visionary" nature of the scientific endeavor.[95] Thus, federal spending for science before the Civil War, although varied, was almost always tied to specific congressional powers.[96] The constitutional question of whether Congress could fund science as part of its power to spend "for the general welfare" remained unresolved.

The major breakthrough came in 1862 when Congress created the Department of Agriculture pursuant to the power to spend for the general welfare, and directed the department to employ "chemists, botanists, entomologists, and other persons skilled in the natural sciences pertaining to agriculture."[97] The same year marked establishment of the land grant colleges, which became centers of scientific agricultural research.[98] As a result of these and related developments, federal scientific research in agriculture increased throughout the nineteenth century.[99]

When the Supreme Court, in 1936, first delineated the scope of the federal spending power, it confirmed federal power to spend for science. In *United States v. Butler*,[100] the Court adopted the Hamiltonian view that federal spending need not be limited to the enumerated powers, but could be for the general welfare.[101] The Court relied on the very passage in the *Report on the Subject of Manufacturers* in which Hamilton supported premiums for scientific advances.[102] The brief for the federal government had urged the Court to take this course in part so that federal science spending programs would not be endangered.[103] The Court cited Madison as supporting the opposing view that spending must be limited to the enumerated powers.[104] With respect to spending for science, however, Madison was no Madisonian; as noted earlier, he favored federal financing of a scientific expedition that could not be justified under any enumerated power.[105]

Butler and later decisions established beyond a doubt that science spending for the general welfare is constitutional. Because scientific advances can provide various benefits for society at large, the general welfare test is met easily.[106] Whereas states also are free to fund scientific research, they traditionally have not been the dominant actors in this area. The federal government's pervasive power over defense, standards, and patents limits the states' role, and federal science spending in those fields as well as for the general welfare has existed for over 100 years. Although state science programs have existed for some time, these typically have been either in partnership with the federal government or minor in scope compared to federal activities.[107] As early as 1846, for example, the federal government provided more than twice as much support to leading scientists than did all state governments combined.[108] In recent years, the ratio has shifted even more in the direction of federal involvement.[109]

Thus federal spending for science is not simply a matter of political preference that shifts dramatically with changing political tides. It is rooted firmly in both Hamiltonian and Madisonian views of the Constitution, and it is tied clearly to historical and institutional realities that stretch back more than a century.

The post-World War II growth of government support for science, spurred by the development of nuclear weapons and the space program, has at times obscured this reality. Yet reference to federal spending levels since the Civil War demonstrates that the federal commitment to science did not begin with the Manhattan Project. In 1884, when laissez-faire and states' right philosophies prevailed[110] and total federal expenditures were only about $240 million,[111] intramural bickering among federal science programs led to congressional inquiry into the need for reorganization.[112] Federal spending for science totalled several million dollars at the time,[113] and various programs had overlapping jurisdiction.[114] For purposes of comparison with the level of federal activity in other areas, it should be noted that this bickering among several science agencies took place three years before creation of the first modern regulatory agency, the Interstate Commerce Commission.[115] By 1904, federal spending for science was approximately $10 million,[116] a figure that grew to about $85 million by 1940.[117]

Today, government science spending has grown enormously to over $75 billion, about $14 billion of which is for basic research.[118] The basic research figure constitutes over 60 percent of all American spending in that field.[119]

Liberals and conservatives alike support government science spending, demonstrating once again the central role of the scientific ideal in the American tradition.[120] The usual American preference for private market forces does not apply when a product produces a large "public good"—that is, a benefit, like national defense, that all share whether or not they pay for it. In such cases, public support for the product is necessary to ensure that those who benefit pay and to avoid the result that too little of the product will be produced because the producers cannot capture all the gains. Most economists agree that science is a classic "public good." [121] An advance can benefit millions in ways that the private sector can capitalize on only with difficulty. Moreover, advances are uncertain and benefits distant, further supporting public involvement.

Distributional concerns are similarly absent from most public debate over science spending. A federal program to subsidize home buyers is debated in terms of which sectors of the society benefit at the expense of others. Science, however, is generally believed to benefit virtually everyone, at least potentially. Science is viewed primarily as a great equalizer, making better health care, energy, and the like more available to all. There are, of course, dissenters from this view. A few view science as reinforcing existing disparities in American society.[122] But the mainstream view throughout American politics is very much to the contrary.

Thus the overall constitutional status of science is favorable indeed. On the one hand, scientists are able to pursue their profession free of government censorship. On the other hand, scientists receive generous government support.

The Tension between Freedom and Funding

There is, however, an important tension in this constitutional framework. In giving out its money to scientists, the government necessarily chooses among competing applicants. Those who lose out are free to pursue their research, but their freedom may often be theoretical, given the costs of research and the federal dominance in funding that research.

Obviously science is treated differently in our constitutional system than religion, because the First Amendment bars government funding of the latter. But the special status of science under our constitution is best illustrated by contrasting it with the status of the arts and politics. Literature and the arts are usually described as enjoying the same First Amendment protection as science, the Supreme Court having held that the First Amendment protects "serious literary, artistic, political [and] scientific" works.[123] Actually, science may fare better when we recall, for example, that novels by Edmund Wilson and Henry Miller have been banned under varying tests of obscenity, whereas sex manuals of rather limited importance have long been protected because they fall into the category of science.[124]

The greatest contrast, however, between science and the arts appears in the relationship between freedom and funding. Federal spending for the arts lacks the built-in impetus of the military and standards clauses, as well as the historical association of science spending with the general welfare. Thus government spending for the arts, although constitutional, has remained quite low, and, even with recent increases, is a tiny fraction of spending for science.[125] Yet even with support for the arts at such a low level, many artists (not to mention politicians) believe that government funding raises troubling questions concerning government domination of the artistic impulse and government support for "popular" rather than "elite" artistic endeavors.[126] By contrast, scientists are relatively comfortable with their status as recipients of federal largess despite the far more intimate relationship between government and science. Questions are raised about whether the right scientists are receiving funding, but science in this country long ago crossed the bridge that the arts confront only in the distance. Science is to a large extent a government endeavor, and yet scientists have continued to enjoy considerable intellectual freedom.

Nothing inherent in the nature of art or science compels this unequal status. In Europe, government support for art historically has been far greater than in this country, with no apparent loss of creativity.[127] In contrast, twentieth-century experience in Germany and the former Soviet Union indicates that government domination of science can have unfortunate consequences for the scientific endeavor. Under the Nazis German researchers had to avoid anything that smacked of "Jewish science," whereas in the Stalinist Soviet Union government support of Lysenkoism hampered the development of biology for years.[128] Thus the role of science in American society does not stem from the nature of science itself but rather, in large part, from its unique constitutional status. Funding is combined with protections for scientific freedom, and scientists routinely call for increased appropriations while vigorously invoking the name of Galileo when restrictions on their private inquiries are broached or when the government tightly controls how its research money is spent.[129]

The status of science under the Constitution also contrasts sharply with the place of political speech in the United States. Politics enjoys the same free speech protection as science,[130] although, as with the arts, science may actually fare better in practice.

In *Buckley v. Valeo,* for example, the Supreme Court upheld a congressional limit on the amount an individual can contribute to a political candidate.[131] The Court found justification for this limit in the corruption and the appearance of corruption when large private contributions dominate an election campaign. The Court specifically cited corrupt practices in the 1972 elections.[132] Given the absence of any similar concerns involving private contributions to scientific research, it is not at all clear that Congress could constitutionally limit an individual's freedom to contribute to another's efforts to communicate a scientific theory.

Furthermore, in politics as in the arts, the biggest contrast with science is the relationship between freedom and funding. Supporting politics through government funding raises important First Amendment problems, even when the amount of money involved is small compared with the amounts spent on science. Thus, in *Buckley* two Supreme Court justices believed that federal funding of presidential campaigns was unconstitutional given the disadvantage this system creates for minor parties who are not funded.[133] Chief Justice Burger even analogized the dangers of political funding to the dangers of establishing religion.[134] Although the majority of the Court upheld the funding scheme on its face, they noted, "we of course do not rule out the possibility of concluding in some future case, upon an appropriate factual demonstration, that the public financing system invidiously discriminates against nonmajor parties."[135]

Federal funding of science is not perceived as raising such questions. The scientists who do not receive funding are certainly disadvantaged in developing and presenting their theories in the marketplace of ideas, but that price must be paid to maintain science's unique dual status as supported and free.

Indeed, even this price is not as high as it might be because of the final episode in the favored constitutional status of science. Typically, when the government funds an activity it has the power to attach strings that might otherwise violate individual rights. But this power has been narrowly construed when it is a science program that is being supported.

The leading modern case on government power in this area is the Supreme Court's 1991 decision in *Rust v. Sullivan*.[136] In a controversial 5–4 ruling, the Court held that recipients of federal family planning money could be prohibited from engaging in abortion counseling and referral. The Court reasoned that recipients could advocate abortion on their own time, but they were bound by the government's restrictions when they were performing services supported by government money. Neither free speech rights nor the right to an abortion could overcome the government's ability to attach strings to its largess.

Shortly after *Rust* was decided, a federal district court was presented with a case that the government maintained was indistinguishable. *Board of Trustees of Stanford University v. Sullivan*[137] arose when the National Heart, Lung, and Blood Institute of the National Institutes of Health decided to award a contract for a five-year research project on an artificial heart to Dr. Philip Oyer of Stanford Medical School. A confidentiality clause in the grant required Dr. Oyer to give a government contracting officer forty-five days advance notice of his intent to publish preliminary findings. If the officer objected to publication, further review by the government was available. But ultimately the doctor would have to go to court if the government continued to oppose publication. The basis for these government regulations was a desire to prevent the Stanford researcher from issuing "preliminary unvalidated findings" that "could create erroneous conclusions which might threaten public health or safety if acted upon," or that might have "adverse effects on . . . the Federal agency." [138]

When Stanford challenged the confidentiality clause in court, federal judge Harold H. Greene rejected the government's argument that this was no different than the restriction on speech upheld in *Rust v. Sullivan*. Greene maintained that whereas the grantees in *Rust* remained free to advocate abortion on their own time, Dr. Oyer was barred from ever discussing his artificial heart research during the five-year grant period. The court noted that, although the confidentiality clause only applied to this government grant, it would be hard to police the statements of Dr. Oyer to see if he was referring to work under the grant, because he had worked for almost twenty years in the artificial heart field. [139] Finally, Greene maintained that the government's standards for restricting speech—"unvalidated findings," "threaten public health and safety," and so on—were too vague to be constitutionally permissible. [140] Thus Greene invoked the full force of the First Amendment's free speech clause to remove this limit on the freedom of a scientific researcher.

It may be that Judge Greene was simply distinguishing *Rust* and protecting free speech as an abstract proposition. But the distinctions he drew are not self-evident. The grantees in *Rust* could advocate abortion "on their own time" because the government interest in that case was precisely that abortion not be advocated in a particular federally funded program. The government interest in the *Stanford* case was that the public not be misled by preliminary and misleading results obtained from federally sponsored research. That danger is just as great no matter when during the day the researcher talks about those results.

In reality, Judge Greene had flexibility in deciding whether the restriction in *Stanford* would be characterized as a reasonable effort to achieve a valid government aim or as a clumsy, overbroad attempt to extend the hand of government too far. A major factor in his decision to take the latter course was the weight he gave to scientific values and the views of the scientific community. He stressed, for example, that it was troubling to have a "non-scientist contracting officer" tell "Stanford University, a premier academic institution, engaged in significant scientific and medical research" what constituted "unvalidated findings." [141] He noted that even "in the Soviet Union, where Joseph Stalin at one time decided what could be published and by whom, the dead hand of government control of scientific research and publication is apparently no more." [142]

It would be a mistake to conclude that the government cannot attach any strings to research projects it funds. It can, after all, attach the biggest string of all—it dictates what sort of research the money is to be used for. But the *Stanford* case shows that in this area of constitutional law, as in others, the science community fares rather well indeed.

Thus government funding plays a central role in the constitutional framework that shapes American science. But precisely how funding decisions are made is not resolved by the Constitution. We must turn to the statutory controls on scientific research to understand that crucial question.

· F O U R ·

The Statutory Framework
for Basic Research

As we have seen, Congress possesses the constitutional power to fund scientific research. But Congress lacks the institutional capability to make the day-to-day decisions concerning who gets that funding. There are simply too many such decisions and they involve too much expertise. Thus Congress has passed statutes delegating its science funding power to administrative agencies. For example, when Congress created the National Science Foundation,[1] it said the agency should "support basic scientific research" and have the work done by those "qualified by training and experience to achieve the results desired."[2] Similarly broad language was used to set forth the science funding job of agencies like the Department of Defense, the National Institutes of Health, and the Department of Energy.[3]

Delegation to Agencies of Funding Decisions

In practice, Congress allocates billions of dollars a year for basic science with the condition that the recipient agencies use the money for research in broadly defined fields. Obviously, the agency itself answers the tough questions in evaluating individual requests for funding: What specific areas of research are most promising? What kinds of qualifications should matter most in making a grant? Thus the difficult decisions on funding are made by full-time agency employees and the outside consultants they retain to evaluate grant and contract applications. The classic

44

method used is a competitive peer review system in which experts evaluate and compare funding requests, and then choose the winners.

The Supreme Court has provided important support for the central role of the agencies by holding that only actual congressional legislation, as opposed to comments found in the legislative history, bind an agency to a particular spending program.[4] Thus a single member's desire to fund a particular science project, expressed, for example at a hearing, is not binding. According to the Court's 1993 decision in *Lincoln v. Vigil*, "the very point of a lump-sum appropriation [by Congress] is to give an agency the capacity to adapt to changing circumstances and meet its statutory responsibilities in what it sees as the most effective or desirable way."[5]

Of course, agency officials will often, as a matter of prudence, heed concerns expressed by members of Congress in hearings, or advice given in a committee report as to how money ought to be spent, even though these inputs are not legally binding. But even these relatively easy forms of guidance are rarely forthcoming in the highly technical field of research funding.

Indeed, agency control over science funding is so well established that deviations from the pattern attract considerable attention. When, in 1984, some universities seeking science funding attempted to follow a different route, the *Washington Post* trumpeted in a front-page headline, "Colleges Bypass Agencies to Get Federal Funds."[6] What shady process had these schools engaged in? According to the article, the schools had sought funds "directly from Congress without going through the usual, laborious route of applying to federal agencies."[7] The notion that the democratically elected Congress would pass legislation setting specific research priorities is generally regarded as "pork-barrel politics"[8] or inappropriate "earmarking"[9] that should not be allowed to subvert the expert review taking place in the permanent bureaucracy.

The continuing controversy over the "earmarking" of scientific research funds is instructive. Beginning in the early 1980s, Congress occasionally passed laws requiring an agency to fund a particular scientific project, usually one involving building a facility at a specific university.[10] Prominent examples included the Soybean Laboratory at the University of Illinois-Urbana and the Waste Management Center at the University of New Orleans.[11] Members of Congress at times justify this practice by saying they want to spread out research money so that it does not all go to the same elite institutions, the notion being that good science takes place in many places. In practice, of course, earmarking has tended to favor the constituencies of powerful members rather than any neutral geographic pattern.[12]

In any event, earmarking has received almost universal condemnation. "Basic and applied research," the newspapers say, "should be determined by peer and merit review, not congressional favoritism."[13] The President's Council of Science Advisors says that earmarking "must cease and must not be initiated or encouraged by universities."[14] One scholar sees in "porkbarrel science" the "corruption of our research enterprise."[15]

One might surmise from this that science funding has been taken over by the great unwashed. In reality, earmarking, even taking the highest estimates and assuming that none of it is done in good faith, accounts for under 1 percent of the federal government's spending on research and development.[16] Vastly more "porkbarrel" spending takes place in countless nonscience areas throughout the U.S. budget.[17]

What is derided as "porkbarrel" is, through another lens, democracy. When representatives spend the taxpayers' money there are at least elections to take them to task. The system is far from perfect, but, outside the realm of science spending, it is at least understood that voters choose people who vote on spending programs. But science is different—here the presumption is that an elite group, the science community itself, decides how to slice up its own portion of the federal pie.

This presumption reflects our belief that science should not be governed by interest group politics. There really is "good" and "bad" science and, even allowing for hard cases, it is safer to have scientists decide which is which. Of course, bureaucracies develop their own pet projects that would not be part of an ideal research program, but it is in fact true that expert agencies are better able to manage incremental decisions in this field than are elected officials. Neither the president nor members of Congress want earmarking to replace peer review as the norm in American science funding.

At this point, constitutional purists might object that, however substantively attractive peer review is, under this approach nonelected officials are making key government decisions, an approach the Constitution does not appear to envision. But this sort of broad delegation of congressional power to administrative agencies is hardly limited to science funding. In many areas of government regulation, such as communications and environmental protection, agencies actually do the day-to-day work. Judicial construction of the Constitution requires only that Congress provide "adequate standards" to guide agencies, and broad language such as "regulate in the public interest" has been found adequate—indeed, not since the 1930s has the Supreme Court found any congressional delegation unconstitutional.[18] Although the Court might revive nondelegation doctrine someday, it will almost surely not be in the area of science funding, where virtually no one believes that Congress or the president can provide meaningfully detailed guidance on technical decisions. Even when modern justices have raised questions about delegations to agencies, they have noted that Congress can delegate if it chooses a general policy and leaves implementation to an agency when a "field is sufficiently technical, the ground to be covered sufficiently large, and the Members of Congress themselves not necessarily expert."[19] Thus delegation in the science funding area has not been seriously questioned.

This is not simply a twentieth-century phenomenon. In the science area, high political officials have never been able to spend their time making detailed judgments. Even Thomas Jefferson fell victim to this reality. As Secretary of State Jefferson personally examined patent applications. But in passing on those applications, Jefferson sought and received advice from professors at the University of Pennsylvania. Moreover, Jefferson himself complained that the job was so difficult that it gave him "from time to time the most poignant mortification" because he was "obliged to give undue and uninformed opinions on rights often valuable, and always deemed so by the authors." After just two years of Jefferson's labors, the patent law was revised to require that the Department of State issue patents automatically if fees were properly paid. Thus the burden of determining the validity of patents fell on the courts. By 1836, Congress passed a new law creating a permanent office of commissioner of patents with a professional staff capable of assessing patent applications.[20] Given the difficulties even Jefferson faced, it is hardly surprising that today science policy of all types is made initially in the federal bureaucracy.

The Absence of a Department of Science

As a consequence of this approach there is no unified federal program for science spending. Various agencies—including the Departments of Defense and Energy, the National Aeronautics and Space Administration, and the National Institutes of Health—fund basic research in areas important to their mission. The National Science Foundation, which funds basic research in a variety of areas, countervails to some extent the practical orientation of the other agencies. But there is no "Department of Science." And, despite efforts in the White House and on Capitol Hill to get an overview of science spending, there is no single "science policy" for the United States.[21]

Moreover, the different agencies have different ways of supporting research. They can do the research themselves by using full-time government employees or government-run national laboratories, as is common with the Departments of Defense and Energy. Often, however, the agencies fund research by private parties, either through grants or contracts. In theory, a grant is given for relatively open-ended research that may provide information of use to the government. A contract, by contrast, is awarded for work done to meet more precise specifications set in advance by the procuring agency.

In practice, however, there is often little difference between a grant and a contract in the area of scientific research. First of all, when an agency awards a grant, it is not making a gift. The agency has certain broad goals it hopes will be accomplished, and it supports those grant requests that seem likely to achieve those goals. Secondly, research contracts are not like contracts to buy nuts and bolts. They are not typically entered into through the process of formal advertising, which includes the publication of detailed specifications, receipt of sealed bids, and award to the bidder who is lowest or otherwise most suitable. After all, with basic research, it would not be possible to set precise specifications in advance. Accordingly, agencies more often use a system of "negotiated procurement" in which a general agency request for proposals leads to negotiations between the agency and interested parties before the research contract is awarded.[22]

In reality, the preference of some agencies (like the National Institutes of Health) for grants, and some (like the National Aeronautics and Space Administration) for contracts, stems more from historical practice than from any substantive difference in the kind of work done.[23] The central fact is that, whether through grant or contract, federal government support of scientific research by private parties is a remarkably ubiquitous aspect of American science. And like so many other areas of American science, it is conducted on an agency-by-agency basis.

None of this is meant to suggest that administrative agencies are wholly autonomous, but they are undeniably the central actors in science funding decisions. To a considerable extent the rest of the executive branch, as well as Congress, reacts to what an agency requests. Bureaucratic power is always important in budget making, but it is particularly so where, as here, it is married to a high level of technical expertise. Moreover, scientists within an agency can often count on support on budgetary issues from scientists in outside groups because of shared beliefs in professional norms.[24]

Limits on Executive and Legislative Control of Agencies

Under the circumstances, executive and legislative control of the agencies is limited. At the White House level, the small Office of Science and Technology policy can advise the president on major science policy issues, but it can hardly manage in detail the funding decisions made by the large mission agencies such as Defense, Health and Human Services, or Energy. The president's science advisor (as the head of this office is known) can, for example, provide input when the effectiveness of a major weapons system becomes a matter of public controversy, but that is a different matter than the ordinary grant and contract decisions made daily in the bureaucracy. The Office of Management and Budget can more vigorously enforce overall spending limits in science as in other fields, but even it cannot scrutinize in every case the key questions concerning precisely who gets the research dollars.

The president's most important effect on the day-to-day conduct of science policy stems from the power to appoint the heads of agencies and their key subordinates. These policymakers work closely with the full-time research establishment and can acquire considerable knowledge about at least some program areas.[25] At the subcabinet level, below most public scrutiny, appointees share authority with civil service scientists who have come up through the ranks.[26]

When Congress considers science spending it faces similar limits.

Because there is no single Department of Science, there is no single science budget. The various agency requests go to numerous committees and subcommittees, hampering the development of an overall policy. The problem is not, as is sometimes supposed, a lack of access to technical information. Congress can and does obtain studies on specific issues from such groups as the National Academy of Science, the Congressional Research Service of the Library of Congress, the Comptroller General, and the Office of Technology Assessment, among others. But these studies tend to be limited to relatively high profile public issues, such as the utility of sending astronauts into space, rather than to the disposition of grant requests.

The president and Congress, of course, cherish science for different reasons than do scientists. The political forces care more about a payoff in practical devices and less about the growth of knowledge per se. Thus, science is rarely immune from budget cutting in hard times, and it is never immune from persistent requests to justify itself in practical terms. A large program concentrated in a single agency, such as the superconducting supercollider, can be ended unceremoniously. But generally money is provided in the broad areas where practical results are most likely, and basic scientists are then allowed to work.

There is even an important sense in which the goals of our elected political officials reinforce the norms of the research community. Politicians have an understandable desire for a scientific "breakthrough." It seems to promise imminent real-world benefits and thus justify the taxpayers' money that has been spent on research. Thus politicians will favor a line of scientific research that will lead to a dramatic scientific result, and leave for later the possibility that the technological payoff is less than ideal. A line of research that will not lead to rapid scientific progress will be of less interest, at least initially, even if its longer term social prospects are admirable. Scientists may, as Snow wrote, "have the future in their bones,"[27] but for legislators the future is now.[28]

The media further reinforce this tendency. News stories tend to focus on dramatic breakthroughs rather than day-to-day research.[29] As Walter Lippman wrote, "[T]he news does not tell you how the seed is germinating in the ground, but it may tell you when the first sprout breaks through the surface."[30]

Thus in the basic research area, the scientists' goal of scientific progress is supported, albeit for other reasons, by political and media forces.

Indeed, scientists themselves are sometimes more cautious about whether a result is a "breakthrough" than are politicians or reporters. But our society's major built-in source of deep caution—the process norms of the lawyer—is not well represented at this stage.

The main risk in this system from the scientists' point of view, at least so long as reasonable funding levels are maintained, is undue pressure for immediate results intruding on sound scientific judgment. Thus political efforts to wage a "war on cancer" in the 1970s led to wasteful spending on projects with political but relatively little scientific appeal. Fortunately, they also led to a backlash in which more meaningful basic research on cancer came into fashion and more practical progress came to be made.[31]

A similar flare-up once marked congressional attitudes toward military research and development. In 1970, spurred in part by the belief that the Department of Defense had been spending too much money on research not directed toward military applications, Congress passed the Mansfield Amendment to the Military Procurement Act.[32] The amendment provided that no research could be undertaken by the Department of Defense unless it had "a direct and apparent relationship to a specific military function or operation."[33] The amendment was not a success. First, it had little impact, as Defense Department officials were adept at pointing to previously nonobvious implications of research funded by the department. Secondly, the amendment was soundly attacked on the ground that, if taken seriously, it would hinder valuable research because good basic science often cannot be shown to have a "direct relationship" to a particular end. In the 1971 procurement bill the amendment was diluted to provide that research must have "a potential relationship to a military function or operation."[34] Through it all, basic research continued in the Defense Department.[35]

Thus, basic science operates free of the day-to-day political constraints common elsewhere in American society. Of course it hardly seems that way to the harried science administrator, confronted with budget pressure from the Office of Management and Budget, facing potential ridicule in the form of a "Golden Fleece" award for research that seems silly, and trying to satisfy or appease the desire for results from everyone in elected office. But these judgments are relative. A single change in Social Security requirements, a single desegregation plan in a local school district, indeed, a single proposed change in postal rates can provoke political and legal frenzies that can make an entire science program seem like a backwater.

All of this could change in either of two ways: if the United States had a single Department of Science, or if the president were given a line item veto. Either change would probably work against the interests of the basic research community.

In theory, a single Department of Science could develop a coherent science policy. Thus there have been many proposals for such a department throughout American history.[36] They have never been enacted, in part because of opposition from those agencies already engaged in science spending. But even if we could write on a clean slate there are two major drawbacks to a Department of Science.

First, putting all science spending in one basket would subject that spending to wide fluctuations. In good times, science might receive quite a boost, but basic research would be in trouble when budget-cutting is rampant. Under the present system basic science is insulated to some extent from budgetary battles because areas like health, energy, and defense are rarely cut all at once, and all of those areas contain substantial basic research programs. Science is spread out across the federal bureaucracy, which makes it a difficult target. Of course, a rational public policy analyst could argue that basic science does not need or deserve any exemption from the type of scrutiny that would accompany creation of a single science budget, particularly given the popularity of science across the political spectrum. But the uncertain and long-term nature of basic research makes it preferable to protect science somewhat from sharp changes in budgetary policy.

The second danger with a Department of Science is more fundamental. As we have seen, under our Constitution, government has the power to fund science in a way that would be very troublesome in areas such as religion or politics. If it chose, for example, the federal government could fund only those cancer researchers who believe cancer is caused by a virus. Those with different theories would be free to publish their views and seek private funding, but in practice they would be at an enormous disadvantage. This approach is unconstitutional in other areas: the federal government could not fund the Catholic Church, and it could not fund the Democratic Party to the exclusion of all other parties. The nature of the scientific endeavor inevitably involves a type of picking and choosing that would cause problems elsewhere. We simply are not willing to fund all individuals who call themselves scientists—judgments on the merits must be made.

But such judgments ought to be made cautiously and with a sense of humility. A single Department of Science might tend to support a single line of basic research, and that would be disastrous if that line proved mistaken. Progress in science is so difficult to predict that a variety of approaches is usually needed in the early days of working on a scientific problem, long before any technology is in sight. A Department of Science could even come under the spell of a political theory that dictates a research path, thus leading to a disaster like Lysenkoism in the former Soviet Union, which hampered the development of biology for years. More likely, but equally dangerous, would be a Department of Science that took a monolithic approach to a problem because it rejected the alternatives on scientific grounds that turned out to be mistaken. As a result, it is a blessing that so many agencies fund scientific research under so many overlapping and inconsistent guidelines that an "American science policy" is hard to discern. Just as the Italians say that the inefficiency of their bureaucracy is the safeguard of their liberty, so too the absence of a Department of Science is a safeguard of free scientific inquiry.

Similarly, the line item veto is a possible reform of the budget process that might bode ill for science. Apart from its overall merits, this tactic could have a negative impact on science spending.

Under present law, the president of the United States can only veto a bill in its entirety; the president lacks authority to veto part of a bill while signing the rest into law. By contrast, the constitutions of forty-three states give governors the item veto, that is, the power to veto parts of certain bills. This power is usually limited to appropriations bills and thus the item veto is seen as a budget-balancing device.[37]

Although doubts about its constitutionality at the federal level have been raised, a variety of liberal and conservative lawmakers have called for giving the president statutory item veto authority so that he could slice "porkbarrel" projects out of massive appropriations bills.[38] From the point of view of science spending, there is a problem because, although the American public supports science as a general proposition, individual research projects are easy for politicians to ridicule. Former Sen. William Proxmire's "Golden Fleece" awards for wasteful government spending often went to relatively inexpensive science projects. For example, in "honoring" a study of aggression in primates, Proxmire focused on the scientist's interest in when the animals clench their jaws:

The funding of this nonsense makes me almost angry enough to scream and kick or even clench my jaw. It seems to me it is outrageous.

Dr. Hutchinson's studies should make the taxpayers as well as his monkeys grind their teeth. In fact, the good doctor has made a fortune from his monkeys and in the process made a monkey out of the American taxpayer.

It is time for the Federal Government to get out of this "monkey business." In view of the transparent worthlessness of Hutchinson's study of jaw-grinding and biting by angry or hard-drinking monkeys, it is time we put a stop to the bite Hutchinson and the bureaucrats who fund him have been taking of the taxpayer.[39]

In fact, studies of primate aggression could have beneficial medical implications for humans. But it is sometimes easier to make fun of the studies than to understand them. In the hands of a politically minded president, any number of science projects could be subject to similar ridicule. Fortunately for the science community, the item veto does not presently seem likely to become a reality.

The Virtual Absence of Judicial Review

Given the absence of a Department of Science or a line item veto, the primary engine of basic science for the present and the foreseeable future is the administrative agency, limited only occasionally by Congress and the president. The question then becomes the role of the courts. In this situation, which arises throughout American life in areas ranging from social welfare to the regulation of health and safety, there is a standard legal approach that defines the nature of judicial control of agencies. The relevant area of the law is called administrative law, and it is familiar to attorneys as one of the most ubiquitous and important branches of our legal system. It is typically here that the cautious process values of the legal profession come into play. Yet as we review the basic ideas of administrative law as they apply to science funding, we will see that such funding receives unusually favorable treatment in the courts.

Pursuant to a variety of statutes, most importantly the Administrative Procedure Act of 1946, agencies must follow certain procedures in making their decisions and must be able rationally to justify the results they reach. To enforce these rules, an agency decision is almost always reviewable in court. Whereas the availability and nature of judicial review is set forth in broad terms by statute, in practice the courts themselves determine in large measure how vigorously they will review agency action. When an agency's decision is challenged, the court will first decide whether it should reach the merits of the complaining party's case. That party must satisfy a number of preliminary doctrines, such as standing and ripeness, designed to assure that the case is being brought by a proper person at a proper time.

If the court does reach the merits it will not hold a trial; that is, it will not replicate the fact-finding work of the agency. Instead the court will see if the agency followed proper procedures and if its decision was within reasonable bounds. On the latter point the court will defer to an agency decision even if it might have come out the other way. The court will step in on a substantive matter only when the agency's decision is so poorly explained or so unpersuasive as to appear irrational. In such cases the court will typically send the case back to the agency with the requirement that the agency either change its decision or provide a better justification for its initial result.[40]

This sort of judicial review is the bread and butter of administrative law. It is entirely consistent with the procedural emphasis that permeates so much of American law. A court does not decide if every agency decision is right or wrong. There are thousands of agency rulings every day, many of which involve technical complexities that would test the resources of any decision maker. A judge, moreover, is a generalist who operates with no staff beyond a secretary and a couple of law clerks right out of law school. Under the circumstances, the preliminary doctrines of administrative law, such as standing, enable the court to select those cases most appropriate for judicial review. If the merits of a complaint are reached, the court focuses on the quality of the process used and the adequacy of the explanation given by the agency—areas where a generalist is the best decision maker.

But it would be a serious mistake to confuse procedurally oriented review with punchless review. Courts have shaped the work of modern federal agencies in areas ranging from ratemaking to communications to energy and the environment precisely by forcing agencies to conform to essentially procedural norms.[41] Of course it would be a myth to suggest that the judges who play this role are utterly neutral on the merits of the agency decisions before them. Being human, they are more likely to look closely at a decision they would have made differently. But those instincts are limited by their professional roles and by their resources. The result has been that courts have become the primary external control over agency behavior. Under the circumstances, we must look to judicial review of agency decisions to fund scientific research in order to understand the relationship between law and basic science.

Potentially, the courts could play an active role in policing science funding decisions. The Supreme Court's decision in *Lincoln v. Vigil*, noted earlier, only insulates from review an agency's decision on allocating resources when neither Congress nor the agency has created standards to be met by applicants for funding. In the science funding area such standards are set forth by the agencies' own rules and practices as they seek to evaluate the thousands of funding requests they receive. Yet when we look at science funding we do not see the ordinary give and take between courts and agencies that marks American administrative law. We see instead abdication by the courts of any control over agency decisions.

We must look closely at the cases that establish this agency dominance in order to understand how extraordinary it is and to appreciate its implications for the overall relationship between law and science. The most important of these cases concern disappointed applicants for research grants.

The starting point in understanding these decisions is an appreciation of peer review—the dominant approach agencies such as the National Institutes of Health and the National Science Foundation use in deciding who receives grant money.

Peer review involves a grant application being sent to a group of leading scientists in the relevant field. These scientists give their views as to whether the application should be granted. The reviewers typically take into account not only the research proposal itself but the scientific reputation of the person seeking the grant and the quality of the institution with which the applicant is affiliated. Thus a well-known scientist from a major university is treated more favorably than an unknown from a minor school.[42]

There are many variations in the peer review system. Some agencies utilize outside experts more than others, some utilize more than one layer of review, in some a favorable peer review makes the award of the grant almost certain, whereas in others additional factors, such as conformance with an immediate agency mission, play a bigger role.[43] Moreover, peer review is not without its critics. The system has at times failed to detect fraud, and it has hardly been foolproof in terms of locating the most worthwhile projects.[44] But peer review remains unchallenged as the dominant way in which decisions are made concerning the funding of basic science, just as it is the dominant method for deciding what articles will be published in scientific journals.[45] Indeed, if anything, the pressure today is to extend peer review even further. Proposals have been made to subject the projects of the national laboratories, such as Los Alamos, to peer review,[46] and to use peer review more extensively in areas relating to the impact of technology.[47]

From a legal perspective, certain features of peer review are particularly striking. There is no adversary process—no one appears before the panel to press the applicant's claim or to oppose it. And there is a willingness, even an eagerness, to take into account the personal stature of the applicant—a factor that would be troubling in many settings. But peer review is a perfect fit for the scientific world view; indeed peer review has been called "a mirror of science."[48] It is the embodiment of the scientific community governing itself. Scientists say what is good and what is bad science. They are not perfectly objective. They are not perfectly accurate. But they are the ones making the decisions. This consensus-based approach is not workable when the basic norms of science are violated; when, for example, it became necessary to adjudicate claims of fraud, more traditional judicial models came into play at the research agencies.[49] But when the question is the usual one of what is promising research, the decisions are made in a nonadversarial setting by the scientific community. And when those decisions are challenged in court, the research agencies who are being sued argue vigorously and successfully that outsiders should stay on the outside.

The logical starting point for examining judicial review of scientific research is with Dr. Harold Kletschka, who brought the first modern judicial challenge to a grant decision.[50] In 1959, Kletschka began work at the Syracuse Veterans Administration Hospital and at the nearby Upstate Medical Center, a New York state medical school. By 1961, he had obtained from the Veterans Administration (VA) a $20,000 grant for research into development of a plastic artificial heart. Before he could use the grant he was called to military service. When he returned in 1962, the VA refused to restore his grant and transferred him to another hospital. Kletschka claimed these events were due to the spreading of malicious and slanderous statements by some of his colleagues at Syracuse. He brought a lawsuit against a variety of defendants, including the VA, claiming that a conspiracy had deprived him of his rights, including his right to the research grant. The defendants responded, in part, that their actions were based on the quality of Kletschka's work.[51]

The district court that initially heard the case did not reach the merits of the doctor's claims. The court found some of the defendants immune from suit and found, as to other defendants, that even if Kletschka's allegations were true they did not entitle him to judicial relief.[52] On appeal, the U.S. Court of Appeals for the Second Circuit stated explicitly why it would not review the VA decision on Kletschka's grant. The court invoked an infrequently used provision of the Administrative Procedure Act that exempts from review agency action "committed to agency discretion by law."[53] The use of that provision was appropriate, according to the Second Circuit, because of the nature of scientific research:

It would not be feasible for the courts to review decisions by the V.A. awarding or refusing to award research grants. Each such decision involves a determination by the agency with respect to the relative merits of the many proposed research projects for which funds are sought. This determination requires considerable expertise in the scientific, medical, and technical aspects of each application. A reviewing court would have to master considerable technical data before it could even attempt to determine whether one application, Dr. Kletschka's for example, was so superior to the others that its rejection by the V.A. was an abuse of discretion. Furthermore, even if these technical aspects were mastered it would be difficult for the court to review the judgments of relative personal competence which necessarily play a role in the agency determination.[54]

The Court was not moved even by the fact that Kletschka's grant had been removed after he was summoned to military service, because the doctor's initial 1961 grant "might have been unjustified in 1962 because of intervening advances in heart research."[55] Keep in mind that the court is not rejecting Kletschka's conspiracy theory; it is saying that even if false and malicious statements cost him his grant, his is not the kind of case a court should review.

If slander does not give rise to a cause of action, perhaps discrimination does. That, at least, may have been the thinking of Dr. Julia Apter who, in 1972, challenged the denial of a research grant on the ground that the denial was based on her gender and her political views.[56] The dispute arose when, in 1971, the Rush-Presbyterian-St. Luke's Medical Center, where Apter was a professor, applied to the National Institutes of Health (NIH) for a grant to train students in biomaterials research. Apter would have been the program director responsible for administering the grant. While the application was pending before an NIH committee, she testified before a Senate subcommittee concerning alleged conflicts of interest on the part of some of the NIH committee members. When NIH denied the grant application, Apter brought suit claiming the denial was because a woman had been designated as program director, because she had participated in feminist activities, and in retaliation for her testimony.[57] The trial court threw her case out without reaching the merits on the ground that she lacked standing because the actual applicant for the grant was not Apter but the Rush-Presbyterian-St. Luke's Medical Center, which had not sued. The court reasoned that because the center was unwilling to challenge the grant denial, the court "should not be in the position of foisting the program on it."[58]

On appeal, the U.S. Court of Appeals for the Seventh Circuit reversed, concluding that the alleged violation of Apter's First Amendment right to testify and her alleged personal economic injury in losing the opportunity to be program director were sufficient to give her standing.[59] The appellate court did not, however, decide in her favor. It simply sent the case back to the trial court for further proceedings. Moreover, the appellate court's decision stressed that the trial court should keep in mind that the NIH has broad discretion in the funding of training programs.[60] The appellate court cited Kletschka's case and emphasized that the trial court should confine itself to looking for violations of an express constitutional or statutory guarantee.[61] Not surprisingly, Apter was unsuccessful when the case went back to the trial court.[62]

With allegations of slander and discrimination having failed, the next lawsuit directly challenged the scientific wisdom of an agency decision.[63] Dr. Davide Grassetti had often received federal grant support in the areas of chemistry, pharmacology, and cancer. In 1975, however, the NIH turned down his request for research money to study a chemical compound, carboxypridine disulphide, which he claimed could impede the spread of existing cancer. The agency believed, among other things, that the lack of detail in Grassetti's application was "indicative of a lack of appreciation . . . for biomedical and pharmacological studies."[64] When Grassetti went to court, claiming in part that the agency's decision was unjustified on the facts, he received a cold reception indeed.

First the court, citing Kletschka and Apter, said it was "probable that the medical merits of agency decisions on research grant applications are committed to the unreviewable discretion of the agency."[65] The ordinary administrative law inquiry into whether the agency decision had been adequately justified would not be undertaken. Only the presence of a direct violation of constitutional, procedural, or statutory guarantees could even be considered. The court admitted that "unfortunate as it might be, it is a fact of life that courts are simply not competent to step into the role of a medical research scientist faced with having to evaluate an applicant's technical expertise."[66] Moreover, the court went on to say that even if something resembling judicial review were to be followed, the agency would win because it adequately demonstrated the reasonableness of its decision.[67] Unsurprisingly, this decision was not appealed.

The next case directly challenging a research funding decision was brought not by a disappointed applicant, but by a relatively disinterested party.[68] In 1978, Roslyn Marinoff brought suit against the Department of Health, Education, and Welfare (now Health and Human Services), the agency that oversees the NIH. Marinoff sought to compel the agency to investigate whether a particular chemical could serve as a cure for cancer.[69] Not only did she lose, but the court, in a familiar refrain, never reached the merits of her case; that is, it never decided whether the agency had reasonably explained why it would not investigate the chemical in question. Instead, the court deployed a few of the many preliminary doctrines available in cases of this type. It noted first that Marinoff's complaint, because it sought to order an agency to take action, was seeking, in effect, a writ of mandamus, a rarely granted form of relief. The court found that the writ was unavailable here because, although the agency had a general duty to undertake cancer research, Congress has "left to the agency's discretion the choice as to what substances purported to cure cancer warrant extensive research."[70] A moment's reflection makes clear the import of the court's statement: because Congress left it up to the agency, the court should leave it up to the agency. Thus, there can be no doubt about where the power has been delegated. Continuing in the same vein, the court went on to hold that even if Marinoff's complaint were viewed not as seeking a writ of mandamus but simply as seeking judicial review of an agency decision not to proceed, the suit must fail because, in light of the Kletschka and Grassetti cases, such decisions are "committed to agency discretion" and not subject to judicial review.[71]

A 1993 effort to challenge the government's AIDS research effort fared no better. Kazmer Ujvarosy sought to persuade the National Institutes of Health to investigate a particular theory concerning AIDS; when they denied his request, he went to court.[72] The judge dismissed his claim, finding that Ujvarosy lacked standing and that, in any event, the matter was committed to agency discretion, both doctrines meaning that the court would not even look at the merits of the claim.[73]

This litany of cases provides reasonably precise guidance as to how courts will respond to complaints about science funding decisions: they will respond negatively. In cases spanning from the 1950s to the 1990s, challengers to the government have been unsuccessful. During this period, judicial review of agency action in other fields has gone through phases of relative vigor and relative calm—there have been eras of "hard look" review and of substantial deference[74]—but the judicial reluctance to second guess science funding decisions has remained constant. There is, of course, the possible loophole—the court's occasional insistence that direct agency violation of constitutional, procedural, or statutory directives will lead to reversal—but such cases simply have not arisen. Scientists and the lawyers they consult know that the odds of success are low. So although a case could be imagined in which the scientist would win—a grant openly denied on the basis of race or gender, for example—in practice, judicial review in this area has not been a successful way of challenging agency action.

The situation is similar if an individual protests her failure to receive a contract as opposed to a grant. As discussed previously, in the research area there is often little difference between contracts and grants. That similarity extends to the difficulty of overturning an agency decision. Theoretically, someone who is turned down for a contract to do research work can protest to the Comptroller General of the United States or to the courts.[75] In practice, if the protest is based on the argument that the agency wrongly evaluated the technical merits of a proposal, the chances of reversal are low.[76]

The Privileged Legal Status of Science

At this point, those unfamiliar with administrative law may be decidedly unsurprised at the result of the cases discussed. After all, it might be argued that a research grant or contract is a privilege and not a right, and it involves technical considerations beyond the competence of judges. These arguments, however, do not go very far toward explaining the judicial abstinence in this field. The right versus privilege notion could be invoked to justify unreviewable government discretion in virtually every phase of modern life. Do you have a right to a sidewalk in front of your house? If not, does that mean the government could omit your sidewalk while providing one for your neighbors without any explanation? And if the sidewalk is a mere privilege, could the government provide you with one only if you promise never to criticize the government while walking on that sidewalk? It does not take long to see the danger of an expansive notion of privilege.

To move closer to the science funding example, consider a truck driver's license. It could, presumably, be described as a privilege—the state could have decided that trucks, which are involved in thousands of deaths a year, are to be banned altogether. Having decided not to ban trucks, the state could decide that it will limit, on a completely arbitrary basis, who will have the privilege of driving them. In fact, however, society, including the judicial system, thinks of truck driver's licenses in a somewhat different way. The state sets standards concerning who shall qualify for a license. If you meet those standards you are entitled to that license—you have a right to it. If the motor vehicle administration denies you the license, you can go to court and the court will determine if the agency had proper grounds for denying the license.

Science funding might be viewed the same way. Suppose the NIH announces that funds are available for worthwhile projects in cancer research. You believe your proposal is more worthwhile than any other the agency has received. You would understandably believe, under those circumstances, that you have a right to a grant. If you do not get one and you argue, for example, that inferior projects were funded because of a personal vendetta against you, you would expect a court to make the NIH explain itself. You do not want the judges to be scientists, but only to assure that scientists are doing their job. You would be furious if the court declined to even look at the merits of your case.

The surprising nature of the judicial abdication in the science funding field can perhaps best be seen by examining a comparable area of administrative law. The Social Security Administration deals with millions of requests each year for disability payments. But whereas disappointed researchers seeking science funding almost never win in court, approximately 10,000–25,000 disappointed disability claimants go to federal court each year, and between one-fifth and one-half of them persuade the courts to reverse the agency's decision.[77] What is the difference? It cannot be explained solely by the technical nature of science funding decisions. Disability decisions often turn on complex medical judgments made by several physicians, yet the courts step right in. They do not act as doctors, of course, but they do find that the agency has not adequately justified its decisions.

Consider, for example, the case of Shirley Ber, a sewing machine operator in New York City. In 1960, at about the same time that Dr. Harold Kletscka was applying for a grant to develop an artificial heart, Mrs. Ber was applying for disability benefits on the ground that severe pain stemming primarily from an arthritic condition prevented her from working. A hearing examiner in the Department of Health, Education, and Welfare (now Health and Human Services) studied reports from at least six doctors and concluded that Mrs. Ber had a mild case of arthritis, could continue her job, and thus was not entitled to Social Security benefits. Mrs. Ber went to court and her case ultimately reached the U.S. Court of Appeals for the Second Circuit, the same court that would later hear Dr. Kletschka's case. But whereas the court would not consider whether there was a sound basis for removing Dr. Kletschka's grant, they plunged immediately into the medical reports that had been relied upon by the hearing examiner in Mrs. Ber's case. The court found that those reports permitted only one reasonable conclusion—that Mrs. Ber experienced such sharp pain that she could not work as a sewing machine operator.[78]

Or consider long-time U.S. Steel employee William Lashen, who left his job after an accident blinded him in his left eye. Lashen sought disability payments because of his visual problems and because he had difficulties holding objects in his right hand.[79] The government, citing conflicting testimony from doctors and an ambiguous report from a vocational expert, denied benefits, finding that there were jobs that Lashen could hold. But in 1993, about the time the courts were rejecting Kazmar Ujvarosy's request for government money to fund research on his AIDS theory, Lashen won a decisive victory when a federal court held that the evidence required that he be granted benefits.[80]

Our concern is not whether the court was right or wrong about Mrs. Ber or Mr. Lashen. The question is why they were treated so differently from Dr. Kletschka and Mr. Ujvarosy, that is, why judicial review is so much more searching in disability cases than in the science funding area. You should not assume that the judicial role in Social Security has been uniformly praised. It has, in fact, been the subject of lively debate, with some contending that the courts contribute little but inefficient and ineffective decisions. Yet the judicial role continues, side by side with judicial abstinence in science funding.[81]

The difference cannot be explained by judicial deference to the grinding need of disability claimants. Many of the disability claimants who go to court are middle class; indeed genuinely poor claimants often lack the resources to sue. Moreover, scientists denied government funding are often sympathetic plaintiffs. If unsuccessful, their entire career may be slowed, even halted.

Can it be that the slippery right versus privilege argument explains the disparity? It would be hard to argue that disability payments, a system not even created until 1956, is an absolute "right." A worker's contributions pay only a small part of the payment received. Income is being redistributed under a program the government was not obligated to create. If there is a right, it is the right to receive payments when you meet the agency's standard for disability. Scientists, who pay taxes and who may spend a good deal of money preparing a grant application, will feel that they have an equal "right" to a grant if the application sets forth a deserving project.

With the contrast to disability payments in mind, we can look back over the cases denying review of science funding decisions with a bit more skepticism. The courts in those cases used a variety of doctrines in ruling in favor of the government. They found the agency decisions to be "committed to agency discretion." Judges and lawyers have quarreled over the precise meaning of that phrase, but all have agreed that it applies only to a very narrow area of decisions. Simply as a logical matter, the fact that an agency is exercising discretion is hardly grounds for judicial abdication. The courts in administrative law cases routinely correct "abuses of discretion." Indeed, given the broad powers given to modern agencies, judicial deference in the face of "agency discretion" would leave no role for the courts at all.[82]

In the cases we surveyed, the courts relied as well on doctrines such as standing and the limited nature of mandamus relief. These doctrines too are flexible—they can be applied stringently or leniently depending on the nature of the case. Courts in administrative law cases have many other such doctrines at their disposal. The court will not hear the merits of your case if it is not "ripe," that is, you have not yet been harmed by agency action fit for judicial review. You cannot sue if you have not "exhausted your remedies" by pursuing available sources of relief within the agency. And so on.

When, as in the science funding area, courts resolve to apply these doctrines rigorously before reaching the merits, suppliants before the courts may feel that they are facing a Kafkesque maze. The adjective is of particular relevance here. Franz Kafka was, in fact, a lawyer who worked in a large social welfare bureaucracy, and he was well aware of the difficulties facing those who sought relief from the Workmen's Accident Insurance Institute.[83] Kafka once remarked, in amazement, "How modest these people are. Instead of storming the institute and smashing the place to bits, they come and plead."[84] Kafka's fiction, of course, conveys a nightmarish vision of the search for justice. But compared to the modern judge bent on avoiding the merits, Kafka was a piker. *The Trial* is a terrifying account, but it relies, from a modern lawyer's point of view, on rather basic maneuvers, like declining to specify the charge against K. A modern-day *Trial* in an administrative law setting would include demands that the hapless applicant satisfy recondite tests for standing and ripeness before the court would even think about discussing whether the agency has adequately explained the charge. "Before the Law" is perhaps a chilling and prophetic universal nightmare, but a mild one indeed for today's lawyers. In this segment of *The Trial*, a suppliant seeking entrance to the law waits for years before a gate. Just as he dies, the gatekeeper announces, "[T]his gate was built only for you and now I am going to shut it." A modern version of "Before the Law" would admit the suppliant through the gate and then dismiss him if he could not prove that he had "exhausted administrative remedies" and then admit him again only to raise the problem of "mootness," and so on.

But the labyrinthian ways of judicial review, despite their appearance, are not, in functional terms, a meaningless maze. Preliminary doctrines such as "standing" and "commitment to agency discretion" enable judges to shield themselves from a flood of cases by picking and choosing those that are most appropriate for judicial consideration. In the science funding area the courts have chosen, with remarkable unanimity, to employ doctrines effectively closing off judicial review, leaving open the possibility of such review only if extraordinary cases, such as those involving racial discrimination, should arise. The real question is why that course has commended itself to so many judges. This judicial abstinence contrasts, after all, not only with Social Security disability cases, but with judicial involvement throughout American society.

The fundamental reason for this abstinence is that the area of basic scientific research is one of the few in American life in which something approaching consensus still exists. As we have seen, science is in some respects a self-governing republic, with scientists deciding what is and is not good work. Of course these are disagreements, hard cases, and uncertainties. But there is broad enough agreement on fundamental issues that nonscientists will generally defer to scientists on questions concerning basic research.[85]

Here, as before, we must be extremely careful about assertions concerning the "scientific establishment." As we saw earlier, science is established in the sense that it is government supported, but there is no "science establishment" in the rigid hierarchical sense. Not only do numerous agencies fund research under varying guidelines, but even within an agency different perspectives exist. Studies have shown that your chances of getting funding depend in part on the particular scientists who serve on your peer review panel.[86] And this is as it should be. There are always at least some prestigious scientists willing to look for new and different ideas. But this does not mean that anything goes. If there is no science establishment, there is at least a science community. Scientists as a whole are willing to view some practitioners as marginal or worse and to act accordingly.

The existence of the science community directly constrains the number of lawsuits that will be brought to challenge science funding decisions. Disappointed applicants who bring suit may be reducing their chances for getting funding in the future. Few people want to be seen as marginal troublemakers when they may have to go back to the same well again. You will recall, for example, that Dr. Judith Apter initially had trouble bringing her lawsuit because the medical center where she worked would not join in her suit. Apter contended, not unreasonably, that the medical center was afraid of losing the opportunity for future grants.

The situation is very different for a disappointed applicant for disability payments who challenges a Social Security Administration decision. There is no coherent community of professional views concerning what is a disability. The medical profession may or may not be able to reach consensus on a given diagnosis for a syndrome, but even if it could the question of what is disabling is too controversial. To many it would seem to be a nonmedical question, but even the addition of vocational experts does not lead to wide consensus. Now to purists, the question of what is a promising scientific research project is not itself a scientific question. But that misses the point—it is a question the scientific community, for better or for worse, is able to deal with in a relatively coherent fashion.

Moreover, scientists seeking funding are members of the very community they are petitioning. By contrast, a disabled worker is not. Indeed, an applicant for disability payments is unlikely to be seeking the same relief from the same people again. Under the circumstances, bringing a lawsuit poses few risks; indeed, it may even nudge the agency in your favor under the adage that the squeaky wheel gets the grease. With science funding, the squeaky wheel may get replaced.

Consider then what courts confront when a challenge to science funding comes before them. There is the normal deference due to an administrative agency that is, after all, a large bureaucracy capable of detailed judgments. There is the esoteric nature of the scientific judgment at issue. And there is, most importantly, a sense that the challenger is not a wronged citizen, but rather an outsider with marginal views challenging a respected community of scientists. It is not surprising that the courts have generally rebuffed such challenges without even reaching the merits of the case.

Thus, from a litigator's point of view, basic science operates in something of a vacuum. Traditional administrative law provides no workable way to challenge decisions of the science community. Thus the favorable statutory status of science meshes perfectly with its favorable constitutional status. The scientific community itself dominates a system marked by substantial support and freedom for scientists, whereas the legal community finds itself with little power. And, as we shall, one of science's traditional rivals—religion—is also outflanked in American law and culture.

• FIVE •

Science versus Religion
in American Law

The power of organized religion has waxed and waned dramatically throughout human history. In many preindustrial societies, the church provided not only answers to what we think of today as scientific questions, but strict guidance to political leaders as well—religion "once could define secular laws in usury, regulate the conditions of production in the guilds, and prohibit what today are normal business and commercial practices. . . . [M]onarchs were brought cringing to religious shrines and matters of personal morality were effectively dictated by pontifical power."[1] In the twentieth-century Soviet Union, by contrast, religion was repressed in the name of an all-encompassing "scientific" view of government and morality.[2]

The Framers' Conception of Religion and Science

From the beginning, America has had a more nuanced relationship between church and state in general, and church and science in particular. The framers of the Constitution, as we have seen, cherished the Enlightenment ideal that science could illuminate everything from chemical reactions to political theory. But the framers were also descendants of people who had come to America in large part seeking religious freedom. The growth of modern science in the eighteenth century did not require the framers to uniformly reject religion:

Religious belief in the New World was by no means repressed by scientific progress as it was in the Old. On the contrary, there emerged an American

69

symbiosis of rationalism and Christianity, technological progress and moral challenge. . . . Franklin, Jefferson, Rush and Priestly all espoused a rationalistic conception of progress, but, unlike Paine, they found that science and reason did not require them to reject completely their Christian heritage. Rather, Christianity supplied them with a comfortable ethical system whose telic projections could be made entirely harmonious with the methods and conclusions of science.[3]

The original relationship between science and religion in America turned in part on the American infatuation with progress. Scholars still debate whether the belief in human progress was known in ancient Greece and Rome, or whether, facilitated by Christianity's linear conception of history, it began in the Middle Ages.[4] There is wide consensus, however, that the idea of progress was dominant among eighteenth-century Enlightenment thinkers.[5] We have already noted the optimism, fueled by Newton's discoveries, that improvement, perhaps perfection, was attainable in all human endeavors.

This notion of progress was particularly strong in America. The people who came to live in the New World often saw themselves as replacing the corrupt institutions of the Old World with a more perfect order.[6] The very acts of creating a nation and writing its Constitution were a kind of "applied Enlightenment."[7]

The Enlightenment origins of the U.S. Constitution reflected and reinforced a particular balance between religion and science. To many of the framers, dogmatic, authoritarian religion, as opposed to a more enlightened deism, was a threat to the idea of progress they held dear. Their views shaped the nonestablishment and free exercise of religion clauses of the Constitution, clauses that have a continuing impact on the relationship between American science and religion.

The First Amendment's requirement that "Congress shall make no law respecting an establishment of religion" was designed for many purposes, some of them conflicting. Certain of the framers, for example, wanted to forbid Congress from establishing religion in order to maintain state establishments they favored.[8] In this century, however, the Supreme Court has interpreted the nonestablishment clause in light of the purposes of Jefferson and Madison, as reflected in their battles to forbid established religion of any kind in Virginia.[9] Moreover, the Court, beginning in 1947, applied the nonestablishment clause to state as well as federal government.[10]

A religion-science skirmish in colonial America gives us a taste of the Enlightenment views that characterized Jefferson and Madison's approach to nonestablishment.[11] After the Boston earthquake of 1755, the Reverend Thomas Prince's sermon, "Earthquakes the Works of God and Tokens of his Just Displeasure," suggested that Ben Franklin's lightning rods might have brought on the earthquake. Prince concluded, "O! there is no getting out of the mighty Hand of God! If we think to avoid it in the Air, we cannot in the Earth."[12]

Harvard professor John Winthrop, a leading Newtonian, immediately published a powerful scientific rejoinder that was widely believed to have made Prince appear ridiculous.[13] Winthrop's response, as well as his writings on comets a few years later, attacked clergy who fostered fear rather than understanding of natural phenomena, and emphasized the consistency of Winthrop's own belief in God with an understanding of Newtonian mechanics.[14] Winthrop's attitude exemplified an important strand of Enlightenment thinking: a combination of attacks on "superstitious" clergy with support for scientific speculation.[15] Leading American scientists joined Winthrop in condemning the "priestcraft" that controlled men's minds.[16] The goal of these scientists was not atheism, but rather a faith illuminated by natural philosophy.[17]

The Virginia supporters of the nonestablishment clause shared Winthrop's approach. They wanted to prevent the suppression of enlightened science by the church. Thus, in his "Memorial and Remonstrance Against Religious Assessments," Madison argued that fifteen centuries of establishment Christianity resulted in "superstition" on the part of clergy and laity alike.[18] The centerpiece of Jefferson's attack on established religion in Notes on the State of Virginia was a pointed history of science and religion: "Galileo was sent to the Inquisition for affirming that the earth was a sphere; the government had declared it to be as flat as a trencher, and Galileo was obliged to abjure his error. This error, however, at length prevailed, [and] the earth became a globe."[19]

Jefferson was not alone in citing the martyrdom of Galileo. Milton, the leading influence on colonial ideas of free speech,[20] was influenced greatly by a visit he made to the exiled scientist.[21] The Areopagitica, a basic source to this day on the evils of licensing speech,[22] describes Milton's trip to Italy where he "found and visited the famous Galileo, grown old, a prisoner to the Inquisition, for thinking in astronomy otherwise than the Franciscan and Dominican licensers thought."[23]

Thus the Jeffersonian wall between church and state was designed in part to protect American Galileos. In this respect, the free exercise and establishment clauses are complementary; the constitutional requirement that "Congress shall make no law respecting an establishment of religion, or prohibiting the free exercise thereof"[24] both protects and enhances science. Whereas some religions may rely on dogma to the detriment of science, others believe scientific inquiry enhances God's glory.[25] Thus nonestablishment combined with free exercise encourages people like Winthrop to pursue their researches. Throughout American history, the religious tolerance built into the First Amendment has bolstered American science. American Quakers, for example, whose faith encourages scientific endeavor, made major contributions to American science beginning in the eighteenth century, and in this century, American tolerance of Judaism led to an influx of Jewish scientists, particularly from Germany.[26]

The Modern Dispute over the Theory of Evolution

The establishment clause has played a decisive role in the twentieth-century successor to the dispute between Galileo and the church. Just as astronomy displaced human beings from the center of the universe, the theory of evolution displaced human beings from their special status among the earth's inhabitants.[27] In the case of evolution, the establishment clause resolved the resulting religion-science dispute in favor of science.

The theory that humans evolved from other primates need not, in the abstract, pose a challenge to one's spiritual beliefs. For example, Darwinism was readily absorbed when it was introduced in Japan in the late nineteenth century. The reason was not that Japanese society was more advanced scientifically; indeed, Japan had much less of a scientific community at that time than did Europe or America.[28] As Edwin Reischauer pointed out, evolution did not cause popular protest because of the nature of the dominant Japanese belief systems:

Because of Shinto ideas, there were no clear lines between natural objects, such as rocks, trees, waterfalls, and mountains, and living creatures of all sorts, vegetable or animal, and humans, or between humans and gods. Buddhism had also brought the idea that the quality of one's present life might bring rebirth as a superior being or as an inferior one, like a bug or a worm. No one recoiled at the idea that humans could be descended from less advanced animal forms. In fact, Darwinism proved a support to the acceptance of Western science.[29]

But when Darwin's theories emerged in nineteenth-century America they presented an enormous shock to many Christians, and for some that shock remains.[30] The shock stems from specific religious teachings. In the Bible people are created separately from other creatures and are given a role and a set of capabilities that set them apart from all others. The Darwinian notion that people are animals is a fundamental challenge to that entire structure. This is not simply an instance where a biblical account appears at odds with modern science. It is to many a threat to the very idea of transcendent morality.

The clash between evolution and science first came to the American courts in the Scopes trial. The trial verdict was mixed. In 1925, John Thomas Scopes was convicted by a jury of violating a Tennessee statute that made it unlawful "to teach any theory that denies the story of the Divine Creation of man as taught in the Bible, and to teach instead that man has descended from a lower order of animals."[31] At the time of Scopes's trial and appeal the U.S. Supreme Court had not yet ruled that the nonestablishment clause of the First Amendment applied to actions of the state, as opposed to federal, government.[32] Thus Scopes's appeal to the Tennessee Supreme Court was severely constrained. And the Tennessee Supreme Court found that the anti-evolution law was within the power of the Tennessee legislature.[33]

But the process orientation of the legal system enables courts to reach compromises, a power of particular importance in highly charged and divisive cases. The Scopes trial, with Clarence Darrow for the defense and William Jennings Bryan for the State, had elicited enormous public attention, much of it consisting of negative publicity directed at the "fundamentalist" supporters of "monkey bills" like the one in Tennessee.[34] Even Christian magazines expressed concern about Bryan's literalist approach to the Bible.[35]

Under the circumstances, the Tennessee Supreme Court seemed reluctant to affirm the Scopes conviction. They seized on the fact that, after the jury verdict, the trial judge had imposed a fine of $100, the minimum amount allowed under the statute.[36] Now it might seem unlikely that Scopes was prejudiced by having been given the lightest possible punishment. But the Court noted that under the Constitution of Tennessee, a fine in excess of $50 must be assessed by a jury, and the Court declined to rectify this problem in any way—it simply said that the judgment against Scopes had to be reversed because a judge, not a jury, had imposed the fine.[37] The Court then went on to note that "the peace and dignity of the state" would be best served if the prosecution of Scopes were dropped so that "this bizarre case" could be ended.[38] And indeed, the case ended at that point.

The evolution controversy did not come before the U.S. Supreme Court until *Epperson v. Arkansas,*[39] a 1968 challenge to the constitutionality of an Arkansas statute prohibiting the teaching of evolution.[40] By this time, the nonestablishment clause had been applied to the states, and in this case the Jeffersonian and Madisonian view of that clause carried the day. In other words, the challenge to the Arkansas law was successful because the case was seen as a dispute between religion and science.

An amicus brief in *Epperson* demonstrated to the Court that science was in fact at stake by including a statement signed by 179 biologists asserting that evolution "is firmly established even as the rotundity of the earth is firmly established."[41] Another brief for the opponents of the statute, in a passage with roots in the eighteenth century, argued that the uninformed use "all forms of physical and mental torture, to maintain the status quo of their unenlightenment and their accepted beliefs."[42] During oral argument, counsel for the State was asked, "What if Arkansas would forbid the theory that the world is round?"[43] And the Court's opinion, in striking down the statute under the establishment clause, featured excerpts from arguments against fundamentalist religion generally.[44]

Commentary on *Epperson* has tended to focus on the doctrinal point that the Court found the statute unconstitutional because it had been enacted for a religious purpose.[45] But the Court's proof of an illegal purpose consisted merely of citation to newspaper advertisements, letters to the editor, and law review articles.[46] No statement of any legislator was included. In other cases where a religious purpose seems likely, the Court has declined to find one or even to look very hard.[47] Academic emphasis on purpose or motive in the usual sense is misplaced here. The Court's scrutiny of the statute was more intense than in the usual establishment case because the competing value at stake was science. Indeed, the Court said as much: "The State's undoubted right to prescribe the curriculum for its public schools does not carry with it the right to prohibit, on pain of criminal penalty, the teaching of a scientific theory or doctrine where that prohibition is based upon reasons that violate the First Amendment."[48] The Arkansas statute's improper purpose was not to aid religion, but rather to aid religion at the expense of science.

The Supreme Court believed in *Epperson* that what it called the "monkey" law might be a curiosity from an earlier era, noting that, apart from Arkansas, only Mississippi had an anti-evolution statute on its books.[49] In 1970 the Mississippi law was struck down on the authority of *Epperson*.[50] But, contrary to the Court's belief, the subject of the teaching of evolution in the public schools has remained a lively one. The fundamental challenge Darwin poses to the beliefs of many Americans cannot easily be put to rest.

Thus litigation has continued as anti-evolutionists try new techniques. But nothing they try can shake the dominance of the scientific world view in this legal arena. In 1975, the U.S. Court of Appeals for the Sixth Circuit struck down a Tennessee statute requiring that the teaching of evolution in public schools be accompanied both by a disclaimer that it is "theory" not "scientific fact," and by an explanation of the Genesis account in the Bible without such disclaimer.[51] The court held that putting science at this disadvantage compared to religion was, under *Epperson*, a violation of the establishment clause.[52]

Epperson was also applied in a 1973 North Carolina case involving a substitute teacher who was asked by a student if he believed man descended from monkeys.[53] The teacher said yes, challenged some other biblical stories as unscientific, and was fired the next day when students complained.[54] The district court held in favor of the teacher on various grounds, including the establishment clause.[55] The court's opinion traced the persecution of Galileo and the contributions of Newton, and concluded that the "United States Constitution was drafted after these and similar events had occurred, but not so long after that they had been forgotten."[56]

Creationism in the Courts

The most recent attack on evolution has come from creationism—the movement arguing that there is scientific evidence that the creation account in the Book of Genesis is accurate.[57]

The first thing to say about creationism is that its very existence is an extraordinary demonstration of the role of science in American society.

The notion that a religious account of reality depends upon scientific verification would come as a shock to many in other cultures and in other times. It is not at all clear that revelation or faith must be subordinate to empiricism. But in America today some fundamentalists have either come to believe—or have been driven to assert—that scientific support for Genesis is of central importance. These creationists have then brought about the passage of legislation requiring that "creation science" be taught along with evolution in the public schools.

But calling something creation "science" does not make it so from the point of view of the scientific community or the courts. The traditional scientific community rallied against creationism,[58] emphasizing that it really was not a scientific theory because it did not admit the possibility that Genesis was wrong. The courts were then confronted once again with lawsuits pitting science against religion, and they ruled once again for science. The process began when a federal district court held in *McLean v. Arkansas,* 529 F. Supp. 1255 (E.D. Ark. 1982), that an Arkansas statute mandating that creationism be taught along with evolution was an unconstitutional establishment of religion. The matter reached the U.S. Supreme Court in the 1987 case of *Edwards v. Aguillard.*[59]

Edwards involved a carefully drafted statute—the Louisiana "Balanced Treatment for Creation-Science and Evolution-Science in Public School Instruction" Act. This act forbade the teaching of evolution in public schools unless accompanied by the teaching of "creation science," which was defined as the "scientific evidences for [creation] and inferences from those scientific evidences."[60] No school was required to teach evolution or creation science, but if either was taught the other had to be taught as well.

The traditional scientific community urged the Court to reject the notion that "creation science" was anything other than religion. Briefs opposing the Louisiana law were filed by, among others, a group of 72 Nobel Laureates in science, and by the National Academy of Sciences. And the majority of the Supreme Court, citing a survey of Louisiana school superintendents, rejected the state's claim that "creationism" was just another scientific theory and concluded instead that it was a religious doctrine characterized by "the literal interpretation of the Book of Genesis."[61] In the end, the Supreme Court struck down the Louisiana law as an establishment of religion because they looked, as they had in *Epperson*, to the state's purpose and found an improper religious infringement on science:

In this case, the purpose of the Creationism Act was to restructure the science curriculum to conform with a particular religious viewpoint. Out of many possible science subjects taught in the public schools, the legislature chose to affect the teaching of the one scientific theory that historically has been opposed by certain religious sects. As in *Epperson*, the legislature passed the Act to give preference to those religious groups which have as one of their tenets the creation of humankind by a divine creator. . . . Because the primary purpose of the Creationism Act is to advance a particular religious belief, the Act endorses religion in violation of the First Amendment.[62]

The blow to some religious Americans inflicted by the *Edwards* case is considerable, but it is an unavoidable consequence of the constitutional status of American science and religion. Even Stephen Carter, who has argued eloquently that American elites wrongly trivialize religion, concedes that "*Edwards v. Aguillard* is correctly, if perhaps tragically decided. The decision is correct because of the difficulty of articulating the precise secular purpose for the teaching of creationism: even if dressed up in scientific jargon, it is, at heart, an explanation for the origin of life that is dictated solely by religion."[63]

It is impossible to understand *Epperson, Edwards,* and the other evolution cases as simply dealing with the establishment of religion. Consider, by comparison, application of the establishment clause to state laws that criminalize homosexual behavior. These laws, like anti-evolution laws, are religious in origin. They derive directly from specific biblical passages,[64] and the offense in question was defined traditionally as "the abominable sin not fit to be named among Christians."[65] Furthermore, anti-sodomy laws cannot easily be analogized for constitutional purposes to other criminal laws, like those against murder, which have religious roots but have taken on a secular purpose.[66] Unlike the laws against murder, laws against homosexuality are retained in part because of religious pressure,[67] and many homosexual crimes affect only consenting adults.[68]

Yet establishment clause challenges to the laws against homosexual behavior have failed uniformly.[69] Moreover, in decisions involving homosexuality, courts often go out of their way to rely on the biblical origins of the laws. Thus in *Doe v. Commonwealth*[70] a three-judge federal court upheld Virginia's right to prohibit private, consensual homosexual acts between adults. The court found that "the longevity of the Virginia Statute does testify to the State's interest and its legitimacy. It is not an upstart notion; it has ancestry going back to Judaic and Christian law." The court then cited Leviticus 18:22: "Thou shalt not lie with mankind, as with womankind: it is abomination."[71] Similarly, when the U.S. Supreme Court upheld a Georgia sodomy statute, Chief Justice Burger's concurrence stressed that "condemnation of [sodomy] is firmly rooted in Judaeo-Christian moral and ethical standards."[72]

Religion is thus deeply involved with our views about homosexuality, yet establishment clause challenges fail while they succeed when evolution is involved. The establishment clause cannot be understood solely as a statement about religion; its content depends upon the context in which religion is operating. When religion shapes our moral standards, constitutional scrutiny is more lax than when religion shapes our scientific standards. Analyzing the evolution decisions without reference to the constitutional status of science is like analyzing a steam engine without reference to the steam.

Not only have the courts kept Genesis out of the public school curriculum, they have prevented individual teachers and students from opting out of the standard course of study. In 1990, a federal appellate court held that a junior high school teacher had no free speech right to teach creationism when that topic was not included in the curriculum.[73] In 1992, when a California high school biology teacher was reprimanded for teaching creationism, he tried a different legal theory. He went to court, arguing that evolution was simply another religion and that his own rights were overridden when he was forced to teach Darwin's theories as required by the standard curriculum.[74] His claim was rejected—the court found that the state could insist that its teachers teach its curriculum and the court rejected the characterization of evolution as "religion," describing it instead as "the widely accepted scientific explanation of the origin of life."[75]

Here again it is important to understand that it is not simply that religion is losing—it is mainstream science that is winning. Thus Stephen Carter, in the course of a sympathetic account of the views of creationists, notes that he "would be distressed were creationism to be offered as part of the curriculum at a public school supported by tax dollars, but it is important to note the reason. I would be distressed because I think it bad science—no more and no less."[76]

Finally, perhaps the sharpest blow to traditional religion in this area came when some Tennessee parents, describing themselves as "born again Christians," went to court in 1983 to argue that their children should be excused from public school classes when material offensive to their religion, including evolution, was taught.[77] They were not seeking the teaching of creationism or anything else—they just wanted released time. But the court rejected their free exercise of religion claim, saying that attending class did not require "affirmation or denial of a religious belief, or performance or non-performance of a religious exercise or practice."[78] The court further concluded that the only way to accommodate the parents' claim would be to eliminate all material offensive to their religion, and "the Supreme Court has clearly held that it violates the Establishment Clause to tailor a public school's curriculum to satisfy the principles or prohibitions of any religion."[79] The *Epperson* case was cited for the last proposition.

The Growth of Civil Religion

The success of evolution in the courtrooms provides a strong measure of protection for science against a possible rival. It does not, however, fully account for the modern relationship between science and religion in American society. Religion has many claims that turn not at all on Darwin, and religion plays a major role in modern American life. Moreover, when science is not directly involved, we have seen that the courts have allowed the church to have considerable influence, as in the regulation of homosexual behavior. Nonetheless, when we examine the role of American religion in public life across the board, we see religion as a smaller presence than is required by logic and law. We also see science playing a larger role in many debates than might be expected.

This is not happening because Americans are flocking to atheism or agnosticism. Rumors of the death of religion in America are entirely unfounded. The percentage of Americans affiliated with a religious group is higher today than in the early 1950s and much higher than it was in the 1780s.[80] Moreover, the fastest growing denominations tend to be those with the most literalistic interpretation of the Bible.[81]

But the other side of the coin is revealing. The mainstream Protestant denominations—such as the Presbyterians, Lutherans, and Episcopalians—are in decline.[82] Moreover, the content of these traditional reli-

gions, as well as others, has become increasingly secularized.[83] Religions
have sought to soften their distinctive teachings in order to appeal to an
increasingly mobile and modernized constituency.

At the same time, America's "civil" or "political" religion has become
increasingly pervasive and hard to distinguish from the watered-down
doctrines of the mainstream churches. Sociologist Peter L. Berger has
defined civil religion as "basic convictions about human destiny and
human rights as expressed in American democratic institutions."[84] At
times, our civil religion in practice becomes a nonthreatening notion that
America and Americans believe in a vague, undemanding sort of God.
As President Eisenhower reportedly said, "Our government makes no
sense unless it is founded in a deeply felt religious faith—and I don't
care what it is."[85] More recently, President Bush spoke of "our Nation's
Judeo-Christian moral heritage and . . . the timeless values that have
united Americans of all religions and all walks of life: love of God and
family, personal responsibility and virtue, respect for the law, and concern for others."[86]

To some extent, American religion is a victim of its own success. The
genuine opportunity for free exercise attracts people with countless beliefs from around the globe. Under the circumstances, public endorse-
ment of any distinctive religious teaching is bound to offend quite a
large number of Americans. It is important to remember that many
objections to government-sponsored religious observances stem not from
the complaints of atheists but from those of different faiths. For example, the 1963 U.S. Supreme Court case striking down Bible readings in
the public schools was brought by a church-going Unitarian who objected, among other things, to the theological doctrine of the Trinity.[87]
Earlier challenges to Bible readings were brought by Catholics who
objected to use of the King James translation of the Bible, which was not
approved by Catholic ecclesiastical authority.[88] In Boston, in 1859, an
eleven-year-old Catholic boy was beaten by his teacher because he
would not read the Ten Commandments from the King James version.
When a court held that this discipline was proper, public outrage led to
changes on the Boston School Committee.[89]

The practices of minority religions remain controversial today. In
1993, the Supreme Court struck down a Hialeah, Florida, ordinance
that forbid the Santeria religion's practice of animal sacrifice.[90] The
Court noted the ordinance had been supported by many Cuban immi-

grants who were familiar with Santeria from their native country, and who applauded the fact that, in Cuba, "people were put in jail for practicing this religion."[91] In America that cannot happen, but clearly it is true that a Santeria-dominated legislature could not impose its religious beliefs on an unconsenting minority.

The net effect is that religion, which can be highly distinctive, must be watered down when it is linked in any way with the government. Thus consider the well-known Supreme Court decisions allowing display on public property of a creche when it is surrounded by a "Seasons Greetings" banner and plastic reindeer,[92] but not when it stands alone.[93]

None of this means that religion cannot influence public debate and legislation. When a secular purpose can be shown, laws that mandate Sunday closings[94] or ban sodomy[95] will be upheld. But the tolerance demanded by the free exercise and nonestablishment clauses has an impact. On many issues, religious leaders, afraid of offending others and of losing parishioners, shy away from strong moral pronouncements. The stability of our pluralistic political community can only stand so much. As John Rawls has put it, the "overlapping consensus" needed if groups with different beliefs are to live peacefully together implies that religious groups themselves must be tolerant of other approaches to the truth.[96]

Stephen Carter argues for greater acceptance by American elites of people with strong traditional faith, but he also envisions a society in which religion remains separate from and critical of the state and in which various viewpoints can flourish.[97] According to Carter, religious groups that would take away the freedom of others should be opposed precisely because of the content of their beliefs.[98] The proper political goal, according to Carter, is the participation of religious and nonreligious groups in a "state that loves liberty and cherishes its diversity."[99]

Science, Progress, and Values

If religion in a pluralistic society is unlikely to be a unified source of values, the scientific community, with its unusual degree of internal coherence, is in some respects better off. Moreover, changes in the American conception of progress have strengthened the influence of science. In its Enlightenment embodiment, progress embraced the idea of improvement throughout human affairs. In this century, however, world wars, totalitarian regimes, and the growth of relativistic philoso-phies have undermined that faith.[100] We are no longer sure that our political ideas are moving forward, but we still like the idea of forward movement. So what remains? The answer is science—the one institution where progress is still the unashamed touchstone. Progressivism has survived today largely because modern thinkers "have divorced it from the 'heavenly city of the eighteenth century philosophers,' tied it to the cause of democracy and abundance, and brought it down to earth."[101] Thus the linkage between science and faith available to the framers has fallen victim not only to Darwinism, but to increased secularization and pessimism:

In its inception when the secular order embraced the vision of a perfected humanity and a new human community, important segments of the community of faith could identify with the efforts to achieve such a goal. In that situation a collapse of faith into the general cultural situation was understandable. But with the decline of that vision and its supersession by the rise to dominance of the "technological imperative" it has become more difficult to find in the secular sphere reflections of a substantive Christian purpose.[102]

Thus in the public sphere appeals to science and its progressive values are common. We may no longer believe we can make better people, but we believe we can always learn more about the natural world, and some type of progress remains better than none.

But we must be cautious about what science cannot do. It is precisely its lack of normative content that makes progress an unproblematic norm in the scientific community. Science does not tell us what we ought to do. Indeed, it disclaims any such authority. If it did otherwise, it would weaken its claims to neutrality and testability. But we often forget that. A discussion of whether a computer can be built or whether a genetic therapy can be achieved quietly slips into an assumption that the computer or the therapy ought to be undertaken. Science, given the absence of a loud voice for traditional religion, often plays a large role in our thinking about the kind of society we ought to build.[103]

The theory of evolution itself offers an excellent example. As a scien-tific theory it has had enormous influence. But it has done much more than that. From nineteenth-century Social Darwinism to modern socio-biology, evolutionary ideas have spilled over into theories about human virtue and morality.[104] The presentation of those theories is perfectly appropriate and understandable—it would be odd indeed if science did not influence our thinking on nonscientific issues. But matters of morality, in the end, are not subject to the scientific method. One can believe, for example, that all of the physical similarity in the world does not prove that human moral choices are indistinguishable from the choices made by other animals. As one twentieth-century theologian wrote, "it is not true that a specific kind of continuity in the natural order affects the life of the human spirit. . . . Sin is not found in the brutes, and anyone who professes to find it there misunderstands the concept 'sin.' "[105] These voices too often go unheard when speculations begin about the implications of the latest scientific breakthrough. Our pluralism makes the voices talking about values so diverse and dilute that they are too easily ignored.

Thus basic science occupies a favorable position indeed in American law and culture. The Constitution shields science from its rival—religion—and from government suppression. It lays the groundwork for generous funding, and statutes assure that the resulting funding is parceled out by the scientific community itself. Meanwhile in our pluralistic culture with traditional religious voices often weak and divided, science even plays a major role in the formation of our values. Throughout the entire process, the progressive ethos of science utterly dominates the cautious process norms of the lawyer. But when we come to applying science to the real world through technology, the tables are turned with a vengeance.

Legal Restrictions on New Technology: The Regulatory Gap and the Emergence of the Science Counselor

When scientific developments lead to commercially important products, the legal situation changes dramatically. Gentle inquiries are replaced by intense scrutiny as technologically complex products are subject to regulation in countless arenas.

The Constitutional Basis for Regulating Technology

Here, as with basic science, the best place to begin an examination of the law is with the constitutional framework. Where in the Constitution is the federal government given the power to regulate technology? After all, the federal government is limited to those powers enumerated in the Constitution and there is nothing there that speaks specifically about the regulation of technology. Indeed, when the Constitution was written, and for many years thereafter, there was doubt about the federal government's power to regulate any local industry—many believed only the states had such power. But the Constitution did give Congress the power to regulate "interstate commerce" and in this century that power has been read so broadly that almost any form of technology is subject to regulation if Congress wishes.[1]

The courts have read the commerce clause broadly because they have come to believe that in a modern integrated economy very little is purely local. Thus, for example, when you buy a thermometer at your local drugstore to be used in your home, you may think the transaction is local, but it is well within Congress' power to regulate. After all, some of the materials that went into the thermometer probably came from other states. Even if they did not, use of this type of thermometer and similar medical devices by many people could affect the cost of medical care or the number of hospital admissions. In turn, this would somewhat affect the movement of doctors, patients, or financial resources across state lines. There is ample precedent under any of these theories for an exercise of congressional power.

If this example seems farfetched, consider an actual case concerning Congress' power to regulate the local sale of drugs. In 1946, a laboratory in Chicago shipped a number of bottles of sulfathiazole tablets to a wholesaler in Atlanta, Georgia. Sulfathiazole was used at the time to combat infections. When shipped from Illinois to Georgia, the bottles had warning labels on them as required by the Federal Food, Drug, and Cosmetic Act of 1938. One label, for example, read "Warning—In some individuals Sulfathiazole may cause severe toxic reaction." Six months after the Georgia wholesaler received the bottles from Illinois, one bottle was sent to Sullivan's Pharmacy in Columbus, Georgia. Three months later, the Columbus druggist removed some tablets from the labeled bottle, placed them in unlabeled pill boxes, and sold them to a Georgia resident. The druggist was then charged with violating the Federal Food, Drug, and Cosmetic Act.

Did Congress have the power to regulate the sale of pills that a Georgia druggist received from a Georgia wholesaler and sold to a Georgia resident? The U.S. Supreme Court said yes, emphasizing that the congressional effort to require labeling for drugs originally shipped in interstate commerce would be undercut if the Georgia druggist could remove the labels with impunity.[2] Given this type of precedent, there are few, if any, developments in modern technology that are beyond Congress' reach.

Nor is the commerce clause Congress' only source of regulatory authority. As we have seen, Congress has the power to fund scientific research because of its power to spend for the general welfare. But the power to fund includes the power to place lawful conditions on the receipt of funds, at least where the conditions are related to the funding.[3] Thus, for example, when the National Institutes of Health funds research involving human subjects, it requires the institution receiving the funds to establish an institutional review board to protect the subjects' rights.[4]

The states also have the power to regulate technology to protect the public. Indeed this "police power" of the state, and of local governments acting on behalf of the state, has been clear from the country's formation. The only major restriction is that state regulation cannot conflict with federal, because of the supremacy of federal law under the Constitution. Thus, if the federal government regulates a new type of aircraft, no state can have conflicting regulations.[5]

But what about First Amendment protection for scientists? As we have discussed, when scientists publish a paper, the Bill of Rights prevents the government from stopping them. But the rules change completely when scientists move from expressing their views to performing experiments or marketing products. In the latter cases, regulation is permissible to protect the public health and safety or for other valid goals.[6] Scientists may claim that performing an experiment is a way of expressing their beliefs, but that claim will be unavailing. The First Amendment protects speech, not action—punching your neighbor in the nose expresses your views, but it is not protected by the Constitution.[7] Thus biologists have no First Amendment right to perform experiments in their basement when those experiments endanger the safety of the neighbors or the environment. Properly drawn statutes, such as those relating to the use of plutonium, can and do limit scientific experimentation to protect public safety.[8]

Moreover, restrictions on experiments are allowed to protect the subjects of those experiments. Thus there are regulations concerning research using human, fetal, and animal subjects.[9]

There can be difficult cases when it is unclear whether government restrictions on research are based on an improper concern for the intellectual content of that research or a proper concern for public safety. Thus the government would not be free to restrict basement biology experiments if, in fact, the experiments were completely safe, and the government's purpose was to suppress the ideas that might grow out of the research. To hold otherwise would allow the government to practice censorship in the name of public safety. This is why the Supreme Court ruled, for example, that flag burning could not constitutionally be punished—the punishment was for the ideas expressed, not to regulate some other harm, such as pollution caused by the smoke.[10] But in the typical case involving technology, the government has ample constitutional power to regulate. There really are valid health, safety, and environmental concerns that come with the development and marketing of new products.

Thus the Constitution empowers Congress to regulate technology, and Congress has not declined that invitation. In a host of areas ranging from protecting the safety of drugs to producing clean energy, our government has imposed regulations that bear directly on the public availability of new technology. These issues undeniably have a high technical component in two senses: the regulators have to understand the nature of the new technology itself, and they have to understand the often technical questions involved when one looks at the consequences of that technology for the natural and human environment.

Right at the outset, it is clear that the issues involved here implicate a broader range of societal forces than the issues involved in funding basic research. In the latter case, to use Harvey Brooks's terminology, we are concerned with "policy for science," whereas in the former we are looking at "science in policy," a situation involving "matters that are basically political or administrative but are significantly dependent on technical factors."[11] In public issues involving new technology, those technical factors play a role, but they are rarely dispositive. Investors, workers, consumers, and other members of the public often have a stake and often have differing goals and values that cannot be reconciled in scientific terms.

Statutory Regulation through Delegation to Agencies

So how does Congress resolve public policy issues with a high technical component? In a few cases, such as those involving the safety of saccharine and the wisdom of building a supersonic transport plane, elected officials take direct action.[12] But generally speaking, as with basic research, Congress has delegated most of its authority over technology to administrative agencies.

The agencies that regulate technology—such as the Environmental Protection Agency, the Nuclear Regulatory Commission, and the Food and Drug Administration—have the power to issue rules, which have the force and effect of law, and to adjudicate individual cases, such as license applications.[13] Just as there is no single "Department of Science" that controls research funding, there is no single "Department of Regulation." Approaches to controlling technology vary from agency to agency. Moreover, as with the spending agencies, the congressional delegations of authority to the regulatory agencies are so broad that it is the agencies, not Congress, that make most of the difficult decisions. Thus, for example, the Toxic Substances Control Act of 1976 gives the Environmental Protection Agency (EPA) the power to regulate the manufacture and use of new chemical substances. The statute says the agency should, in considering whether to regulate, weigh the costs and benefits of the substance, the economic consequences of the regulation, and act when there is "an unreasonable risk of injury to health or the environment."[14] Obviously the EPA, not Congress, has to make the hard choices.

To some extent, Congress delegates regulatory matters to the Environmental Protection Agency for the same reason it delegates funding matters to the National Science Foundation—the number of cases and the complexity of the technical issues involved outstrip Congress' institutional capabilities. But past that point, there is a central difference in the two areas of delegation. With science funding, as we saw, Congress was calling on the scientific community to govern itself. With regulatory policy, Congress is giving matters to agencies designed to consider a host of factors, including not only technical expertise, but the claims of competing interest groups. Indeed, it is precisely the explosive political nature of regulatory issues that sometimes encourages Congress to pass the buck to a government bureau. Thus the agencies, not Congress, often formulate and implement government policy. This may be wise or unwise, it may undermine or strengthen democratic principles, but it is undeniably the case throughout American government.[15]

When the issues become those of accommodating the interests of competing public groups rather than determining the will of the scientific community, attorneys begin to come to the fore. The relative role of lawyers in the regulatory as opposed to the funding agencies can be sensed by simply looking at who works where. The Nuclear Regulatory Commission, for example, has roughly the same number of employees as the National Science Foundation, but the commission employs over a hundred attorneys, whereas the foundation employs fewer than fifteen.[16] Within the regulatory agencies generally, lawyers, economists, and other nonscientists play large roles, with lawyers being the dominant professional group.[17]

Lawyers have this role because, as we have seen, they are the principle agents for the peaceful resolution of social disputes in American society, and agencies are a microcosm of that society. There is a feedback mechanism at work here: as we will note later, our culture insists on vigorous judicial review of regulatory agency decisions. Judicial review means that lawyers argue in court about agency policies, and it means further that when agencies begin their work they must plan for those court cases and thus they must rely heavily on lawyers.

Thus when regulatory agencies go about their business, they do not stress the consensus-oriented peer review model that the science community brings to the National Science Foundation or the National Institutes of Health. The agencies instead tend toward the adversary approach that mirrors legal norms. The stress is on having every viewpoint represented openly and vigorously. Consensus is seen as a chimera—the goal is giving people their say and reaching a politically acceptable solution, bounded by technical factors but not finally determined by those factors. One important effect is that scientists who enter the process are split apart rather than brought together because they often appear as representatives of particular points of view. Thus, for example, studies comparing American cancer policies with those in other countries find that "the formal and adversarial style of American regulatory decisionmaking . . . polarizes scientific opinion."[18]

Even if the scientific community happens to be in unanimous agreement on the technical aspects of a regulatory issues, that does not mean the scientists will agree on the appropriate policy. People can agree on how much radiation will escape from a reactor, but disagree on whether it makes sense to spend a million dollars to reduce that amount by 5 percent.

Most importantly, even if the science community happens to have a consensus on a particular regulatory policy, that hardly determines the agency's position. The scientific community may, in fact, be inclined in many cases to be supportive of new technologies compared to the public at large, because technology may be the fruit of research and technological success may lead to more research funding. But the validity of a regulatory policy is not a scientific question. Regulatory issues concern, in the end, value questions: how many jobs is it worth to slightly improve the health of a thousand people? How much should consumers pay to reduce the risk of auto accidents by 1 percent?

Questions like these can only be resolved through politics, broadly understood. When the Food and Drug Administration declines to approve a new drug, or when the Nuclear Regulatory Commission defers approval of a new reactor fuel, it is quite possible that most of the scientists in the relevant field would disagree. Regulatory agencies are regularly accused of being "captured" by industry, consumer groups, members of Congress, and bureaucratic inertia. They are never accused of being captured by scientists. The reason is that although scientists work for the agencies, the agencies reflect, to a greater or lesser degree, the whole spectrum of interest groups in American society, and the scientific community is hardly the most numerous or powerful of such groups.

It is true that regulatory agencies such as the Environmental Protection Agency and the Food and Drug Administration often call on science advisory committees to inform them by providing relatively unbiased technical data. There are several hundred such committees reporting to scores of federal agencies in a variety of ways.[19] But even these experts cannot turn political judgments into technical ones; they cannot make differences in values disappear. As Sheila Jasanoff concluded in her pathbreaking study of science advisors in the policy process:

[A]gencies and experts alike should renounce the naive vision of neutral advisory bodies "speaking truth to power," for in regulatory science, more even than in research science, there can be no perfect, objectively verifiable truth. The most one can hope for is a serviceable truth: a state of knowledge that satisfies tests of scientific acceptability and supports reasoned decisionmaking, but also assures those exposed to risk that their interests have not been sacrificed on the altar of an impossible scientific certainty.[20]

The Stringent Judicial Review of Regulatory Decisions

The most dramatic contrast between the science funding and the regulatory agencies comes in the area of judicial review of agency action. When we looked at science spending, we were able to canvass virtually every judicial opinion handed down. There were, after all, only a handful of cases and every one upheld the agency making the funding decision. In the regulatory arena there are thousands of cases, many of them reversing agency conclusions. At the federal level, modern environmental law cases fill volumes. Major projects, from nuclear power plants to pipelines, have been slowed or stopped by litigation. Food and drug law is an entire area of study that includes cases where new products have been delayed in reaching the market or prevented from doing so altogether. In other areas ranging from communications to computers, regulation is a fact of modern life. At the state level, statutes and judicial decisions—in areas ranging from malpractice to products liability to tort suits for exposure to radioactive materials—have subjected technology to close scrutiny.[21]

When judges become involved in regulatory matters involving emerging areas of technology, they do not suddenly talk and act like amateur scientists, openly second-guessing the decisions made by those with technical expertise. Indeed the approach utilized by the judges is, on its face, the same whether the agency action being challenged is a funding decision or a regulatory one. Parties challenging the agency must first overcome various barriers to review by convincing the court that they have standing, that the matter has not been "committed to agency discretion," and so on. When the court does reach the merits, it will look to see if the agency has followed proper procedures and if the agency's decision is "arbitrary and capricious" in the case of a rulemaking, or supported by "substantial evidence on the whole record" in an adjudication. These formulations assume the agency will only be reversed in unusual cases, and, indeed there is still much talk by the courts of deferring to technical expertise. But the judges are acutely aware that the regulatory issues before them combine scientific and policy matters. They want to be sure that controversial policy decisions are made openly and persuasively, not under the guise of scientific neutrality. Thus, the courts apply the same verbal formulations with far more vigor in regulatory than in funding cases.[22]

Moreover, even when a court declines to resolve a technical issue, it still may cause a regulatory delay. In many cases involving judicial review of agency action, the court, if troubled, will remand the case to the agency to enable the agency to change its mind or to provide a better justification for its first decision. Thus, the court is not directly resolving the matter. But in such cases the court is often causing delay, and when the issue is whether to move forward, a delay is a decision. When, for example, a new drug is not available for a certain period of time, those who favor marketing it are losing profits, and potential users of the drug are losing health benefits. But the groups that oppose selling the drug are delighted—the harmful side effects they fear are being avoided, and the market situation may change, making the drug less attractive. That is why, in almost any litigated regulatory dispute, at least one side is happy with delay. Lawyers may not seek delay for its own sake, but if by making every credible argument they drag out a proceeding, they may make their client very happy. An ancient story, well-known to lawyers, illustrates the point. A man sentenced to die at noon, tells the king, "If you'll postpone my execution until tomorrow, I will teach your horse to talk." After the king agrees and leaves for the day, the man's friend asks, "What in the world is your plan?" The man replies, "Who knows? By tomorrow, I may die—the King may die—the horse may talk."

The centrality of the judicial role in regulation did not happen by chance. With science funding there were no important counterweights to the science community itself and thus no major role for the courts. With regulation, countless individuals and groups are immediately affected. But the agencies that make the initial decision are not fully trusted. Agency officials are not elected—they are appointed by the executive at the highest level and chosen by the civil service system below that. They use expertise as well as make value judgments. For most day-to-day issues direct involvement by Congress or the president is unrealistic. In the end, our society insists that judges vigorously review regulatory agency action. As James Q. Wilson concluded in reviewing a study that considered, among other things, judicial reversal of benzene and clean air standards formulated by agencies:

This very diffusion of political supervision of regulatory agencies has facilitated a striking growth in judicial supervision of them. The courts provide a ready and willing forum in which contending interests may struggle over the justification and interpretation of specific rules and practices, matters that ordinarily are of little interest to congressional committees or the White House. . . . And though both industry and its critics grumble about the burdens of litigation, especially when a decision goes against them, one suspects that each finds court appeals of regulatory decisions an economical way to advance or protect its interests.[23]

Thus in our complex, heterogeneous nation, with many citizens possessing legally protected interests, technological change is not allowed to proceed regardless of its impact. Indeed, the notion that somehow technology could proceed "without legal control" is virtually meaningless. A system of property laws is necessary if a new invention is to be worth anything, and legal protection of the public health and safety is a precondition to a functioning society.

Obviously, legal control of technology is not something new and different from the lawyer's point of view. From the railroad to the automobile to the airplane and beyond, legal doctrines have been shaped by technology and have, in turn, shaped technology itself. The law had to adjust to new issues raised by airplanes passing over property; airplanes had to be built with legal notions of tort liability in mind. The American legal system's adjustment to the industrial revolution suggests that it will adjust to the technological revolutions that lie ahead. Thus we see again the contrast between the scientists' sense of a world making progress and the lawyers' sense of a more or less endless process of mediating social disputes. J. D. Watson exuberantly described his path-breaking work in formulating the double helix model for DNA as "perhaps the most famous event in biology since Darwin's book."[24] Yet in an early discussion of legal controls on recombinant DNA research, the prominent attorney and legal scholar Harold Green reported that he was "happy to say" that nothing "unique or novel" in such research insulated it from regulation.[25]

Thus, from the scientists' point of view, legal control of technology provides quite a jolt. The centrality of the science community in funding decisions gives way when the broader society becomes involved in decisions on the application of technology. Previously marginal scientists, with little impact on funding, move to center stage because of their involvement with citizen groups on technological issues. No longer do they fear ostracism from the science community because they now play a role in a new community dominated by non-scientists. Most often the jolt for the science community comes when a technology it regards as reasonably safe and valuable meets vigorous resistance. Nuclear energy provides an example. But the problem can arise in the other direction as well, when something viewed by the science community as pseudoscience (such as laetrile) gains public support.

The Regulatory Gap

Thus, the stage is set for what I call the *regulatory gap*—a gap between research and application that has enormous practical consequences. The gap stems from the fact that basic research receives unusually little public scrutiny while applications of that research receive an extraordinary dose of public involvement. We have discussed why basic research is largely left to the science community. Why is technology treated so differently? There is always, of course, less interest in theory than in application. When matters impinge directly on your personal life you obviously become more concerned. But something sharper is going on with modern technology. The level of public scrutiny is extraordinarily high; debates over novel energy sources, genetic engineering, new medical procedures, and other developments take on the characteristics of holy wars. The societal consensus represented by the views of the science community on research is utterly shattered.

Some of the reasons, of course, stem from factors we have already considered. The American legal framework provides freedom for scientific inquiry and invites public support for basic research, while limiting judicial review. With technology, the legal framework allows vigorous regulation supervised by equally vigorous judicial review. As a result, scientists and lawyers, two professional groups with varying value systems, dominate research and regulation respectively. Thus the stage is set for a gap when ideas become products and when peer review and consensus give way to adversary procedures and interest group politics.

But the regulatory gap is even deeper than this model would predict. The legal framework provides broad guidelines within which social conflict is resolved. If our culture were more comfortable with new technology the gap would, in practice, be reduced. Fewer interest groups would fight the latest technological developments and fewer judges would deploy the weapons of judicial review in an aggressive manner in this field. There would still be a gap, but it would be more modest.

Instead, the regulatory gap created by our legal structure is exacerbated by twentieth-century attitudes toward progress and technology. As we saw in our discussion of religion in American life, the unified

Enlightenment ideal of progress has fragmented. Whereas science still appears to make progress, the human condition does not. The horrors of twentieth-century totalitarian regimes and of modern war have engendered a deep pessimism about the human future. And technology has hardly been exempt. Indeed, since the atomic bomb, technology has been particularly implicated in many minds with the failures rather than the successes of the human race. Spurred by the Vietnam War and the growth of the environmental movement, the decades since the 1950s have seen ever-sharper questioning of technology.[26] At the same time, the continued march of theoretical science provides an endless stream of ideas that play a major role in American life. We are happy to learn of discoveries about the nature of the universe and to ponder their implications; we are more cautious about the actual products that appear in the marketplace.

Cultural patterns of this type are not the result of logical syllogisms. Countless Americans enjoy the conveniences of modern technology while remaining convinced that technology has "gotten out of hand." Whether rational or not, the transition from theory to practice in the realm of science and technology is remarkably rocky.

Comparisons with other fields illustrate the point. Of course, science is not the only area where theory is less controversial than practice. But the regulatory gap in science is far wider than in other areas.

Consider health policy. Since the Truman administration, the American polity has, at various times, debated the broad issue of medical coverage. Should basic care be provided for the needy, for the aged, for everyone? This debate—the "basic science," if you will—has involved wide segments of the public. We have not delegated to a narrow professional group (such as economists or doctors) the task of shaping policy. When government agencies such as the federal Department of Health and Human Services promulgate broad guidelines for programs like Medicare and Medicaid, judges do not shrink from active judicial review.[27] As a result, when agencies make individual determinations as to who is eligible for a particular benefit and the courts review that decision, the system continues to function. Of course there are controversies about the application of broad guidelines in many cases, but we do not see the system grinding to a halt as happens when an entire power plant or even an entire mode of energy production never makes it on-line.

Or consider zoning law. Zoning decisions, although they may affect the quality of life of many citizens, rarely have the broad, dramatic impact of, for example, a development in communications or energy. Yet initial zoning policy—broad, "theoretical" planning—undergoes far more public scrutiny than basic science policy. Comprehensive planning documents for various communities may be the subject of public forums, debates, and newspaper editorials that would be unheard of for, say, initial research in computer science. Moreover, there is a growing number of jurisdictions in which legislation provides that individual land use decisions must be consistent with broader zoning plans.[28] The "technology" must fit the "science." Thus, in zoning, although not everything proceeds smoothly, there is at least some reason to expect continuity between theory and practice.

There is no point arguing whether the regulatory gap in science is different in degree or in kind from the gap between theory and practice in other fields. The fact remains that the gap is vast. Moreover, it has tremendous consequences for public policy in America today. Perhaps the most dramatic example to date has been that of civilian nuclear energy.

The Case of Nuclear Fission

After World War II, an enormous government research effort was devoted to the development of nuclear reactors for the generation of electricity. Optimism was so high that President Eisenhower could say in 1953 that with adequate uranium resources nuclear energy "would rapidly be transformed into universal, efficient and economic usage."[29]

The fission reactors developed by the early government and industrial effort were largely acceptable to the scientific community. Tremendous support was placed behind one particular approach, the so-called light water reactor. Relatively little support was given to other approaches. Beginning in the 1970s, however, years before the 1979 accident at Three-Mile Island, public concerns over environmental, safety, and economic factors led to a tremendous slowdown in the civilian nuclear program. Regulatory issues came to the forefront, as countless lawsuits added to the licensing time for reactors. The nuclear industry was buffeted by complaints concerning cost, safety, waste disposal, vulnerability to terrorists, and the political costs of large, central power plants. State and federal regulation tightened in response to these public concerns.[30]

The nuclear industry did not lose every courtroom or legislative battle, but at times it must have seemed as though the battles would never cease. Consider state regulation of reactors. In 1976, California passed legislation placing a moratorium on certification of new nuclear plants until a state commission determined that there was a demonstrated way to dispose of high level nuclear waste. The industry went to court, arguing that the California law conflicted with federal laws pervasively regulating nuclear energy and setting up a process for the development of nuclear waste storage technologies. The U.S. Supreme Court ruled in favor of the California law, finding that federal law regulated the safety aspects of nuclear energy but not the economic aspects. The California law, the Court said, was motivated by concern that waste storage might make nuclear energy uneconomic.[31] The industry was, of course, disappointed with losing the case, but it felt that at least the court had established that the federal government regulated nuclear safety. The industry thus had reason to be confident when the Karen Silkwood case reached the Supreme Court.

Karen Silkwood was a laboratory analyst in a Kerr-McGee plant that fabricated plutonium fuel pins for nuclear reactors. She was contaminated by plutonium under controversial circumstances. After her death in an automobile accident, her estate sued under state law to recover damages due to her contamination. The jury awarded the Silkwood estate punitive damages, in effect punishing Kerr-McGee for endangering Silkwood. On review in the Supreme Court, Kerr-McGee argued that the Court's decision in the earlier California case established that federal law had sole authority in matters of nuclear safety. But the Court disagreed, finding that Congress intended federal regulation of nuclear safety to coexist with state tort laws. The Court concluded "there is tension between the conclusion that safety regulation is the exclusive concern of the federal law and the conclusion that a state may nevertheless award damages on its own law of liability," but the Court concluded that "Congress intended to stand by both concepts and to tolerate whatever tension there was between them."[32]

We saw before how disappointed grant applicants challenging actions by the dominant scientific community felt they were facing a Kafkaesque maze. Every corridor of potential judicial relief led to a dead end. Now, on the other side of the regulatory gap, it is the proponents of a new technology, often supported by the dominant scientific community, who themselves face an endless course of regulatory obstacles, where surmounting one leads only to another. The result is not that nuclear power suddenly stops. There is no public consensus to forbid new developments, however controversial. But there is a full dose of public control, slowing technological process.

The dramatic change in nuclear power's fortunes from the days of early research to the present is due in large part to the regulatory gap. More attention in the early years to social concerns that would accompany commercialization would have reduced later regulatory problems. As one scientist has written:

As soon as we found a concept that worked reasonably well, powerful forces drove that machine, the L[ight] W[ater] R[eactor], to prominence. We did not take the time to test, modify, and finally choose the "best" nuclear reactor among many competitors. Now we know that safer, smaller, and probably cheaper fission reactors can be built.[33]

Some members of the public would have opposed nuclear energy in any form, but there is considerable evidence that other reactor designs, ignored in the early years, might have proven more acceptable to many citizens. In particular, early attention to waste disposal and to the health effects of radiation would have paid off. It appears possible, for example, that a design known as the modular high-temperature gas-cooled reactor, used in other countries for decades, might be socially superior to the conventional light water reactor.[34]

Another nuclear technology—the breeder reactor—is also a victim of the regulatory gap. The breeder is a fission reactor that runs on plutonium. While it is operating, it converts a relatively common form of uranium into more plutonium.[35] This increases the availability of fuel, but plutonium is a more dangerous fuel than that used in conventional reactors. Nonetheless, because of its fuel efficiency, the construction of breeder reactors was "an almost unanimous ambition of civilian nuclear scientists" after World War II.[36] Given its origins in the insulated world of science, it is not surprising that the Clinch River Breeder, a demonstration project that received billions of dollars before being slowed by litigation and stopped by Congress, represented a design far from optimal for meeting social concerns, such as the need to safeguard plutonium from terrorists who might fashion it into bombs.[37] Other designs, potentially superior in social terms, were slighted.[38] The breeder thus fell victim to the regulatory gap.

Computers and Regulation

If nuclear energy is the most dramatic example of the regulatory gap it is far from the only one. Virtually every technology that comes on-line must struggle with legal requirements that stem from a process-oriented system in which countless groups have a say. Perhaps the clearest way to see this is to consider the computer industry, one of the fast-growing segments of American technology. Here the regulatory gap has been nowhere near as destructive as with nuclear energy, yet it has taken a toll.

We tend to think of the computer industry today as a rapidly growing consumer-oriented portion of the private sector. But as with so many areas of modern technology, a major spur for initial research came from the federal government. The rising tide of immigration made the government's task of taking the 1880 census extremely difficult. It was becoming hard to complete one census in the ten-year period before the next had to begin. Thus in 1889, the superintendent of the 1890 census held a competition to find an improved way to handle census data. The winner was an electrically powered calculating machine developed by two men, John Billings and Herman Hollerith, who had previously worked for the census office. Computers were given a tremendous boost when this machine successfully handled the 1890 census.

The federal government continued to support developments in computer sciences, particularly because of the need for computers in World War II and in the immediate postwar era.[39] Today, an enormous private computer industry serves much of the American population in areas ranging from finances to communications. But having made the transition to the commercial sector, developments in computer science that are perfectly acceptable from a technical point of view have increasingly run into regulatory issues not on the agenda of the basic researchers. As a result, development of the computer industry, although still rapid, is not trouble-free.

A series of Supreme Court cases concerning the patentability of computer programs provides a classic illustration of the often rocky relationship between regulation and new technology. Patents give the inventor a seventeen-year monopoly for certain useful nonobvious inventions. Once you have a patent, your monopoly is good even against others who later come up with the same idea. Can a computer program be patentable? To a nonlawyer that might seem like a yes or no question. But it turns out to be a good deal more complicated, and thus the matter of providing incentives to those who write programs turns out to be a difficult regulatory issue.

In October 1963 the patent office received a patent application for a method of converting numbers from one form to another. The inventors, Gary Benson and Arthur Tabbott, had written an algorithm—a step-by-step procedure—for taking numbers written in a traditional format and converting them into binary numbers. In the binary system—which is often used in computers—all numbers are expressed as combinations of the two digits zero and 1. The number one for example, is expressed as 001, the number two is 010, the number three is 011, the number four is 100, and so on. The inventors' algorithm was designed for use in computers. In effect, the inventors were seeking to patent a particular computer program—one that used mathematical techniques to put numbers in binary form. The patent office rejected the application, and when the inventors' challenge to that decision reached the Supreme Court, it unanimously agreed with the patent office. The Court referred to the familiar rule that one cannot patent a law of nature or mathematics, and said that a patent for Benson and Tabbott would, in effect, preempt the use of a particular mathematical formula. The fact that the formula was set forth as a step-by-step computer program was irrelevant.[40]

But matters soon became more complicated. In 1978, the Court considered Dale Flook's application for a patent on a method for calculating "alarm limits." In oil refining and other industries, various operating conditions, such as temperature and pressure, are constantly monitored while certain chemical conversion processes take place. When the monitoring reveals that an inefficient or dangerous condition exists, the "alarm limit" is reached and an alarm goes off. Because conditions change as a chemical conversion process starts up or slows down, the "alarm limit" must be updated so that the alarm will only sound when there really is a problem. Flook sought a patent on a three-step method for updating alarm limits: (1) measure the present value of the variables, such as temperature; (2) use an algorithm, that is a step-by-step procedure, to calculate an updated alarm limit based on those variables; and (3) replace the old alarm limit with the updated value. The algorithm

Flook devised for step 2 was designed to be used by a computer—it was, in effect, a computer program.

A majority of the Supreme Court, in an opinion by Justice Stevens, held that no patent should be awarded to Flook. Stevens reasoned that the only new thing in Flook's process was step 2, the computer program for calculating the alarm limit. Allowing a patent for this program would be allowing the patenting of a mathematical formula, in contravention of the binary conversion case and earlier precedent.[41] But three members of the Court, in a dissent by Justice Stewart, saw it differently. To them, Flook was trying to patent a new three-step process. He should not be barred because one part of that process involved the use of a formula. After all, Stewart reasoned, thousands of processes involve, at some point, an unpatentable formula.[42]

Just three years later, the dissenters in the Flook case found themselves in the majority. The patent application of James Diehr and Theodore Lutton concerned a method for converting raw, uncured synthetic rubber into a cured and therefore usable final product. Their method involved using a mold to shape the uncured rubber under heat and pressure for just the right amount of time. Diehr and Lutton used a standard formula that revealed, based on the temperature, time, and so on, when to open the mold. They devised a way to constantly measure the conditions inside the mold, feed those figures into a computer, and have the computer continually update the standard formula until the formula indicated the mold should be opened. The patent office declined to grant a patent. However, this time, in 1981, the Supreme Court reversed. Justice Rehnquist, who had dissented in the Flook case, wrote for a majority of the Court that this patent application was different than Flook's. Whereas Flook was seeking simply to patent a formula, Diehr and Lutton had devised an entire improved process for curing rubber in which a computer program simply played a part.[43]

Justice Stevens, who had written the Flook opinion, was joined by three other justices in dissent. The dissenters saw no difference between Flook's method of calculating an alarm limit for chemical conversions and Diehr and Lutton's method for calculating how long to cure rubber.[44]

It is important to note that Rehnquist, in the rubber curing case, did not overrule the Flook case even though he had dissented there. The difference in the two cases, in terms of the attitudes of particular Justices, was that Justices White and Powell voted to deny Flook a patent but to grant one to Diehr and Lutton. By distinguishing rather than overruling Flook, Rehnquist won the support of White and Powell and left the Court room to maneuver in the future.

Before you become too critical of the Court's efforts in this area, consider the difficulties of the task. The patent monopoly is a tremendous incentive to inventors but it is costly to others who seek to enter a field. Precisely how much incentive is desirable in a field like computer programming? Moreover, what does it mean to allow or disallow patents for programs, when those programs are imbedded in complex products and processes? As the progression from binary number conversion to curing rubber indicates, these cases can become more and more difficult.

Today the issue of the patentability of computer software remains intensely controversial. Litigation is extensive, and the costs of that litigation include, at times, a slowing of the innovation process.[45] Companies like to know how they will protect their intellectual property rights before investing, and the uncertain state of the law makes that difficult. Moreover, many computer scientists believe that when computer software is involved, the patent process makes progress less rather than more likely.[46]

Indeed, the patent question is simply the tip of the iceberg of incentive issues for computer scientists. The computer field moves so rapidly that even when patents are available, getting one may be too slow a process to be worthwhile. And having one may provide little of value when the field rapidly shifts course. Accordingly, a good deal of attention, including regulatory attention, has shifted to copyright law, another way of protecting the computer scientists' intellectual property.

A copyright is much more easily obtained than a patent and the protection lasts longer. But a copyright, unlike a patent, does not protect you against someone who independently comes up with the same idea. Should copyrights be available for various types of computer programs? After much debate, Congress and the courts have generally said yes; however, regulatory issues remain, concerning, for example, whether and how copyrights should cover the "look and feel" of a program—its interface with the user—as well as its internal codes.[47] Here, as with patents, uncertainty has bred litigation and delays.[48]

Thus although the computer industry has moved fast, it has been slowed by legal disputes over intellectual property, and grumbling by computer scientists has inevitably followed. In principle, the regulatory gap here could have been narrowed. From the beginning, computer software did not easily fit into existing categories; indeed, it blurred the distinction between patent and copyright.[49] In recent years, scholars have suggested that a new form of intellectual property protection should be tailored precisely for software.[50] But these proposals come after years of litigation and delay and they plunge into a world in which caution and compromise inevitably rule. There is little support for having computer software "unregulated"—with no legal protection, thefts would be so common that the incentive to innovate and market would fade. But regulation when it comes is something of a cold shower to a new technology. Understandably, the early writers of computer software did not focus on the protection of intellectual property.

The Emergence of the Science Counselor

The regulatory gap is a deeply entrenched feature of the modern American legal landscape. It will never disappear entirely, because the difference in world view between scientists and lawyers will never disappear entirely. But can the gap be narrowed? Developments in recent years suggest that some narrowing will take place as an increasing number of scientists become what I call *science counselors*.[51]

Narrowing the regulatory gap is a matter of self-interest for the scientific community. When a technology slows or grinds to a halt after billions have been invested, the pessimism and discontent that follows is widespread. It could eventually poison public support for basic research itself. Pure scientists may love science for its own sake, but the public funds it because of potential payoffs.

Science counselors are scientists doing research who shape that research, early on, to increase the likelihood that the resulting commercial product will encounter a relatively calm regulatory climate. They are not cheerleaders who proclaim that science will solve the world's ills at no cost. They are cautious and prudent researchers who bring social factors into the research process.

Science counselors are not a panacea. Nothing can remove the pinch of regulation entirely. Any new product alters rights in ways that create disputes, but the most wasteful outcomes can often be avoided. Scientific research need not produce the type of product that is least acceptable to society. That outcome follows from the indifference of researchers to commercialization. If research is guided by a socially conscious hand from the outset, choices can be made that improve the product's chances of relatively smooth commercialization. Scientists increasingly realize that taking these steps is in the interests of science. Doing research today without concern for the ultimate legal consequences is like doing a high wire act without the wire.

"Science counselor" is not, of course, a precise job description. There have always been scientists more or less attuned to the social implications of their work. The trend, however, is in the direction of more researchers giving greater weight to those implications.

Perhaps the best way to understand the role of the science counselor is to contrast that role with the others scientists play when they seek to shape public policy.

For decades, American scientists have participated in public debate on large issues such as arms control and the environment. As recently as the immediate post-World War II era, relatively few played this role. For every J. Robert Oppenheimer there were thousands who stayed out of the limelight. As the years went by, more scientists (such as Edward Teller and Linus Pauling) became familiar figures in public debate. Today, on issues like global warming, scientists like Carl Sagan are increasingly prominent participants.

The activities of these "visible scientists,"[52] to use the term popularized by Rae Goodell, have not been free of controversy. Theoretically, scientists enter public debate as expert witnesses, advising politicians, legislatures, and citizens' groups on the technical aspects of public issues. In practice, it is often hard to separate technical advice from personal viewpoints as scientists sometimes offer views in areas far removed from their specialties and seem to arrive at those views through political rather than technical reasoning. Some have condemned scientists for seeking to expand their influence beyond their expertise, whereas others have praised them for going beyond narrow laboratory concerns and entering into wider moral and political discourse. A major motivation for some of these visible scientists has been a sense of moral obligation born of the scientists' role in building the atomic bomb.[53]

The visible scientists, so prominent on television and in other mass media today, tend to be senior figures in their fields, including Nobel laureates. They have often abandoned scientific research altogether as they devote essentially all their efforts to their current political concerns.

Akin to the visible scientists are the "regulatory scientists" analyzed by Sheila Jasanoff and others.[54] These individuals provide advice to government agencies through service on countless advisory committees. They are typically less prominent than the visible scientists, but their efforts are ubiquitous. Like the visible scientists, when they provide advice they are not doing research; they are attempting to provide input into social decisions. They also have to confront the question of whether one can really separate technical from political advice in the policy arena.

There is an inexorable progression from the few presidential science advisors of the World War II era to the scores of "visible" and "regulatory" scientists prominent today to the full-blown emergence of "science counselors." Science counselors, unlike visible and regulatory scientists, do not leave the scientific community to participate in public debate and decision making. They are ordinary researchers in government, in universities, and in private institutions who become informed about potential social issues raised by their work and shape their work in light of those issues. Whereas visible and regulatory scientists are doing policy work, science counselors are doing science.

Because of this difference, the closest analogue to the science counselor is not the visible or regulatory scientist. Rather, it is the science manager who is concerned with budgets and the laboratory's output.

Much research depends on government funding, so the writing of grant and budget requests has become an art. Budgetary decisions shape the type of research done, and science managers are often at the interface, urging their labs to do work that looks attractive and urging agencies to see the lab's work as irresistible. Science managers in government have considerable experience in dealing with the sometimes probing questions of the Office of Management and Budget. Managers in industry, by the same token, must show that scientific work will someday, somehow lead to profits.[55]

Scientists working on this borderline find the job difficult, but budgetary constraints act in a broadbrush manner. When cancer research became enormously popular, a great deal of science became known as cancer research. The science counselor is going a step beyond the traditional science manager who says "fund my lab—it will pay off." Science counselors tell their lab not to follow the road most likely to produce a new source of energy but to follow the road most likely to produce a new, nonpolluting source of energy using raw material available in America.

More fundamentally, science counselors may not head a lab or a research team. They may be ordinary scientists who have absorbed the notion of social constraint into their very concept of what a scientist does. Instead of grumbling about environmental or economic restrictions being imposed on their work by outside forces, they have made those restrictions part of their professional ethic.

Pursuing science for its utility, rather than for the pure expansion of knowledge, has always caused tension for scientists. The tension becomes greater as regulatory requirements sharply define the notion of utility.

The value system of the science counselor can be contrasted with the value systems of traditional scientists and lawyers. The traditional pure scientist is primarily concerned with testable knowledge about the natural world. Progress is defined as growth in our collection of that knowledge, and honors go to the scientist who establishes priority in adding something to that collection. The results of scientific research are ultimately put at the disposal of society for good or ill. When traditional scientists work on a mission-oriented project, their search is for the most scientifically attractive solution—the one that most quickly and neatly resolves the scientific problems presented. Traditional scientists may have strong moral concerns. They may, for example, decline to work in a field because of its implications for weaponry. But this is an all-or-nothing judgment—once scientific work begins, scientific values dominate.

Lawyers in a science policy dispute or elsewhere are primarily concerned with representing their client and protecting the integrity of the decision process itself. Progress in the scientific sense is not a major factor—lawyers are often indifferent to whether the world is better off if their client wins. They may even doubt whether "social progress" is a meaningful phrase. Lawyers believe, instead, that society can best peacefully resolve its disputes if process values are paramount.

The science counselor rejects the lawyer's agnosticism. There must be progress if science is to be worthwhile. But the science counselor also rejects the traditional scientist's notion of progress as simply the expansion of knowledge. For the science counselor, progress is social progress—the creation of socially acceptable technology that serves the public by making life, on balance, more comfortable and serves science by assuring a continued demand for research. The science counselor can argue at times that the search for socially acceptable progress will lead to interesting new areas of scientific research, but the desire for social acceptability may lead to an emphasis by scientists on areas that are scientifically not very interesting but socially quite important. The bottom line is that progress has been redefined away from the pure scientific model.

For generations, engineers have chided scientists for framing great theories with little concern for how they could be applied. In building a skyscraper, engineers are a lot more useful than scientists. The science counselor, in a sense, is responding to this kind of criticism, but from the legal not the engineering point of view. Science counselors are, in part, trying to make science fit social constraints.

Science counselors, nonetheless, must be scientists. A lawyer in this role would lack credibility with scientists, lack intimate knowledge of research, and lack the faith in progress, however dilute, that marks the work of the science counselor. The science counselor embraces, however reluctantly, the legal constraints that mark modern American society. By altering research to fit those constraints, the science counselor seeks to mesh science and society.

The science counselor's work should not be confused with technology assessment. As generally practiced, technology assessment comes too late.[56] Various early warning systems are used by technology assessment organizations to foresee and shape technological development. Scientists, engineers, lawyers, and social scientists engage in technology assessment, whereas Congress relies on technology assessment to narrow the regulatory gap.

Technology assessment, however, is caught in the middle. It comes after millions have been invested in research and development and momentum has begun behind various approaches. Moreover, by the time technology assessment gets underway, real regulation, whether through legislation or litigation, has often begun. Under these circumstances, it is not surprising that technology assessment organizations, such as the congressional Office of Technology Assessment, typically have only advisory powers. They do valuable studies and aid public debate, but the vital public decisions are made elsewhere. The science counselor, by coming onto the scene earlier and shaping the research itself, will avoid the irrelevance that is often the fate of technology assessment. As one public policy analyst has said, in the future the best scientists must master policy issues, even though this will "take time and energy away from their scientific work."[57]

Superconductivity and the Science Counselor

The emergence of the science counselor has been and will remain a gradual process. The origins of the modern science counselor can be traced most directly to the late 1960s when the regulatory gap grew and the threat to science sharpened, partly as a result of the environmental and antiwar movements. In recent years public debates on a variety of issues have been informed by the participation of science counselors. A good example is the emerging field of superconductivity.[58]

Superconductivity is electricity without resistance, the transmission of electrical current without energy loss. Discovered in 1911 by a Dutch physicist, superconductivity was for seventy-five years observed only at near absolute zero temperatures. By 1973, for example, the phenomenon was possible only at minus 418 degrees Fahrenheit, sharply limiting technological applications.

In April 1986, however, two physicists at the IBM Zurich Research Laboratory submitted for publication experimental results showing that in a ceramic compound superconductivity had been observed at minus 397 degrees Fahrenheit. Other scientists joined the search using similar compounds, and the relevant temperature began jumping upward. Although it is not certain, there is now hope that superconductivity may become available under proper conditions at temperatures achievable with ordinary commercial refrigerants, and perhaps even at room temperature.[59]

Various agencies of the federal government—including the Departments of Energy and Defense, and the National Science Foundation—had long funded superconductivity research. But with the recent advances, funding levels have increased sharply.[60]

The potential practical benefits of superconductivity are considerable. At present when electricity is transmitted, as much as 20 percent of the energy is lost in the form of heat generated by resistance in the wire. A superconductivity cable could eliminate that loss, reducing the cost of electricity. Eliminating the heat caused by resistance could also make possible smaller and faster computers, because presently efforts to scale down computers are limited by heat production. Superconductors could also be used in electromagnets to generate intense magnetic fields, opening up possibilities, including magnetically levitated trains.[61]

There has been no shortage of media excitement over superconductivity—the media typically emphasizes scientific breakthroughs and often presents them in the most glowing form.[62] And indeed, the race to make progress in superconductivity was an extraordinarily exciting human as well as scientific process, as ably conveyed in Robert Hazen's *The Breakthrough*. But there will, of course, be difficult decisions down the road as superconductivity moves into technological applications.

For example, some of the recent advances in superconductivity have relied on materials that contain yttrium, a so-called rare earth. Yttrium is not, in fact, rare, and increased uses of superconductivity will require increased production of it. Yttrium is often found in monazite ore, which is presently mined and processed for various purposes. If superconductivity turns out to mean increased work with monazite ore, a rather dramatic example of the regulatory gap is in the offing. Monazite ore is a low-level radioactive compound. In April 1986, the same month the IBM physicists submitted their findings on ceramic superconductors, a federal court handed down a decision in ongoing litigation brought by William Merklin, an employee of Raw Earths, Inc.[63] None of the breathless press accounts on superconductivity mention Mr. Merklin; indeed he did not work with superconductors or even with yttrium. But he did work on processing monazite ore and he did contract cancer of the larynx, throat, and lymph nodes, perhaps from his exposure to the radioactive ore. In the course of its decision, which held that Mr. Merklin might have a viable claim for damages, the court found that "radioactive monazite ore and its refined derivatives are dangerous products" for purposes of certain legal theories.[64]

Of course, this particular risk with superconductivity may never come to pass. But it is quite likely that in practice the applications of superconductivity will raise a variety of health and safety issues. Thallium and mercury, for example, are other possible components in commercial superconductors, and both are quite toxic.[65]

So unless something changes, the regulatory gap will take its toll once again. Some scientists do not see it coming; after all, some of them reacted to developments concerning mercury-based superconductors with enthusiasm, saying these materials have "both intrinsic scientific interest and overlapping technological potential" without ever mentioning the toxicity of mercury.[66] But there does appear to be change on the horizon. With superconductivity, science counselors have begun to emerge. In fact, with all the hyperbole surrounding superconductivity it is primarily scientists who have sounded notes of caution. Dr. John Hulm, for example, director of corporate research and planning at Westinghouse, has said that he had "never seen the country so hysterical about a new technology. It's puzzling and a little dangerous. We are creating expectations that may not be realized."[67] Consider as well the views of Massachusetts Institute of Technology (MIT) professor H. Kent Bowen and of Dr. Siegfried Hecker, director of the Los Alamos National Laboratory. Both have stressed that if the United States is to be competitive in end products using superconductivity we must link scientific progress with manufacturing technology to aid in ultimate commercialization. Bowen has stressed the need to minimize uncertainties about commercial applications, and Hecker has said explicitly that we cannot "disconnect" research from manufacturing and marketing.[68] In the same vein, R. J. Cava, a researcher at AT&T Bell Laboratories, has questioned whether toxic superconductors will ever be widely usable and has discussed the relative public acceptance of mercury as opposed to thallium.[69]

The most dramatic development concerning the social implications of superconductivity has been the creation of a consortium linking American Telephone & Telegraph, International Business Machines, the Massachusetts Institute of Technology, and the Lincoln Laboratories, a government-sponsored MIT lab. This organization is designed to give the United States the lead in commercializing superconductors. It grew out of the recommendation of a White House Science Council Committee, chaired by Ralph E. Gomory, IBM senior vice president for science and technology.[70] That White House committee concluded:

We believe the optimal way to proceed is to take advantage of the scientific strength at universities and government laboratories and infuse it with detailed knowledge of applications. This knowledge is resident in industry. This is best done if the three institutions, university, industry and government, work together to develop goals and to jointly support them, manage them, and review them for progress.[71]

Saying that we should take the scientific strength at universities and government and infuse "it" with a detailed appreciation of applications obscures a basic point. It is people—basic scientific researchers—who will be infused with this practical knowledge. And it is their work—their science—that will be altered.

Thus with superconductivity we are seeing the beginning of a system in which science counselors shape research for social ends. At present, we are in a transitional stage. In the chapters that follow, we will see scientific developments in genetics, fusion, and artificial intelligence that are heading for the regulatory gap. Although science counselors are attempting to soften the blow, it remains true that promises of dramatic technological impact far outstrip the reality. At the same time, these scientific advances are shaping our values even as their practical consequences remain surprisingly distant.

The Human Genome Initiative
and Human Responsibility

The Human Genome Initiative is a massive government undertaking designed to determine the structure of every gene in the human body. It has been presented to the public as a concentrated scientific effort aimed directly at knowledge that will cure disease. In reality it is a controversial multiagency set of programs with unclear medical implications but with a growing impact on how we think of ourselves as individuals.

From its scientific origins to the present, the Human Genome Initiative has illustrated the fundamental relationship between science and society. At the outset, the basic research that made the initiative possible was typical in that it followed an erratic course driven by scientific norms and resistance to political controls.

The Development of Modern Genetics

The story of modern genetics began over a century ago and proceeded with discoveries that followed anything but a straight line.[1] In 1866, the Austrian monk Gregor Mendel published a paper concerning the breeding of sweet peas. Presumably few people in history have failed to notice that living organisms pass on traits to their offspring, but Mendel made an unusually systematic inquiry into the process. When he bred tall peas with tall and short with short, the offspring were true to type—the tall begat tall and the short begat short. When he bred tall and short, the offspring were all tall. But when these mixed ancestry tall plants were crossed, 75 percent of their offspring were tall and 25 percent were short. From these and similar results, Mendel was able to deduce that inherited traits were determined by two heredity units, one from each parent, and that the agents of inheritance might turn out to be dominant or recessive.

Mendel did not, however, know the mechanism through which inheritance took place; indeed, the word *gene* did not exist in his day, nor did he coin it. Unbeknownst to Mendel, at the same time he was crossing sweet peas, the Swiss scientist Friedrich Miescher was determining that what we now call deoxyribonucleic acid (DNA) was found in the nucleus of cells. Miescher was unaware of Mendel's work, and, even if he had been, it is unlikely that any connection between them would have been made. Although Miescher sensed that his work had implications concerning cellular growth, the science and technology of his day were unable to uncover the basic structure of DNA, let alone its relationship to the mechanism of inheritance.

These modest beginnings of modern genetics demonstrate the folly of efforts to force basic research to produce precisely defined social ends. Imagine a regulatory agency that somehow had jurisdiction over farflung researchers such as Mendel and Miescher and that sought to shape all science for specific social ends such as better medicine. Even if such hypothetical masterplanners were indifferent to both the freedom of the researcher and the value of knowledge for its own sake, they would founder on the sheer unpredictability of scientific progress. After Mendel and Miescher it simply was not knowable which characteristics of human beings were inherited, how if at all such characteristics could be changed, and at what cost such changes could be made. It was not even immediately clear if their work related to health or if it had any practical implications at all. Although as research progresses its technological implications become more evident, at the very beginning the future is nearly invisible.

Indeed, the next steps in the unraveling of the human genetic code were not even inspired by Mendel's work, which was published but lay unread for decades. Instead it was Charles Darwin's theory of evolution that sparked the rediscovery of Mendel's ideas and subsequent progress. Darwinian evolution required, of course, that organisms pass on certain traits; otherwise the survival of the fittest would last exactly one generation. Yet Darwin, unaware of Mendel's research, wrote that "[t]he laws

governing inheritance are for the most part unknown. No one can say
... why the child often reverts in certain characteristics to its grandfa-
ther or grandmother or more remote ancestor." [2]

In the latter part of the nineteenth century, controlled experiments in
botany confirmed Darwin's idea that mutations leading to fitness en-
hanced survival. Finally, in 1900, unknown to each other and unaware
of Mendel, three botanists rediscovered Mendel's laws. Each of the
three—Karl Correns of Germany, Erich von Tschermak of Austria, and
Hugo de Vries of Holland—searched the literature, found Mendel's
paper, and credited him for the discovery. Thus we speak today of
Mendel's laws and Mendelian inheritance rather than Correns's laws or
de Vries's inheritance.

Not every scientist has been as gracious as Correns, von Tschermak,
and de Vries, but their reference to Mendel does illustrate the fundamental role priority plays in the value system of science. It's coming in first
that counts—not how well-written your paper is or even how clever you
may be. An independent rediscovery might take as much sheer brilliance
as the original discovery, but it does not generate equal fame. Indeed,
even if the trio of researchers in 1900 had not cited Mendel, we still
might invoke the monk's name if later research had uncovered his work.
By rewarding priority science puts progress first. A researcher seeking
recognition within the scientific establishment is on notice that repeating
old work will not lead to the greatest rewards. Finally, the emphasis on
priority supports the cumulative nature of science. One reads earlier
work to avoid repetition, and one is then in a position to build on
that work.

The contrast with law is striking. Consider the development of the
idea of privacy, a concept that, as we will see, has important implications
for individuals' control over information about their genetic makeup.
Most lawyers and legal scholars associate the early development of
modern privacy law with U.S. Supreme Court Justice Louis D. Brandeis.
It was, after all, Brandeis who wrote the famous dissent in the 1928
Olmstead case in which he called for extending the constitutional protection against unreasonable searches and seizures to wiretapping,[3] a
position the Supreme Court ultimately adopted in 1967.[4] In the most
famous passage in *Olmstead*, Brandeis said that the makers of our
Constitution "conferred, as against the Government, the right to be let
alone—the most comprehensive of rights and the right most valued

by civilized men."[5] Thus we associate Brandeis with "the right to be let alone."

Careful scholars have noted that when Justice Brandeis discussed the "right to be let alone" he was drawing on a law review article, "The Right to Privacy," he had coauthored in 1890 while practicing law.[6] But even here there often seems to be an assumption that it was Brandeis rather than the coauthor, Samuel D. Warren, who was the primary force behind the article. In fact it was Warren, whose marriage to a prominent woman had led magazines to report on his life "in lurid detail," who proposed to Brandeis that the piece be written.[7] In any event, it was neither Brandeis nor Warren who first spoke of privacy as the right to be let alone. As they noted in their article,[8] this idea was drawn from a passage in Thomas Cooley's 1888 *Treatise on the Law of Torts:* "The right to one's person may be said to be a right of complete immunity: to be let alone."[9]

Now Cooley was not an obscure man in his day. He served on the Supreme Court of Michigan, he was a professor of law, and he was a prolific writer on legal topics.[10] If scientific conventions governed, law students today would speak of Cooley's right to privacy. But there is nothing surprising or inappropriate about the use of Brandeis's name instead. Brandeis wrote more powerfully, he applied the idea more broadly, and his position on the U.S. Supreme Court gave his words special importance. Priority alone is hardly decisive in the law.

After the rediscovery of Mendel's laws in 1900, the focus shifted to finding the chemical basis for heredity. By 1940 a series of scientists had established that the units of heredity were contained in sausage-shaped structures called chromosomes in the nucleus of every cell. These chromosomes carried genes that determined an organism's biochemical characteristics. Chromosomes, it had been determined, came in pairs, with each parent providing one of each pair. Genes were known to produce proteins and enzymes, the source of the structure and chemistry of living matter.

In the early 1940s researchers at the Rockefeller Institute in New York found evidence that genes were made of DNA, the substance found decades earlier by Friedrich Miescher in the nucleus of cells. The puzzle was that DNA seemed too simple to carry out genetic instructions while replicating itself for the next generation. The mystery was solved by the 1953 publication of James Watson and Francis Crick's paper setting forth the double helical structure of DNA. A rapid series of later discoveries filled in the precise nature of the genetic code.

The discovery of the double helix is a classic example of the role of aesthetics in science: the double helix was an elegant structure, inspiring Watson to write that he and Crick were convinced that "a structure this pretty just had to exist." [11] A scientist cannot force the world to fit his image of beauty. But that image can inspire his efforts to find something that will later stand up—as the double helix did—to verification by others.

The discovery of the double helix also points up again the centrality of priority in the scientific endeavor, although it is an aspect of priority that is less attractive than the trio of researchers independently crediting Mendel's earlier work. Priority can also mean winning a close race against someone you know is working in your area. Watson was aware that the great scientist Linus Pauling was also seeking to find the structure of DNA. When Watson, immediately after the discovery of the double helix, wrote to professor Max Delbrück about his breakthrough, he urged Delbrück not to tell Pauling:

I was still slightly afraid something would go wrong and did not want Pauling to think about hydrogen-bonded pairs until we had a few more days to digest our position. My request, however, was ignored. Delbrück wanted to tell everyone in his lab. . . . Then there was the even more important consideration that Delbrück hated any form of secrecy in scientific matters. [12]

Watson's experience with the tension between priority and secrecy is typical. Trying to keep matters secret is, if nothing else, difficult. In the end, prompt publication is typically the best guarantee of priority.

As we have seen, the role of priority changes radically when one moves from science to law. Indeed, it is not simply a matter of crediting Brandeis rather than Cooley for the right to privacy because of the former's greater eloquence and prestige. At times, coming in second is better for a judge or a lawyer. Being the first to confront an issue can happen by chance and a result initially reached often has to be amended in light of experience.

Consider, for example, the admissibility in criminal trials of evidence from what has come to be called DNA typing. [13] Apart from identical twins, any two people differ, albeit very slightly, in terms of their DNA. Criminals often leave behind hair follicles, blood stains, or other substances from which DNA can be extracted. A suspect's DNA can then be compared with the crime scene evidence to see if they match. The system is not foolproof. Typing the DNA in the laboratory must be done very carefully so that errors do not creep in. Moreover, with present technology, it is only possible to type a portion of an individual's DNA, so there is a small chance that when two samples match they are, in fact, from different people—the match is simply a coincidence. The odds of such a match between samples from two different individuals' DNA are higher if the two are related, or of the same race, or otherwise more closely linked genetically than two people chosen at random from the world's population.

The first appellate decision ruling on the admissibility of DNA evidence in a criminal trial was a 1988 Florida judgment upholding the use of such evidence.[14] But just being first hardly granted this court any special status. The case reached the court when it did because of the size of the appellate docket, not because of any wisdom on the part of anyone. Moreover, a judge's decision that a certain kind of evidence is admissible does not resolve an issue in the way that a scientific discovery does. In our federal system, other states can take other views and a given court can even reverse itself if relevant value choices or social mores change.

In fact, the 1988 Florida decision has been strongly criticized, particularly on the grounds that the court did not consider thoroughly enough the possibility of laboratory errors or the chances of a coincidental match.[15] A later New York decision that was more careful on these points and excluded the evidence before it has been better received.[16] The point is not that it was a mistake to admit DNA evidence—at present such evidence is admissible in most jurisdictions if it is carefully obtained and analyzed.[17] The point is that the first judicial decision is often the recipient of potshots rather than praise.

In the decades following the discovery of the double helix, the model of inheritance that underlies the Human Genome Initiative came into sharp focus.[18] The term *genome* is used to refer to all the genetic material in the chromosomes of a particular organism. Each human has twenty-three pairs of chromosomes; one in each pair from the father, one from the mother. Each chromosome contains a long strand of DNA, the chemical that makes up the genes. The DNA is a two-stranded chemical polymer with each strand composed of four nucleotides: A (adenine), G (guanine), C (cytosine), and T (thymine). DNA, as Watson and Crick found, is a double helix in that each nucleotide on one strand is precisely paired with another nucleotide on the other strand: A will only bond with T and G will only bond with C. During cell division the double helix "unzips" and each strand can serve as a template for the creation of a complementary strand. Because of the specific bonding between nucleotide pairs, precise replication of the DNA is assured, resulting in two perfect copies.

A given chromosome contains an average of about four thousand genes whereas a given gene consists of anywhere from two thousand to two million nucleotide pairs. Thus a complete description of the human genome would contain about three billion nucleotide pairs. It would appear to be a long list, filling over a million pages in a book, made up entirely of the letters A, T, G, and C.

This list is valuable because gene sequences are consistent within species. Thus a particular gene on a particular human chromosome controls the same trait in all humans. In genetic terms we are more alike than we are different; according to current estimates, the DNA sequences for two randomly selected individuals are likely to be over 99 percent identical—the remainder accounts for the genetic differences between the two.[19] Indeed, the current belief is that human and chimpanzee sequences are about 98 percent identical.[20]

The Human Genome Initiative is not going to actually take a single person and list his or her three billion nucleotide pairs—it will instead be a composite drawn from cell lines of people around the world over several decades. The effort, which is underway but will require further advances in technology to be practical, is expected to cost about $3 billion over the next ten years. The result will be in essence a reference set, enabling, for example, comparisons to be drawn with people suffering certain ailments in an effort to find a genetic cause.

The Political History of the Genome Initiative

It would be hard to imagine a more unitary goal than mapping the human genome. One might expect that here at least a single federal agency would do the job. But fragmentation, not unity, is central to American science spending, and that truth holds true here.

The political history of the Human Genome Initiative reveals the strengths and weaknesses of our decentralized approach to government science.[21] As early as the 1970s there were discussions concerning whether it would be sensible to map the human genome. At first, the federal government did not show much interest. Those efforts that did take place were found largely in the private sector, particularly at the philanthropic Howard Hughes Medical Institute.

In 1984, however, the Department of Energy held a conference in Alta, Utah, which began substantial federal involvement. As a successor agency to the Atomic Energy Commission, the Department of Energy had a special interest in the effects of radiation. The Alta meeting focused on whether advances in DNA research could improve the government's ability to detect increases in mutations among survivors of the atomic bombings of Hiroshima and Nagasaki. Participants in the meeting discussed the possibility that a reference sequence of the human genome could be helpful in this endeavor. By the time of a 1986 conference in Santa Fe, New Mexico, enthusiasm for sequencing the genome had grown; shortly thereafter, officials at the Department of Energy reallocated a few million dollars of previously appropriated money to begin the Human Genome Initiative. Support was then sought and won for congressional appropriations to keep the project going. The initial reallocation was not unusual in terms of the reality of how large agencies, particularly in the technical field of science spending, operate and, as we have seen, it is not the sort of decision typically subject to judicial oversight.

As word spread in the scientific community about the Department of Energy effort, officials at the National Institutes of Health inevitably became interested. The NIH, after all, is the leading supporter of biomedical research in the United States, and it could see implications of the genome initiative in health areas far removed from mutations caused by radiation. By 1987, NIH had created its own office of genome research and had begun to receive federal funding.

In its early stages, both in the Department of Energy and in NIH, the genome initiative was pushed by research scientists. As one commentator has noted:

The history of the genome project makes it clear that scientists played a crucial role in starting it, and they were the sources to which policymakers turned for advice along the way. . . . A few pivotal scientific figures—the scientists who took the trouble to learn about the policy process and to interact with it—

clearly had enormous influence. Watson was preeminent among these, but Hood, Gilbert, Bodmer, Baltimore, Berg, Dulbecco, Alberts, Cantor, Olson, and others had major effects at critical junctures.[22]

The attraction of scientists to the genome project stems in part from adherence to purely scientific values. If it is desirable, as many scientists believe, simply to know as much as possible about the way the world is, then knowing the genetic makeup of humans is a worthy goal. There is a kind of elegance in a finite list of four letters in various combinations representing the complete genetic identity of the human species. Surely this helps explain the desire of many scientists to map and sequence the entire human genome, even though 90 percent of the base pairs appear to have no genetic function and the money used in this endeavor could obviously be used in other ways.[23]

Today the Department of Energy and NIH coordinate their genome efforts, and seek to coordinate as well with efforts in the private sector and overseas. Nonetheless there is unavoidable inefficiency in having two major agencies working together in this fashion. This is most dramatically demonstrated in Congress. Because no one agency (let alone a Department of Science) runs the genome show, no one committee has jurisdiction over authorizing the spending of the taxpayers' money. Thus in the House of Representatives, authorization for the Department of Energy's genome program goes through the Science, Space, and Technology Committee, whereas the NIH seeks genome money from the Labor, Health, Human Services, and Education Committee. On the Senate side, things are no better organized: the Department of Energy genome project answers to the Energy and Natural Resources Committee, whereas NIH genome requests are analyzed by the Health and Environment Committee. Indeed, even this catalogue is not exhaustive; some genome money is spent by still a third federal agency, the National Science Foundation, which answers to its own pattern of oversight on Capitol Hill.

To someone new to American science, this approach would seem at least odd, and almost surely controversial. But here as in other areas of science we are comfortable with inefficiency because of our fear of centralization. Different agencies means different approaches, and new technologies for analyzing genetic material will have to be developed if the Human Genome Initiative is to be finished without unreasonable expense. Moreover, disparate funding sources provide some protection against sudden reductions in government support. Thus the Congressional Office of Technology Assessment rejects even designating a lead agency for the genome effort: "if there were a single lead agency controlling genome projects, the choices would be limited, diminishing the pluralistic funding that has been a mainstay of American biology."[24]

And so the Human Genome Initiative moves forward in typical American fashion: in an array of agencies the scientific community, motivated in large part by the ethos of pure science, shapes the direction of research. Supervision by Congress is limited, and control by the judiciary is essentially nonexistent. The result is that the Human Genome Initiative, like much of American science, lumbers forward a bit slowly but it does keep moving; indeed, it becomes close to unstoppable once it is fully underway.

Big Science versus Little Science in Genome Research

This account should not be taken to suggest that there are no divisions in the scientific community concerning the genome initiative. In general, scientists support large budgets for scientific research more or less across the board. Most would rather see cuts in nonscientific programs before cuts are made in science. This approach enabled the scientific community to remain largely unified concerning federal support for research in the decades following World War II. But the budgetary pressures that began to grow in the 1980s brought increasing pressure on scientists to pick and choose concerning which projects they would support before Congress. A key event in this process was a 1988 speech by Frank Press, president of the National Academy of Sciences and former head of the Office of Science and Technology Policy, in which he explicitly called on scientists to provide guidance to politicians on research priorities so that important work could be protected as budgets tightened.[25]

It was in this environment that the Human Genome Initiative began to take shape. Moreover, the initiative was subject to a very specific complaint within the scientific community—it was said to represent "big science" over "little science," a criticism that requires a bit of explanation.

Whereas scientific research may once have been largely the province of the individual or small teams, the twentieth century has seen the growth of activities (such as the Manhattan Project and the space program) that involve hundreds, even thousands, of people and vast sums of money. The classic description and analysis of this trend is *Little Science, Big Science* by Derek J. de Solla Price.[26] Of course, there is a continuum between large and small projects, and there is no reason science programs of various sizes cannot be simultaneously funded, as indeed they are today. But at the extreme ends of the spectrum, undertaking one gigantic project may in reality foreclose funding for hundreds of smaller research grants, while bestowing money on a wide array of small research programs may make it impossible to undertake one or more big ones.

The little science, big science controversy has been largely fought out within the scientific community itself. From the beginning, the Human Genome Initiative has been attacked by some scientists, particularly younger ones, as a misguided intrusion of big science into biomedical research, a field that has been characterized by small initiatives heading in many directions.[27]

A key supporter of these concerns in the early days of the initiative was Ruth Kirschstein, director of the National Institute of General Medical Sciences, a branch of the National Institutes of Health and the largest source of funds in the world for small-scale genetic research.[28] But the initiative was not sidetracked by these concerns, in part because of the important scientists who supported it, and in part because it was not big science in the same way as the superconducting supercollider. The initiative is a centralized effort, but it is carried out in numerous laboratories around the country. Moreover, it involves the development of automated technologies for mapping the gene and of computerized approaches to information problems, both of which are techniques of broad value to biologists doing other, smaller scale research jobs.[29] In the end, the arguments for the initiative carried the day within the scientific community; indeed, the initiative ultimately won the public support of Ruth Kirschstein.[30]

So the scientific community, as is typical, called the shots in the formation and execution of this major research effort. Of course, a continued refrain that helped keep the genome initiative politically palatable was the promise of a payoff down the road, in particular an "immense benefit to the field of medicine."[31] Such claims are certainly plausible. But, as always, these payoffs will be slower in coming and more piecemeal than it appears when the basic research is underway, because it is here that the regulatory gap inevitably comes in. When science leads to technology—when biomedical research leads to medicine—the road is not smooth. In the case of the Human Genome Initiative, the medical payoffs will be slow in coming and controversial, and even the increases in our knowledge about ourselves will lead to problems concerning personal privacy.

Science Counselors at Work

Before turning to these difficulties, however, it must be noted that the gap between science and social impact has been narrowed in the genetics area, at least as compared with our experience with nuclear power. Indeed, the nuclear experience made a difference. In the early 1970s, before there was any Human Genome Initiative, DNA researchers began to work in the related area of recombination. Scientists began to understand that they could alter genetic material and create new biological entities. These scientists themselves saw the possibility not only of better medicines or crops, but of new diseases and new threats to the public safety. One reason they had this level of concern was their sense that they were working in the shadow of nuclear power and nuclear bombs. Thus as early as 1971 cancer researcher Robert Pollack believed that lax safety standards in laboratories doing recombinant DNA research posed a " 'pre-Hiroshima condition—It would be a real disaster if one of the agents now being handled in research should in fact be a real human cancer agent.' "[32] In 1974, future Nobel laureate David Baltimore explained his concerns about biohazards by noting that "we all grew up with the question of the correctness of using the atomic bomb as one of the great moral dilemmas of the second part of the twentieth century. And I don't think that any of us are untouched by that."[33]

The analogy between atomic bombs and recombinant DNA is hardly precise. The first involved a conscious decision by government and scientific leaders to build a weapon of war, and a subsequent decision by the president to use that weapon. By contrast, the main early concern with genetic engineering was that an accident might lead to tragedy; although recombinant DNA research presumably could be used in warfare, that was not the concern Pollack and Baltimore were addressing.

In a larger sense, however, the nuclear experience was relevant. It pointed up the inevitable social consequences when science becomes technology and it dramatized the ways in which those consequences could be negative. Moreover, the debate over the civilian uses of nuclear power, a debate that had already begun by the 1970s, made clear to many scientists and others that weapons were not the only unwelcome consequence of science.

In the recombinant DNA field these heightened concerns had real results. For about seven months in 1974 and 1975, scientists themselves observed an international moratorium on certain DNA research.[34] Subsequently, the scientific community drafted voluntary research safety guidelines that became the basis of later government regulations.[35] In helping to shape the restrictions under which their own research would take place, scientists acted as science counselors, shoring up public acceptance of their work and attempting to pave the way for greater public use of technology.

And this is the way it will be for genetic engineering from now on. Not a moratorium by any means, but a lengthy back-and-forth process in the agencies, courts, and legislatures as the new technology simultaneously adjusts to and alters existing rights and values. The result has been a small but growing industry built on the results of DNA research; a promising field for some investors, but not an instantaneous boom stemming directly from the work of Watson and Crick.[36]

Science counselors have been at work as well with the Human Genome Initiative, and thus, here too, we can expect steady if relatively undramatic commercial progress. In 1989 the government created a working group of scientists and others on the ethical, legal, and social issues related to the initiative, and the government has continued to fund conferences and studies undertaken by this group.[37] These endeavors have undoubtedly illuminated the future to some extent. But even advance warning cannot make the road ahead completely smooth, as the following survey of issues identified by the working group makes clear.[38]

The Regulatory Issues Ahead: Gene Therapy and Privacy

Consider first the matter of gene therapy, the most highly publicized benefit from compiling genetic information. As our knowledge of the human genome has increased, there have been discoveries relating to the genetic basis of disorders such as cystic fibrosis, Huntington's disease, and amyotrophic lateral sclerosis (Lou Gehrig's disease). These discoveries are generally accompanied by the statement that genetic engineering may someday lead to therapies, either for the affected individual or for that person's offspring.[39] But the key word here is "someday." Our actual experience with gene therapy suggests that patience should be the watchword.

The key figure in the first use of human gene therapy was Dr. W. French Anderson, who conceptualized and brought into play a treatment at the National Institutes of Health for two children with severe combined immunodeficiency (SCID).[40] People with SCID are born with a genetic defect that destroys their immune systems and leaves them vulnerable to countless infections. At one time, SCID victims were put in plastic bubbles to protect them from the world around them; more recently, drugs and other treatments provided some relief. Dr. Anderson's approach involved removing blood cells from the victims, using retroviruses to insert normal genes into them, cultivating the repaired cells and then reintroducing them into the body.

This procedure avoided the most controversial application of gene therapy because it did not involve the patient's germline cells; in other words, the changes in the patient would not be passed on to children. Still, when the proposal was formally put forward in 1990, it had to undergo an arduous process of review. There was, after all, the background debate over genetic engineering led by Jeremy Rifkin, as well as the ordinary concerns about the risks of a new treatment. The proposal had to be approved by the Recombinant DNA Advisory Committee of the National Institutes of Health, as well as by the Food and Drug Administration. Dr. Anderson's test received approval and has proceeded with encouraging results. Other proposals have since received approval from the same federal agencies.

Thus the current situation with gene therapy is one where a cautious case-by-case approach is in place for a list of genetic ailments. As the Human Genome Initiative moves forward, new information will be gained that will increase the list of potential defects subject to gene therapy. But as Dr. Anderson himself has explained, this type of therapy as presently practiced will hardly revolutionize modern medicine—it simply is too cumbersome to reach far into the lives of most people:

How much impact will gene therapy have on medical practice in the future? Not a great deal so long as the technique is carried out as it is today, where cells are removed from patient, the desired gene is inserted, and the gene-corrected cells are returned to the patient. This procedure is too dependent on specialized technologies, is too expensive, and requires too much scientific and medical expertise to be used extensively except in major medical centers.... [G]ene therapy will be applied to a broad range of diseases over the next several years, but only thousands, not millions, of patients are treatable by current techniques.[41]

Dr. Anderson speculates that gene therapy will become more widespread when we develop a way to inject vectors that will repair cells into patients just as drugs like insulin are injected now, although he cautions, as a science counselor should, that "[a]lthough the medical potential is bright, the possibility for misuse of genetic engineering technology looms large, so society must ensure that gene therapy is used only for the treatment of disease."[42] Thus gene therapy will move forward slowly, given not only the complex technology involved, but the absence of a societal consensus on what needs to be repaired. Huntington's disease is an easy case, but extreme lack of height, for example, is not.

But what about the benefits the Human Genome Initiative will bring apart from therapy? Surely there is much to be gained in simply knowing one's own genetic code, completely apart from the question of changing that code. The initiative holds out the possibility that someday individuals will be able to find out their own susceptibility and that of their children not only to ailments like cystic fibrosis, but to syndromes like heart disease and certain types of cancer. Even if we assume there are environmental components to these illnesses, and even if we assume there is no magic genetic therapy, surely people would want to know what they are facing so they can, to the extent possible, take precautions.

Actually, we already have evidence that many people simply will not want to know. Consider the case of Huntington's disease, a genetic condition for which the symptoms do not become visible until the carrier reaches middle age. The symptoms are devastating, including dementia, a severe loss of physical control over oneself, and a wasting away as dramatic as that caused by cancer.[43] At present, with Huntington's disease being detectable but not treatable, over half of the at-risk adults advised of the test for its presence decline to take it.[44] Moreover, most geneticists will not test children at all for this ailment, given the possibility that the child, when grown, may not wish to know.[45] In general, with a variety of genetic ailments, researchers have found that revealing the existence of the ailment can cause anxiety, depression, and a feeling that one has been stigmatized.[46]

Even those individuals who want to know all they can about their own health prospects may hesitate before undergoing genetic screening. The reasons are not hard to fathom. First of all, if your genetic information is knowable, insurance companies will want to know it. They will want to charge higher premiums for those likely to get heart attacks than for those who are not predisposed to heart disease. Most importantly, insurance companies will not want to sell their product at all to people who know a lot more than they do about their odds of getting sick. Insurance company representatives have quite predictably and quite appropriately been involved in the discussions to date of the initiative. They and others have already begun to debate whether genetic testing should be required, allowed, or forbidden in the insurance world and how all of these issues intersect with questions relating to national health insurance. No one can presently predict the outcome of any of this, but clearly there are important reasons why society may want to go slowly in gathering and disseminating genetic information.

And insurance issues are small compared to those surrounding employment. Should an airline be able to look at the genetic profile of a potential pilot? What about a school board interested in whether a prospective teacher is likely to contract cancer in the next ten years? Here notions of individual privacy and autonomy will militate strongly against those seeking to gain genetic information about others. Working out the appropriate boundaries will take decades of legislation and litigation. In the meantime, the safest course for many individuals will be to avoid obtaining information about themselves.

So the practical impact of the Human Genome Initiative—the technology that flows from it—will not quickly reshape society. Gene therapies for diseases are likely to remain rare for decades, and those that are proposed will have to undergo years of testing and regulatory approvals before use. The initiative will yield information that can lead to predictions of disease if not cures for many individuals, and this information will have an impact when people plan their careers and their childbearing decisions. But even here concerns about insurance and employment will retard the acquisition and dissemination of information as our legal culture slowly works out an accommodation between privacy and efficiency concerns.

Determinism and Human Values

Yet the Human Genome Initiative already has had an impact on our society. For if the regulatory gap means a delay in technology, the road between basic research and the formation of values remains wide open. Stressing the most dramatic implications of basic research serves the funding goals of science administrators and the professional norms of popular journalists. Thus the mainstream media have already seen the initiative as opening up the possibilities of the most dramatic sort of manipulation of human nature. *Time* magazine headlined a story on the initiative, "Seeking a Godlike Power: Science Promises to Deliver the Blueprint for Human Life."[47] The story referred to genetic technology as giving humankind the "awesome ability," indeed, the "almost godlike power to improve its condition."[48] In another story, *Time* told us that genetic research will give us "the genetic tool kit for building such intellectual traits as musical talent, mathematical genius and, above all, personality."[49] A book reviewer in *Fortune* magazine was no less modest: "In essence, genetic engineering will make humanity mutable. . . . Our great-grandchildren may be more like designed artifacts than random genetic mixes like ourselves."[50]

There are more than a few problems with these formulations; indeed most geneticists recoil from the simplistic determinism that underlies these ideas.[51] Even the terminology is misleading, because most popular accounts seem to assume there will be "a gene" for some trait, when, in fact, monogenic disorders are rare—most common genetic disorders involve the interaction of several genes, often genes on different chromosomes. More importantly, most traits, whether monogenic or multigenic, are shaped by both heredity and environment. Even when Mendel bred tall peas with tall, the offspring would not do very well if they were tossed in vats of acid. All we can typically say is that certain traits are likely to be inherited in an appropriate environment. Most human diseases are genetically linked only in the sense that genes make us more or less susceptible to them; whether we actually get them depends on a host of environmental factors. That is why the periodic discoveries of a "gene for alcoholism" are misleading; some genetic factors may explain why some people drink too much, but many other factors, including everything from family structure to religious practice, play a role in countless cases.[52] This is all the more true with personality traits, not to mention complex ideas like "intelligence." One group of scientists and poli-cymakers concluded that "[t]he number of combinations that 100,000 genes can form interacting with one another and with the environment is essentially infinite, so we do not now foresee [the Human Genome Initiative], at any rate, leading to fundamental changes in what we regard as the nature of the self."[53]

The notion that our knowledge of the gene can lead to "a genetic tool kit" to remake humanity enjoys currency in part because it plays into deep-seated American ideas about the inevitability and desirability of progress—ideas that closely fit with scientific norms. Americans have always tended to believe that our condition can be bettered, including the condition of ourselves. In an earlier era improving the human species was called eugenics, an idea with considerable influence in this coun-try.[54] Indeed, it is precisely the science counselors involved in the Human Genome Initiative who are trying to perform the important function of calming down public expectations about what genetics can do and of pointing up some of the dangers in pushing genetic capabilities to their limits. After all, even if a trait is controllable by genetic manipulation, that hardly means it should be so controlled. Curing Huntington's dis-ease is one thing; "curing" "shortness" is another. As one commentator put it, a "counterattack of technically knowledgeable" voices has tended to subdue "the new eugenics."[55]

Finally, at the deepest level, the public debate about genetic explana-tions of human nature reflects the extraordinary impact of scientific models on the formation of our values. Keep in mind that, for many, the "moderate" position is to temper genetic theories with a recognition of the importance of the environmental factor in human behavior. But even to accept a complex interaction of environment and genes as an explanation of what it is to be human is to accept what remains deeply problematic from nonscientific perspectives. Attributing behavior to genes plus environment is still inherently deterministic. It may make human behavior hard to predict, it may mean that certain behavior can only be explained probabilistically or as the result of chance, but it means that free choice is out of the picture. For the work of scientists that is certainly understandable, and that work has illuminated human actions along with the actions of planets and electrons. But for humans the possibility of free will remains, and the related ideas of responsibility, praise, and blame remain as well. The public discourse about what it is to be human should not be restricted to the scientific world view.

From a philosophical perspective, the Human Genome Initiative adds little if anything to the age-old debate about free will and determinism. It has always been possible to imagine physical causes for human actions, and it has always been possible to argue that nonetheless our sensations of freedom and choice are real and meaningful. Determinists have had their champions, from Hobbes to Hume, as have the opponents of determinism, from Aquinas to Kant to the present.[56] Long before the Human Genome Initiative, the determinist Robert Fearey argued that "[m]an's variegated character and wide capacities have blinded us to the fact that he is in fact as passive to his creation and development, and hence as unaccountable for his actions, as an inanimate machine."[57] Long after the implications of modern genetics became clear, a secular philosopher, Stuart Hampshire, argued that "[o]ne may say that the sense of freedom that men undoubtedly have is to be identified with their power of reflection and with the self-modifying power of thought. The intuition that when we are thinking of ourselves as thinking beings, we are excluding deterministic explanations of our performances, can be justified, so far at least."[58] And these hardly exhaust the positions of what remains a lively area of philosophical debate. Theological scholars continue to analyze the ideas of freedom and responsibility, with some contending, for example, that Christianity holds an individual "responsible for his actions not only to secular authorities and his fellowman, but also to God,"[59] whereas a secular school of thought called compatibilism maintains that deterministic causation is not incompatible with ideas of responsibility. As Michael Moore has argued, when you show that glaciers caused Lake Michigan, you are not showing that Lake Michigan does not exist.[60]

Our public consideration of who we are as humans should be open to purely scientific perspectives, but it should not and it need not be limited to those perspectives. Nothing in the substance of the Human Genome Initiative or in the structure of American law is to the contrary. There is nothing in our ban on established religion or in our settled traditions that prevents discussion of the secular and theological dimensions of the issue of free will in our classrooms as well as in our media. The pathway for scientific influence on our value formation is wide open, but the pathway for other influences can be just as inviting.

Nuclear Fusion: Boundless
Optimism and Limited Energy

The front page of the *Washington Post* trumpets, "U.S. Makes Major Advance in Nuclear Fusion," with the first paragraph quoting a government expert saying this "could lead to the production of the first practical working fusion reactors."[1] This was not a reference to the short-lived hope for "cold fusion," but rather to the long-standing billion-dollar government project to tame the power of the sun for peaceful use. But this headline appeared in 1978, and "working fusion reactors" remain decades away.

The *Washington Post* story was neither the first nor the last time that breakthroughs have been breathlessly announced in the effort to produce energy for electricity by the same process used in the hydrogen bomb. In the late 1950s newspapers in Great Britain wrote about early fusion research with the implication that reactors would soon be on-line.[2] In 1992, the chair of the House Committee on Science, Space, and Technology spoke of a recent "breakthrough" in fusion research while calling for continued American funding of the fusion program.[3] All of this in the face of a program that has yet to achieve "breakeven"[4]—the point where more energy comes out a controlled reaction than goes in—and a program for which the government itself now projects that commercial reactors will not go into operation before 2040.[5]

Clearly fusion has promise. Only the prospect of extraordinary benefits could sustain enthusiasm for a program that has been underway for forty years and is still more than forty years away from commercial reality. The ready availability of fuel and the possibility of safe and environmentally sound reactors has convinced many that fusion could someday outperform not only the nuclear fission process used in current reactors, but other sources of energy as well.

Fusion may someday play a role in American energy supply, but those expecting miracles will be disappointed. Even forty years from now, there will be no magic end to legal and economic constraints on major sources of energy. In the meantime, fusion provides an illuminating view of the hazards of doing big science in a single agency and of the prospects for international cooperation. And it illustrates how even the distant prospect of limitless energy can affect our thinking about the appropriate scale for human technology.

The Underlying Science

The basic science that underpins nuclear fusion goes back more than a hundred years and displays a familiar pattern of unpredictable twists and turns.[6] Discussions of the science of nuclear power usually begin with Albert Einstein's 1907 assertion that, in theory, any tiny bit of matter can be converted into an enormous amount of energy. Although the equation $e = mc^2$ represented a quantum leap in the development of nuclear power, it is arbitrary to regard that formula as the first step. The idea that mass contains energy grew out of Einstein's 1905 paper on the theory of special relativity, which in turn drew in part on the work of the nineteenth-century Scottish physicist James Clerk Maxwell. The progressive nature of science ensures that even the most astonishing ideas have antecedents and even the most ordinary observations may have surprising consequences. Neither Maxwell nor Einstein had the slightest idea when they published their work that it would someday lead to nuclear power.

In the twentieth century the practical task of liberating energy from mass developed along two lines, fission and fusion. In 1938, uranium atoms were split by neutron bombardment, a process quickly termed *nuclear fission*. Splitting the atom left less mass than had existed before the bombardment, the remainder having been given off as energy in accordance with Einstein's equation. Fission served as the source of power for the atomic bombs dropped on Hiroshima and Nagasaki as well as for the civilian nuclear reactors that now provide about 15 percent of the electricity in the United States.

The theory underlying nuclear fusion, the other line of development, emerged before fission, but its practical impact appeared later. As early as 1927, scientists speculated that stars, including our sun, were fueled by the forcing together, or fusing, of two lightweight atoms and this fusion diminished mass and released energy, again in accordance with Einstein's equation. The precise process that powers the stars was determined by Hans A. Bethe in the late 1930s. After World War II, the United States developed the hydrogen bomb, which uses fusion to create destructive capabilities far beyond those of the fission-powered atomic bomb.

In the 1940s, many scientists realized that fusion, like fission, might be harnessed for civilian use. The basic method of generating electricity from fusion parallels that used in generating electricity from fission, coal, or any other heat source. You begin by generating heat, which boils water, thus producing steam to turn turbines that produce electricity.

Producing heat in a controlled manner from fusion is terribly difficult. Because the nuclei of light elements are positively charged, they repel each other electrically. In the enormous gravity of the sun, the nuclei of hydrogen atoms are fused together to the point that a heavier element, helium, is formed and energy is released. On earth, we lack the sun's gravity, so scientists need to achieve temperatures many times hotter than the sun's core while containing the colliding nuclei at those temperatures for a sufficient length of time and at a sufficient density in order for significant amounts of energy to be given off. Fusion researchers discovered in the 1950s that forcing hydrogen isotopes to achieve the necessary temperatures of over 100 million degrees Celsius and the necessary densities was even more difficult than expected. At the temperatures involved in fusion, most atoms are stripped of their electrons with the result that matter becomes a mixture of positively charged nuclei, called ions, and free electrons. Matter in this state is known as plasma and behaves differently from solids, liquids, or gases. An enormous amount of basic scientific research on plasma physics has been and remains necessary for determining how to control a fusion reaction.

Research on fusion has been taking place since the 1950s in the United States, Europe, Russia, and Japan. Some of the most promising results to date took place in late 1991 when the Joint European Torus facility in Great Britain put out about two million watts of energy, and in late 1993 when a Princeton University laboratory produced over five million watts.[7] These tests, however, lasted only a few seconds each and, more importantly, they produced less energy than they consumed.[8] Clearly scientists are still short of the "breakeven" point, where fusion produces more energy than it uses up, and they are even further away from making the reactions "self-sustaining," in other words, capable of keeping themselves going while remaining under control.[9]

Obviously, controlling fusion is an extraordinary undertaking—the head of the American program once described it as "probably the most difficult technical task that has ever been attempted, bar none." [10] But the promise at the end of the road is considerable. The most promising fuel for the fusion reaction is a combination of two isotopes of hydrogen: deuterium and tritium. Deuterium occurs naturally in ordinary water and thus supplies are far more ample than for oil and gas. Tritium, which is radioactive, is produced from lithium, another readily available substance.[11] Moreover, the amounts of deuterium and tritium in reactors would be so small that a malfunction would not cause a major calamity. If something went wrong, the plasma would strike the walls of the containment vessel and quickly cool down.[12] The waste disposal problems also seem less daunting than with nuclear fission. The only radioactivity associated with reactor operation would come from the tritium and from neutrons striking the reactor structure. Neither source is expected to be a major problem. Finally, like nuclear fission, fusion involves no fossil fuels and thus no combustion products that contribute to global warming.[13]

The American Fusion Program

Although it is now seen as a civilian energy program, the American efforts to control fusion began in secret and in the shadow of World War II.[14] Because of the wartime link between nuclear energy and national security, the Atomic Energy Act of 1946 created a nearly complete government monopoly over nuclear matters and set up a new agency, the Atomic Energy Commission, with authority over both the military and civilian aspects of nuclear power. In 1951, the commission created Project Sherwood, a secret program under which laboratories around the country took diverse approaches to the problem of controlling fusion reactions. In 1958, the United States, the former Soviet Union, and Great Britain simultaneously made their fusion programs public.

Today, the American fusion program is run by the Department of Energy, a successor agency to the Atomic Energy Commission. Although a few other agencies play a minor role, fusion is for all practical purposes a Department of Energy operation.[15] At present, that operation is funded at a level of about $300 million a year.[16]

Science counselors have become abundant in the fusion field, as researchers have sought to avoid the sort of overpromising that was so costly to nuclear fission. It is generally politicians and journalists who talk repeatedly of fusion breakthroughs and of solving the energy crises. Dr. William Happer, Director of the Office of Energy Research in the Department of Energy, speaks cautiously of fusion as "an important, long-range element of the National Energy Strategy" and of the need "to improve the environmental and safety characteristic of fusion."[17] His most optimistic goal is "having an operating demonstration power plant by about 2025 and an operating commercial power plant by about 2040."[18]

Even with the appropriate cautions of science counselors, the regulatory gap will be a dramatic one if nuclear fusion ever enters the marketplace. Solving the scientific problems and creating efficient, self-sustaining reactions will be an impressive achievement, but it will not guarantee an economically and environmentally sound technology.

Consider first the costs of fusion energy. Every discussion of this topic begins by noting how inexpensive the fuel will be for fusion reactors. But fuel costs are only a small part of the costs of generating electricity.[19] The high capital costs of building fission reactors contributed to their decline, and fusion will face at least comparable problems. According to Robert L. Park of the American Physical Society, even if "tritium were free and we could use it tomorrow the capital costs of a fusion reactor would make it financially impossible to build in the near future."[20]

Moreover, fusion energy does inevitably involve radioactivity, and thus some public opposition is likely. The radioactivity problem will be less than with fission, and the risk may in any event be far less than numerous societal risks from nonradioactive sources. But unless attitudes change, there will be public opposition on this score.

As noted earlier, radioactivity will be created by two sources in fusion reactors.[21] First, neutrons produced in a fusion reaction will make reactor components radioactive. The extent of this problem will depend on the type of materials used in the components. Second, the radioactive tritium used as fuel diffuses through most metals at high temperatures. Even if tritium were to escape, it is less hazardous than the radioactive materials used in fission reactors and it has a half-life of only twelve years.[22] But people do not necessarily evaluate radiation risks in that fashion. The public outcry that followed an accidental 1979 release of tritium indicates that many people fear radioactivity per se. An Arizona plant made glow-in-the dark watches and self-illuminating signs; when tritium leaked, demonstrators carried signs reading "Tritium Spells Death" and the state ultimately seized the tritium held by the plant.[23] In 1992 and 1993, similar public opposition to tritium contamination flared up in South Carolina and Arizona.[24]

To scientists, these fears may simply be irrational and thus of no consequence. But to politicians, if voters are afraid, that fear in and of itself is a reality that must be dealt with. Of course public education and discourse can change attitudes, but at any given moment public fears are an important element in the real equation of how public policy is formulated.

Alternative Approaches to Fusion

Attention now to these economic and environmental factors could narrow the regulatory gap if fusion ever entered the commercial world. There is more than one way to build a fusion reactor, and the varying approaches may not be fungible from a social point of view. A description of magnetic confinement and inertial confinement—the two basic approaches currently under study—will demonstrate some of the choices now being made and the difficulties in assuring that social factors play a role in those choices. Magnetic and inertial confinement do not exhaust the options available in bringing about controlled fusion,[25] but they illustrate the choices that lie ahead.

In any fusion device, the key problem is to build a container that can hold the plasma when it is at temperatures of literally millions of degrees. Magnetic confinement systems rely on the fact that the plasma consists of charged particles that can be contained by magnetic fields. This approach dates all the way back to Project Sherwood in 1951. The most successful magnetic confinement systems to date are the Soviet-invented doughnut-shaped magnetic bottles called *tokamaks,* a word that comes from the Russian acronym for torodial magnetic chamber.

The alternative approach to fusion containment, one that does not use magnetic fields, is *inertial confinement.* Inertial confinement dates back not to Project Sherwood, but to the 1958 invention of the laser, a device that initially had nothing to do with fusion. Lasers generate powerful and coherent beams of light that can be focused on a spot a few hundred-millionths of an inch wide. By the late 1960s, nuclear scientists were theorizing that a laser could create fusion in tiny pellets of deuterium and tritium. This work had weapons implications and much of it was classified. But the same principles have given rise to research on civilian energy generation. Inertial confinement devices have been built in which several laser beams are focused for less than a billionth of a second on microscopic deuterium-tritium pellets. By crushing the pellet core, the intense pressure achieves very high temperatures and densities. As with magnetic confinement, fusion has been achieved, but not yet in an efficient manner.

Lasers are not the only inertial confinement system. In such systems the pulsed energy source, called the driver, can be heavy or light ion beams rather than laser beams.

The social consequences of magnetic and inertial confinement systems are not identical. Neither is clearly superior and it is difficult to project how either would look in actual operation as part of an electric utility grid. With tokamaks it will be necessary to maintain the large superconducting magnets used to confine the plasma. Lasers, on the other hand, have to be shown to be sufficiently durable to actually work on a day-to-day basis. It seems likely that a given tokamak reactor would generate more electricity than a single laser system, so depending on one's views about centralization of energy production, one system might be better than the other. As to radioactivity, it is plausible that laser systems would involve smaller inventories of tritium than tokamaks.

In an ideal world, different fusion systems would compete so that the most socially desirable option would ultimately be chosen. It may even be that some utilities would choose magnetic confinement systems whereas others would opt for inertial confinement. But the nature of the fusion research program makes it unlikely that both technologies will be available for public scrutiny.

First of all, fusion research takes place, for all practical purposes, in one agency—the Department of Energy. As budgets have tightened, it has become impossible to fund every avenue of research. Magnetic confinement has the enormous advantage of being closer to demonstrating breakeven, or scientific feasibility—in other words, getting out more energy than you put in will probably happen first in a tokamak rather than an inertial confinement device. This result, and the likely follow-ups involving the creation of a self-sustaining reaction, will have important scientific consequences in terms of our understanding of plasma physics. It is unsurprising that scientists want to stress the most scientifically promising approach.

At present, over 80 percent of the roughly $300 million spent annually on fusion goes to magnetic confinement approaches.[26] Although there was a brief period in the 1980s when Department of Energy officials tried to foster more direct competition between magnetic and inertial confinement systems, that ended rather abruptly.[27] At present, Energy Department officials will only assert that commercialization of inertial confinement is a decade or two behind magnetic systems.[28]

In practice, of course, this means that if society ever judges fusion, that judgment will be based on magnetic confinement systems. The enormous investment, both economic and political, necessary to bring a new technology on-line has long-lasting consequences. The situation will be precisely like that with nuclear fission. Light water reactors of a particular design came on-line first and shaped public and political attitudes toward fission. The fact that many believe that alternative reactor designs available today would be superior does not mean that those designs are immediately tried out. Too many people and too many utilities have soured on fission to give other approaches a fair shot. After decades pass, a new style of fission reactor may get a hearing, but the costs in the meantime will have been enormous.

Thus fusion faces the possibility of a dramatic regulatory gap. Of course, it is possible that the first fusion reactor brought on-line will be the best possible from a societal point of view. It is also possible that inertial confinement systems, even if they are societally desirable, are simply not technically feasible. Being socially desirable does not make something scientifically possible. But there is the very real chance that we will miss out on socially promising and scientifically plausible approaches to fusion because they are not presently the leading approaches in the Department of Energy bureaucracy.

The science counselors at work in that bureaucracy have made a difference. There is far more concern today with the social consequences of tokamaks than there ever was with the social consequences of light water fission reactors in the 1950s. But a more thoroughgoing infusion of social values in the research process is not likely in the current bureaucratic environment.

The National Environmental Policy Act and Fusion Research

The current legal regime is not structured to pressure the science bureaucracy to consider alternatives to magnetic confinement more seriously at an earlier date. As we know, it is generally the case that courts exhibit great deference to decisions by the science establishment in the research phase—it is when technologies come on-line that legal norms come to predominate. There is one statute, the National Environmental Policy Act (NEPA), that, on its face and in its conception, might have altered this balance and injected a study of alternatives more forcefully into the current fusion program. But the development of the law under NEPA demonstrates once again how the views of the scientific community hold sway in American research.

The National Environmental Policy Act, passed in 1969, requires that federal agencies prepare environmental impact statements for "proposals for legislation and other major federal actions significantly affecting the quality of the human environment."[29] The references to "major" and "significantly" have been read quite broadly by the courts, so an enormous array of federal actions are subject to the statute; an early case held, for example, that building a jail triggered NEPA's requirements.[30] Moreover, NEPA requires that an environmental impact statement include an analysis of alternatives to the proposed action so that comparisons can be made.[31]

It is unclear whether Congress intended NEPA to be a technology assessment statute.[32] The language is sufficiently vague that it has fallen to the courts to give content to it through litigation. In terms of science policy, the central issue is whether NEPA could be interpreted to mean that the government has to study the environmental implications of and the alternatives to entire research programs, or whether it is sufficient to do separate and discrete impact statements on individual facilities without ever evaluating the overall program.

In the context of the fusion program, the issue plays out as follows: When the federal government builds or licenses a particular test facility, it must do an impact statement on that facility. Thus, for example, when the Department of Energy funded construction of the Tokamak Fusion Test Reactor in Princeton, New Jersey, in the 1970s, it prepared a statement analyzing the effects on the local environment of building and operating the facility, including a study of radiation releases under normal conditions and in case of an accident. The statement even discussed how the 780 people employed at the site would affect local housing conditions and school enrollment.[33]

What the statement did not discuss, however, was the overall direction of the fusion program. The Tokamak Fusion Test Reactor was just one part of a total program that included inertial confinement fusion, albeit at a lower level than magnetic approaches. Should the Department of Energy ever have to prepare a programmatic environmental impact statement for the whole fusion program, a statement that would consider, for example, the alternative of giving greater emphasis to inertial confinement approaches?

In the early years of NEPA litigation, the question of when agencies had to do programmatic impact statements was a major issue. At one time, the Court of Appeals decision in *Scientists' Institute for Public Information, Inc. v. Atomic Energy Commission* (SIPI),[34] imposed serious duties on agencies in this regard—duties that might have actually pushed agencies to at least consider issues they tend to side-step during research. The rise and fall of SIPI illustrates the limits of judicial involvement in basic science.

In SIPI the U.S. Court of Appeals for the District of Columbia Circuit ordered the Atomic Energy Commission, a predecessor of the Department of Energy, to prepare an environmental impact statement for the breeder reactor program. The breeder reactor—later largely abandoned—involved a fission technology in which the reactor, during operation, bred new fuel for other reactors. At the time of SIPI the breeder program was further along than the fusion program is today, but nonetheless it remained years away from having a direct impact on the public.

When SIPI was decided, the commission had begun building a demonstration reactor it hoped to have in operation in about seven years, and an impact statement had been completed for that reactor. The court concluded that at some point an impact statement would also be needed for the entire breeder program; the program came before Congress every year as a "proposal for legislation" in the form of appropriation requests and it would inevitably affect the environment in the future. From the court's perspective, the fundamental issue was determining when the statement for the breeder program had to be prepared. The court thus focused on the central dilemma in controlling scientific research: an impact statement at the beginning of a research program would be meaningless, whereas a statement on the eve of commercialization would be too late. The court quoted from the trial judge's statement to counsel in the SIPI litigation to highlight the problem:

I say this: I say there comes a time, we start out with E equals MC squared, we both agreed you don't have to have the impact statement then. Then there comes a time when there are a thousand of these breeder plants in existence all over the country.

Sometime before that, surely as anything under the present law, there has to be an impact statement, a long time before that, actually.

But the question is exactly where in this chain do we have to have an impact statement.[35]

To solve this problem, the Court of Appeals formulated four factors to be weighed in determining when a statement is necessary:

How likely is the technology to prove commercially feasible, and how soon will that occur? To what extent is meaningful information presently available on the effects of application of the technology and of alternatives and their effects? To what extent are irretrievable commitments being made and options precluded as the development program progresses? How severe will be the environmental effects if the technology does prove commercially feasible?[36]

Applying these factors, the court concluded that an impact statement on the entire breeder program was necessary at that time.

The elements delineated in SIPI represent a substantial effort to guide the application of NEPA to research and development. Of course, this particular formulation could be challenged. The final factor, for example, is phrased in a seemingly negative way ("How severe will be the environmental effects . . . ?"), lending credence to the notion that technology assessment is antitechnology. It would be easy to reformulate this factor by inquiring how substantial the positive or negative environmental effects will be if a technology does prove commercially feasible.

There is no reason early analysis cannot provide a spur to certain areas of scientific research that seem particularly promising from a social perspective.

But, more importantly, SIPI represented a deviation from the usual laissez-faire attitude of the courts and the legal system to basic research. And because of the broad language of NEPA, SIPI had the potential to alter the status quo in a wide variety of areas. But the Supreme Court put an end to that possibility when it rejected the SIPI holding and thus brought NEPA into conformance with the law's usual approach to basic science.

The relevant case was *Kleppe v. Sierra Club*,[37] which involved the Department of Interior's coal leasing program in the Northern Great Plains region. In *Kleppe,* environmental groups brought suit against the Department of the Interior claiming that a comprehensive environmental impact statement was necessary to assess the government's program of issuing coal leases, approving mining plans, and otherwise licensing private companies and public utilities to develop coal reserves on federal land. The plaintiffs maintained that only by looking at the program as a whole could serious environmental analysis be done. The Court of Appeals for the District of Columbia Circuit adapted its four-part SIPI test to include all federal actions, not just technology development programs, and it concluded that enough information was already available on the overall program to do environmental analysis and that the potential environmental effects of the program were severe. The U.S. Supreme Court, however, squarely rejected the SIPI approach:

The [appellate] Court's reasoning and action find no support in the language or legislative history of NEPA. The statute clearly states when an impact statement is required, and mentions nothing about a balancing of factors. Rather . . . under the first sentence of 102(2)(C) the moment at which an agency must have a final statement ready "is the time at which it makes a recommendation or report on a *proposal* for federal action." [38]

The Supreme Court did recognize that in some circumstances a variety of agency actions might be so closely connected to each other that it would be irrational for an agency to deny that it had made a proposal for a broad program and thus an agency would have to do a programmatic environmental impact statement. But the Court emphasized that ordinarily the question of whether an agency had to do a programmatic statement was up to it, because "[r]esolving these issues requires a high level of technical expertise and is properly left to the informed discretion of the responsible federal agencies." [39]

Commentators swiftly noted that *Kleppe* weakened NEPA's ability to inject environmental values at an early point in the decision-making process. [40] Subsequent cases in the basic research context have hammered home the point that it is now the agency—not the courts—that decides when to take a broad look at the implications of a research program, and that agencies rarely are inclined to do that. In *Foundation on Economic Trends v. Lyng*, [41] the plaintiffs wanted the Department of Agriculture to prepare a programmatic impact statement on agency efforts to use recombinant DNA techniques to enhance animal productivity, but the Court rejected the claim, finding that the agency had discretion in this area and the plaintiffs were inappropriately using NEPA as a political weapon to try to force the Department of Agriculture to reevaluate its research priorities. In a similar case, the Court rejected efforts to force the National Institutes of Health to analyze its overall program on the release of genetically engineered organisms into the environment. [42]

Finally, the Supreme Court has squarely rejected as well the alternate theory under which the Court of Appeals in SIPI had imposed a duty to do a broad environmental study—in *Andrus v. Sierra Club* [43] the Supreme Court held that Congress did not intend to reach through NEPA appropriation requests as "proposals for legislation" or "proposals for . . . major Federal actions."

The net effect is that courts will not be in a position to force the Department of Energy to do a programmatic environmental impact statement on the nuclear fusion program. When and if such a statement is done is almost entirely within the control of the agency, as is the scope of any statement that might be prepared.

Now NEPA is simply a statute, not a part of the Constitution. Congress could amend it to both require that agencies do impact statements when the four-part SIPI test is met and to empower courts to engage in searching review of whether agencies are following that mandate. But that is not going to happen. The Supreme Court's rejection of SIPI was hardly idiosyncratic. It fits with our overall societal judgment to leave policy decisions relating to basic research with the scientist-dominated agencies that conduct that research. Neither Congress nor the courts are likely to second-guess the potent combination of bureaucratic and technical expertise that an agency represents.

Funding Problems for Fusion

So the Department of Energy fusion program plows ahead with its focus on the tokamak. But freedom from oversight on tokamaks versus lasers does not translate into massive funding for the program as a whole. On the contrary, the fusion program has proven to be enormously vulnerable to the budgetary constraints that have marked federal policy since the early 1980s. The Department of Energy's annual fusion budget has dropped from over $500 million a year in 1980 to about $300 million at present, a tremendous cut when inflation is taken into account.[44] A particularly telling blow was struck in the early 1990s when the department cancelled plans for the $1.8 billion Burning Plasma Experiment, which was to have been the next major step in the tokamak program.[45]

Several factors have combined against fusion. First of all, the promise of distant payoffs cannot be sustained forever. When a research project seems always to be decades away from commercialization, support will erode. There are benefits to pure science in learning about fusion, but fusion has always presented itself as an energy program first and foremost. Some observers have argued that because it is so unlikely that we could maintain political support for fusion at the level and for the time necessary to produce commercial electricity, the program should be halted.[46]

Moreover, fusion has all of its eggs in one basket—the Department of Energy. Most American science is spread around among numerous agencies, a prudent system in times of tight budgets. This is how science spending generally weathered the 1980s, when a rise in defense-related research offset declines elsewhere. As a big science project centered in one agency and in a few large facilities, fusion also has been cut off from broader support in the community of university scientists.[47] It runs the risk of congressional termination in a single vote—the fate of the superconducting supercollider.

Fusion's rough road politically demonstrates the need to refine the usual division between "big science" and "little science." The Human Genome Initiative is big, in the sense of involving millions of dollars in the pursuit of a single goal, the mapping of the human genome. But the work is spread among many universities, the funding comes from several agencies, and a variety of disciplines, including molecular biology and computer sciences, are involved. Fusion is big, but it is also monolithic. It has increasingly become a single program in a single agency emphasizing a single technology. As such it is a sitting duck for budget cutters.

The reaction of the fusion community to these fiscal problems has been dramatic. The major focus of the program has shifted to a multinational project, the International Thermonuclear Experimental Reactor (ITER). Begun in 1987, ITER is a joint effort by the European Community, Japan, Russia, and the United States to build the largest and most powerful tokamak in history. All four powers have long supported fusion research; indeed, a European tokamak, the Joint European Torus (JET), has enjoyed considerable success. The American fusion community now places great stress on our involvement in ITER.[48]

There is a certain irony here. For decades, in fusion and elsewhere, American science was supported in part on the grounds that we wanted to lead the world, both because of the cold war and for national pride. With the cold war over and budgetary constraints making pride a bit expensive, we now look for other nations to share the financial burden.

There certainly are positive features in this development. If we can spend less money, but end up in the same place technologically, the nation is well served. And working with Europe, Japan, and the former Soviet Union on peaceful projects builds ties that can help international relations generally.

But ITER is no panacea. Even reduced budget requests will continue to come under scrutiny, and the American willingness to spend substantial money for many years on a project in which we are not the unquestioned leaders is uncertain. Moreover, the problem of distant payoffs remains. ITER is still in the design phase; actual construction is years away. If it is built and works to perfection, its supporters say that the next step would be construction of a demonstration reactor, "perhaps within the next three decades."[49]

The Solar Comparison and the Dream of Limitless Energy

So the ability of fusion to provide electricity to our homes remains very uncertain. But fusion has nonetheless already provided fuel for the formation of American values and expectations. Fusion is invariably presented as a potential godsend for our energy needs, and, as such, it plays a role in a familiar story. The scientists' belief in endless progress becomes a central theme in our consideration of our future.

The sharp debates that have already taken place over the desirability of fusion do not undercut this reality, because those debates are invariably in terms of other wondrous technologies that are said to be preferable to fusion. The usual candidate is solar energy. Thus Department of Energy fusion officials are often asked whether their program could compete with "a cheap, efficient solar cell." [50] With solar energy, we are always told, the fuel is free. But as fusion itself illustrates, fuel costs are a small part of total energy costs. A closer look at solar energy reveals the persistence of the American faith in progress.

Solar energy takes a variety of forms. For the production of electricity it is usually associated with the photovoltaic cell. Photovoltaic devices are among the most attractive forms of solar energy because they convert sunlight directly into electricity. Photovoltaics may someday play a central and desirable role in our energy picture, but they are no more magical than fusion reactors. Indeed their development follows the pattern we have seen before and they will face the same challenges as other energy sources.

First of all, the initial development of photovoltaics demonstrates the unplanned nature of scientific progress. [51] In 1839, Edmund Becquerel, a French scientist, observed that when light fell on one side of a certain type of battery cell an electric current was produced. Neither Becquerel nor anyone else could explain this "photoelectric effect." In this century, scientists came to understand the effect in terms of atomic structure— when a photon of light strikes an atom, it can be absorbed by electrons with the added energy driving off one of the atom's outer electrons. The stream of electrons set free in this fashion forms an electric current. In the early part of this century scientists used this knowledge to build the first simple photovoltaic cells. The cells, made of selenium, were so costly and inefficient they had no practical use.

In 1954, researchers at Bell Laboratories accidentally discovered that certain silicon devices produced electricity when exposed to sunlight. Bell Labs pursued the matter because it was interested in finding a way to generate electricity for telephone systems in remote areas not connected to power grids. It turned out that silicon solar cells were much more efficient than selenium. Still the cost of generating electricity with silicon cells was enormous compared with conventional methods. It looked as though photovoltaic devices were again going to be without practical use, and research slowed.

At this point, as is so often the case with basic research, the federal government began to play a major role. Scientists working on the space program needed a power source for satellites. Silicon solar cells filled the bill, particularly because twenty-four-hour sunlight is available in space. By the late 1950s, satellites had solar cells and the National Aeronautics and Space Administration (NASA) had begun funding research into photovoltaics generally.[52]

Today federal support for photovoltaic research continues in several agencies, including NASA and the Department of Energy. Although some photovoltaic devices are in use in remote areas and in demonstration projects, costs are still too high for routine residential use.

Thus research continues on several fronts. There is basic scientific work aimed at a better understanding of the fundamental properties of photovoltaic devices, and there is more applied work aimed at improving production of existing types of devices.[53]

On the surface, photovoltaic devices may seem like an unlikely candidate for the regulatory gap. After all, solar energy is generally described as nonpolluting and inexhaustible. President Carter, for example, said that "[e]nergy from the sun is clear and safe. It will not pollute the air we breath or the water we drink."[54] If costs come down, won't photovoltaic devices march unimpeded into the marketplace?

The short answer is no. President Carter's quote is similar to President Eisenhower's 1953 statement about nuclear energy: "peaceful power from atomic energy is no dream of the future. That capability, already proved, is here—now—today. [With adequate material] this capability would rapidly be transformed into universal, efficient, and economic usage."[55] Just as nuclear fission and fusion do not get a free ride, photovoltaics will not either.

Consider the matter of pollution. Silicon cells remain the leading type of photovoltaic device. Large-scale production of silicon cells would not be entirely benign. It is well-known that exposure to silicon dust, smoke, or fumes poses a health hazard. In particular, inhalation of silicon smoke leads to silicosis, a chronic lung disease. When silicon is present on a small scale, as in glass blowing, the problem is handled by using adequate exhaust ventilation. Large-scale production of silicon cells, however, could mean that exhaust would have an effect on air breathed by the general public.[56]

Other materials used in silicon cell production also could raise problems. Small amounts of boron and phosphorus, which are highly toxic, are used. Freon, used in the cleaning of silicon cells, has raised environmental problems in a variety of settings.[57]

Researchers, seeking higher efficiency for photovoltaic devices, have developed alternatives to silicon. But the leading alternatives do not do away with environmental problems. Cadmium sulfide cells, which are relatively inexpensive to manufacture, rely in part on cadmium, a toxic element that often accumulates in the body, leading to kidney or liver problems. Gallium arsenide cells, which are highly efficient, rely in part on arsenic, which is not only poisonous, but potentially carcinogenic.[58]

None of this means that photovoltaic energy is an environmental disaster. The dangers may well be controllable and they may be far less than the dangers from other ways of generating electricity, including fusion. The point is simply that photovoltaics will not get an exemption from the regulatory gap when they enter the commercial world. Painful and controversial calculations concerning threats to life and health will have to be made. And if a casual approach to photovoltaic safety is taken, the regulatory gap will take its toll. The Occupational Safety and Health Administration, the Environmental Protection Agency, and other regulatory mechanisms are already in place, and thus photovoltaics will automatically be subject to searching review when widespread commercialization begins. Fortunately some science counselors have undertaken to narrow the gap; researchers at Bell Laboratories and at federal laboratories have begun environmental assessments of photovoltaics.[59]

This is not to say that photovoltaic cells and nuclear fusion are comparable sources of electricity in the sense that one could simply add up the costs and benefits and pick a winner. There is a fundamental difference in that solar cells could be placed individually on houses, whereas fusion power would be centralized and then linked to homes by a traditional electricity grid. To use Amory Lovins's influential terminology, solar energy offers the possibility of a "soft" path to our technological future, whereas nuclear takes us down the "hard" path.[60]

Now to some, this is a distinction without a difference—they want reliable electricity at the lowest cost with the fewest environmental problems, and whether the source is on the roof or at a plant miles away makes no difference. But to others, the soft versus hard path debate has important political and cultural implications relating to the centralization of governmental power and citizens' sense of control over their lives. Thus Lovins himself, as early as 1976, described fusion as a "complex, costly, large-scale, centralized high-technology way to make electricity—all of which goes in the wrong direction."[61] Of course, the hard path has its supporters as well, because to some putting an energy source on a rooftop is a nuisance and a recipe for an unhealthy relationship between an individual and the community.[62] Moreover, when your energy source is on your roof, your neighbor's decision to plant a large shade tree takes on new consequences. American courts and legislatures have only begun to work out when homeowners should be able to prevent their neighbors from cutting off access to the sun.[63]

Similarly, widespread use of photovoltaics on residential rooftops will raise issues concerning the structure of the energy distribution system. Should individual homes receiving electricity from the sun be required or allowed to hook up with traditional power grids? How should electric bills be determined when individuals want to be linked to the grid at all times but only use it when their solar system is inadequate?

So, in the end, solar energy, like fusion, will emerge as something less than an instant solution to our problems. But we still hear references from groups like the National Academy of Sciences to solar and fusion energy as offering "the potential for indefinitely sustainable energy supply. That is, each could supply up to ten times our present energy requirements for thousands of years (or much more)."[64] And whereas the academy goes on to discuss the economic and other choices that have to be made, the image of endless plenty is left.

There is and should be a place in American culture for images of endless progress. But we are enriched as well by images that portray our limits. Years ago, E. F. Schumacher, drawing explicitly on the Sermon on the Mount, urged us to remember in the context of our energy debates that "we are poor, not demigods. We have plenty to be sorrowful about, and are not emerging into a golden age."[65] This turned out to be more prophetic than a bushel of headline stories on energy "breakthroughs." Our sense of who we are should draw on human frailties as well as human potential. Keeping such ideas in mind has nothing to do with an establishment of religion; it has everything to do with a more rounded sense of who we are. As research moves on, life may become easier in some ways. But, the human condition is not something to be cured by technology.

NINE

Artificial Intelligence and the Essence of Humanity

Spectacular developments in the far reaches of computer science are announced almost daily. And the most striking advances concern not the brute power of ever faster machines, but artificial intelligence. Computers that appear to think will, we are told, revolutionize the workplace and the schoolroom. This field has so far produced relatively little in the way of usable technology, but it has triggered an enormous debate on philosophical questions about the nature of intelligence. As with so many debates in our society, most of the participation on both sides has taken the scientists' view of the world, even when implicit value questions cry out for the addition of other perspectives.

The Origins of Artificial Intelligence

Artificial intelligence, the discipline that seeks to build thinking computers,[1] traces its origins back to early efforts to have machines do mathematics. In the nineteenth century, Charles Babbage's "difference engine," built with financial support from the British government, was able to calculate the values of certain polynomials.[2] Babbage later conceived an "analytic engine," a general-purpose computing machine. Although never completed, its design anticipated many features of first-generation computers.[3]

In Chapter 6 we traced the development of modern digital computers in this century. As the power of these machines grew and their size shrank, comparisons with the human brain became ubiquitous. The theoretical groundwork for thinking about the ultimate capability of computers was largely laid by Alan Turing, the brilliant British mathematician and codebreaker. Turing played a key role in developing the symbolic computation that is central to modern efforts at artificial intelligence. In 1936 he devised a hypothetical logic machine that consists of an endless piece of paper divided into squares, where each square is either blank or marked. A scanning device moves along the paper and either makes a mark, erases one, or moves one square forward or one back. Turing was able to show that this machine could compute anything that could be computed by any machine, no matter how complex.[4] In other words, logic problems, and any problems that can be formulated logically, can be reduced to a series of yes or no steps.

Modern research in artificial intelligence was energized by a pivotal summer conference at Dartmouth College in 1956.[5] John McCarthy, assistant professor of mathematics at Dartmouth, coined the term *artificial intelligence* while writing a proposal for the conference. At the gathering, McCarthy, Marvin Minsky, Allen Newell, Herbert Simon, and others exchanged findings and ideas about computer languages that were suited to flexible problem solving and about programs they had written that could, for example, prove mathematical theorems. To artificial intelligence researchers, computers are not number crunchers. They are machines that can mimic human behavior in areas ranging from conversation to chess.

Two major approaches characterize current work in artificial intelligence (AI). Symbolic AI relies on serial processing in which software operates on hardware in a single track approach to problems. Neural network AI, which is modeled more on how the human brain functions, uses parallel processing and does not distinguish as sharply between hardware and software.[6] Both techniques pursue the ultimate goal of building machines, including robots with an array of sensory devices, that can learn and think in a human fashion.

Artificial Life

In recent years, a rival conception of computer intelligence has begun to challenge traditional AI. The artificial life movement is more concerned with computer programs that mimic birds in flight than with those that play chess. Although often described as a subset of artificial intelligence,[7] the history and goals of artificial life are somewhat distinct.

The intellectual forbearer of artificial life is John von Neumann, a mathematician who was born in Budapest and came to the United States in 1930. After World War II, von Neumann was one of the creators of the modern concept of the computer, in particular the linkage between a memory unit and a central processing unit. Von Neumann wrote quite generally about what he called *automata,* or self-operating entities, which could proceed "in light of instructions programmed within itself."[8] Von Neumann included both machines and biological organisms in this category of "automata."[9]

This concept evolved in the late 1960s with the creation of computer games, such as Life, in which simple instructions when played out at length led to fascinating patterns of "cell birth" and "death" emerging on a sort of checkerboard on the computer screen.[10] Influenced by these and other developments, Christopher Langton of the Los Alamos National Laboratory coined the term *artificial life* and gave the field definition by organizing the first artificial life conference at Los Alamos in 1987.[11]

As presently practiced, artificial life involves writing programs that create flexible computer entities. These entities are given a few simple rules to follow that govern such matters as mobility and reproduction. When their environment changes they adapt. Thus computer-simulated "birds" have evolved "flocking" behavior that is remarkably similar to that of biological birds.[12] Artificial life proponents maintain that what they have created will someday deserve to be called "alive" every bit as much as creations made of DNA. As Langton has put it, "microelectronic technology and genetic engineering will soon give us the capability to create new life forms *in silico* as well as *in vitro.*"[13]

At one level, the contrast with traditional AI is sharp. Artificial life seeks to replicate biological organisms from the bottom up through evolution, whereas AI operates from the top down by creating machines that undertake sophisticated activities like playing chess. Langton has written that the first conference on artificial life revealed that the participants shared "a very similar vision, strongly based on themes such as *bottom-up* rather than *top-down* modeling, *local* rather than *global* control, *simple* rather than *complex* specifications, *emergent* rather than *prespecified* behavior, *population* rather than *individual* simulation, and so forth."[14]

At another level, however, artificial life shares a great deal with artificial intelligence, and it is not surprising that at many universities they are grouped in the same department. The goal, after all, is to have computers, all of which operate within the limits set by Turing's theoretical work, take on a variety of tasks previously thought to be the sole province of biological organisms.

The Practical Impact of Artificial Intelligence

The potential impact of artificial intelligence, broadly defined, ranges over fields like machine translation, medical diagnosis, modeling of diseases, and operation of aircraft. The U.S. government has been sufficiently intrigued to support AI with funding from a variety of sources. The Advanced Research Projects Agency within the Department of Defense has provided support, as have the individual services through the Office of Naval Research, the Army Research Office and the Air Force Office of Scientific Research. On the civilian side, the National Science Foundation funds and coordinates a variety of endeavors. The National Aeronautics and Space Administration, for example, is interested in the use of intelligent robots in space missions. And the National Institutes of Health has supported efforts to search for a cure for AIDS using artificial life techniques.[15]

Government support for AI has had its ups and downs but it will persist. Much of it is "little science," spread out, in classic fashion, among a variety of agencies and in the civilian and military sectors. There is enough intellectual interest to engage the research community and enough promise of practical payoff to satisfy the legislature.

Of course, here, as elsewhere with basic science, the practical payoffs are more elusive than they first appear. AI has not been immune to the overpromising that so often occurs when the scientific ethic of progress is expressed in the public realm. In 1949, for example, the director of natural science at the Rockefeller Foundation proposed that computers be used to solve "worldwide translation problems," reasoning that because they had broken codes in the war, they could "decode" one language into another.[16] But language turned out to be a good bit more subtle and context dependent than supposed, and machine translators have so far solved rather little. More recently, the U.S. Army's prize AI project, the "Autonomous Land Vehicle" ran off the road. Plans called for an armored transport vehicle that could deliver supplies under combat conditions without a human driver, but five years of work produced a vehicle unable to drive at adequate speeds even under test conditions, and the program was cancelled.[17]

At present, although many computer programs claim to be "intelligent" or to use "artificial intelligence," actual uses of computers for flexible problem solving typically done by humans have been rare in the commercial sector. Although many were launched with great fanfare, very few companies specializing in artificial intelligence have survived, and many of those are struggling.[18] The main successes have been in narrow areas such as credit verification.[19] Moreover, we can confidently predict that when products do arrive in large numbers, the regulatory gap will take its toll. If, for example, clever programs are written to diagnose diseases, that does not mean they were written with the sorts of questions that arise in malpractice actions in mind. And, as noted in chapter 6, the protection of intellectual property in computer software remains a formidable problem. Given the paucity of actual artificial intelligence products on-line, it is difficult to say exactly where other regulatory problems will come in, but there is no reason to believe they will be absent.

Consciousness and Human Uniqueness

All of this means simply that artificial intelligence is likely to follow the normal path to usable technology—rockier than anticipated. But as with other developments in science, the limited commercial impact does not mean limited impact on our values. Indeed, the prospect of thinking computers has created an extraordinary amount of public debate on remarkably philosophical issues. As computers have apparently become more like humans, we humans have struggled to retain our distinctiveness. This has resulted in a new emphasis on the importance of human consciousness and self-awareness, and a growing debate over whether machines can possess those traits. But, remarkably, even this debate is dominated, on both sides, by the scientific world view.[20]

The observation that advances in science can diminish an individual's sense of uniqueness is hardly new. Sigmund Freud, for example, wrote that "[h]umanity has in the course of time had to endure from the hands of science two great outrages upon its naïve self-love."[21] Freud identified these "outrages" as Copernican astronomy, which displaced the earth from the center of the universe, and Darwinian evolution, which posited a continuity between animals and man.[22] Freud believed that resistance to his own theories stemmed from the fact that he further insulted humanity by "endeavouring to prove to the *ego* of each one of us that he is not even master in his own house, but that he must remain content with the veriest scraps of information about what is going on unconsciously in his own mind."[23]

If Freud correctly identified three blows to our pride, two of them have to some extent been absorbed. Man has ceded his place in the physical center of the universe with reasonable grace. And if Freud's own theories have not achieved the acceptance of those of Copernicus, that may simply be because they do not deserve that acceptance on scientific grounds. In any event, many people today can comfortably concede that they sometimes have, as Freud argued, unconscious motivations.

Darwin's theory of evolution remains much more controversial in some sectors of society, and that may be precisely because it continues to threaten human self-esteem in the way that Freud suggested. Although evolution is widely supported by the scientific community,[24] its inclusion in the curriculum remains a contentious subject in many schools, as we saw in chapter 5.[25] Too much continuity between mankind and other animals can be quite upsetting.[26]

Even for many of those who believe in evolution, the human trait of self-awareness preserves a distinction between people and at least some animals. Consider, for example, the position of Peter Singer, the influential advocate for animal rights, whose *Animal Liberation* has been termed "the bible of the animal liberation movement."[27] Singer presents a strictly utilitarian argument; following Bentham, he says the relevant question is not whether an animal can reason or talk, but whether an animal can suffer.[28] He thus stresses the abundant evidence that animals can feel pain and argues that this pain must be taken into account in human decision making.[29] But he expressly rejects the notion that humans are like all other animals in terms of self-awareness:

To avoid speciesism we must allow that beings who are similar in all relevant respects have a similar right to life—and mere membership in our own biological species cannot be a morally relevant criterion for this right. Within these limits we could still hold, for instance, that it is worse to kill a normal adult human, with a capacity for self-awareness and the ability to plan for the future and have meaningful relations with others, than it is to kill a mouse, which presumably does not share all of these characteristics.[30]

Indeed, Singer argues generally that nonhuman animals are not capable of making moral choices, thus making irrelevant the question of the propriety of their behavior toward each other.[31] It is no criticism of animal rights advocates to note that some of them might find it more difficult to subscribe to a doctrine that did not retain such a special role for humankind. There are, after all, many in the emerging field of cognitive ethology who, on thoroughly Darwinian grounds, find evidence for animal consciousness and awareness and planning in animals ranging from birds to rhesus monkeys to honeybees.[32]

In any event, whether or not humans feel comfortable being grouped with animals, a new challenge to human uniqueness has arisen with the development of the computer. As Bruce Mazlish put it, if Copernicus, Darwin, and Freud placed man on a continuous spectrum with the universe, the animal kingdom, and his own psyche, modern technology seeks to eradicate the final discontinuity—that between man and machines.[33]

Preserving this discontinuity has become important to many people. As soon as machines master one task done by humans, there are those who say that some other task involves the really essential aspect of humanity. It is this progression that has led to the modern preoccupation with self-awareness.

The story of chess-playing computers, an important area of artificial intelligence research, is instructive. Although the rules of chess are easily taught to a computer, and although a computer can calculate much more rapidly than a human, it was long believed that certain essential intuitive aspects of the game would always give human players an advantage over a machine. As recently as 1987, one commentator claimed that "it has been calculated that a computer big and fast enough to beat a world class chess master would have to be approximately the size of the solar system."[34] By 1990 this claim had been falsified rather dramatically by the program Deep Thought, which has defeated several grandmasters and can run on any powerful computer.[35] Although Deep Thought has been defeated by the world champion, the program is better than all but about one hundred players in the world.[36] Deep Thought plays much better than the five graduate students who developed it, and it will continue to improve.[37] According to one grandmaster who lost to it, "Deep Thought combines enormous speed and computational power with sophisticated analysis, itself developed by computer, of the relative values of the chess pieces depending on where they are and what stage the game has reached."[38]

Yet some now explicitly reject the notion that grandmaster-level chess programs represent a milestone in the development of artificial intelligence.[39] To them, conscious self-awareness is a key aspect of the human brain's activity, and, they assert, such consciousness has not been achieved by current chess-playing machines.[40] In other words, Deep Thought may play a mean game of chess, but, unlike humans, it does not know it is playing chess.

Thus to many, the utterly internal, subjective sense of consciousness represents a safe harbor from the march of progress:

Science has revealed the secrets of many initially mysterious natural phenomena—magnetism, photosynthesis, digestion, even reproduction—but consciousness seems utterly unlike these. For one thing, particular cases of magnetism or photosynthesis or digestion are in principle equally accessible to any observer with the right apparatus, but any particular case of consciousness seems to have a favored or privileged observer, whose access to the phenomenon is entirely unlike, and better than, the access of any others—no matter what apparatus they may have.[41]

Thus the human capacity for self-awareness—the capacity to be conscious of our own existence—is still celebrated in modern culture. Even a fancy computer cannot think about itself the way we can ponder ourselves. Indeed, self-reference has been described as "America's latest social and pop-intellectual trend,"[42] a trend exemplified by phenomena ranging from the "Gary Shandling Show" to Pulitzer Prizes for media coverage of the media.[43] Even law review articles have begun to appear that contain footnotes citing themselves.[44]

The Debate over Computer Consciousness: Science versus Science

But to many proponents of artificial intelligence, consciousness is not a safe harbor inaccessible to scientific progress. They have argued explicitly that digital computers cannot be assumed incapable of any mental activity:

> Minds exist in brains and may come to exist in programmed machines. If and when such machines come about, their causal powers will derive not from the substances they are made of, but from their design and the programs that run in them. And the way we will know they have those causal powers is by talking to them and listening carefully to what they have to say.[45]

Thus the proponents of what has come to be called "strong" artificial intelligence believe that a properly programmed computer "would not only think but know it is thinking."[46] The philosopher John Pollock, who is engaged in the OSCAR project to build a thinking machine, has written in *How to Build a Person* that "[t]here is no obstacle to building consciousness into an intelligent machine."[47] Most dramatically, Hans Moravec, the director of the Mobile Robot Laboratory of Carnegie Mellon University, has maintained that he already sees evidence of awareness in his computer-driven mobile robots that use sensors to obtain information about their location and movements:

> In our lab, the programs we have developed usually present such information from the robot's world model in the form of pictures on a computer screen—a direct window into the robot's mind. In these internal models of the world I see the beginnings of awareness in the minds of our machines—an awareness I believe will evolve into consciousness comparable with that of humans.[48]

There has been a strong public reaction to claims such as these, and the growth of a remarkable and popular set of sophisticated arguments designed to show that digital computers are not conscious. By examining three of these opponents of strong artificial intelligence—the philosopher John Searle, the mathematician Roger Penrose, and the neurobiologist Gerald Edelman—we can witness the surprising role of science in value formation. Surprising, because the opponents of computer consciousness, no less than the proponents, stress the scientific world view.

John Searle's analysis of the problem requires an understanding of the so-called Turing test. In 1950, when computers had very little power in modern-day terms, Alan Turing devised an operational test to determine when a computer could think like a human.[49] Under the Turing test, as this approach was inevitably named, a computer and a human are hidden from the view of a human interrogator.[50] The interrogator puts questions to the computer and to the human with a mechanism such as a keyboard and screen. Any questions at all can be asked. The computer and the human answer through the keyboard and screen mechanism, but they have different goals. The computer has been designed to pretend that it is a human; the human is simply being him- or herself. At the end, interrogators have to decide which of the two entities they have been communicating with is the human. If they consistently get it wrong, that is, if the computer has consistently fooled them, we say the computer has passed the Turing test.

No computer can currently pass the Turing test, and a moment's reflection will persuade you that it will be quite a feat if a computer ever does. Obviously the interrogator will not rely on simple informational questions where a computer can be easily programmed to give a humanlike set of responses.[51] (A set that might include, of course, incorrect answers to difficult math problems.)[52] The skillful interrogator will rely instead on dialogues in which the computer will be forced to respond persuasively to questions about earlier parts of the discussion, to sarcasm, and to context-based comments on a variety of topics.[53] Nonetheless there are computers today that can engage in a reasonably sophisticated dialogue with humans, and they have fooled some people in Turing tests on limited topics.[54] Unsurprisingly, there are many in the artificial intelligence community who believe that a computer will someday pass a generalized Turing test.[55]

The philosopher John Searle does not debate whether a computer could ever pass the Turing test. Instead he challenges the notion that it would be terribly meaningful if one could. Philosophers and others have long discussed the implications of having a machine that could pass the Turing test.[56] Searle's powerful contribution to the debate has made an unlikely appearance in popular books,[57] periodicals,[58] and even daily newspapers.[59] Indeed, Searle's "Chinese room" argument has become a flashpoint in the dispute over whether human consciousness is unique. With computers making human reason seem decidedly ordinary, there is a dramatic upsurge in interest in the question of whether computers can understand what they are doing in the sense that humans do. This interest is so strong that Searle, through no fault of his own, has had his views badly misrepresented at times. Indeed those who look to Searle for a vindication of human uniqueness are looking in the wrong place indeed. To understand why this is so, we have to begin in the "Chinese room."

Imagine, says Searle, that programmers have written a program that enables a computer to "understand" Chinese in the following sense.[60] If the computer is given a question written in Chinese characters, then it can produce an excellent answer written in Chinese characters. The computer is so good at this that it cannot be distinguished in a blind test from a native speaker of Chinese. This computer can be said to have passed a form of the Turing test, but is it correct to say that the computer understands Chinese in the way that the native speaker does? To answer this question Searle proposes the following thought experiment: Imagine you do not understand a word of Chinese. You are locked in a room with a large basket full of Chinese symbols written on bits of paper. Also in the room is a large book written in English that gives a series of rules for manipulating Chinese symbols. The rules say nothing about the meaning of the symbols; they simply say things like "if you are given a squiggle-squiggle symbol from outside the room, find a squoggle-squoggle symbol and pass it back out under the door." While you are in the room, someone outside starts passing Chinese symbols on bits of paper under the door. You follow the rule book and pass the appropriate bits with Chinese symbols back out under the door. As it happens, the bits coming in contain questions and the rule book you are following is cleverly designed so that you are sending out excellent answers. But you know none of this; moreover, you have no knowledge of what any of the symbols mean. Nonetheless, to an outside observer you will seem to have passed the Turing test. Just like the outstanding computer, your answers will be indistinguishable from those given by a native speaker. Yet, Searle concludes, you surely do not understand Chinese in the same sense as a native speaker; indeed, you do not understand Chinese at all. You are mindlessly manipulating symbols according to a book of rules. Similarly, Searle argues, the computer does not understand Chinese. It too is simply manipulating symbols according to a set of rules. Searle summarizes his point by saying that syntax alone is not sufficient for semantics.[61]

Searle's argument has created a firestorm of protest among the proponents of strong artificial intelligence.[62] His argument is important in part because it is so general. It is not subject to persuasive criticism on the grounds that future advances in computer speed or in parallel processing will change the terms of the debate.[63] Searle has stressed that the essence of the strong artificial intelligence position is that binary processing per se—breaking everything down into yes-no questions manageable by a digital computer—can give rise to consciousness.[64] Searle notes that, in principle, digital computers can be made out of anything at all—beer cans connected by strings, for example.[65] Proponents of strong artificial intelligence are committed to the position that a beer can computer of sufficient complexity could pass the Turing test and would be as conscious of what it is doing as a human.[66]

The objections to the Chinese room argument are legion. Some contend that whereas the individual in the Chinese room does not understand Chinese, the whole system does.[67] Just as a single neuron does not understand anything, but the brain does, the individual does not understand Chinese, but the system—the individual, plus the rule book, plus the room, plus the slips coming in and out—understands Chinese.[68] Others argue that there is simply no way to know whether any other individual understands anything except by what they say or do, so we simply must assume that the person in the Chinese room understands Chinese just as we assume that sort of thing about each other.[69] Still others directly challenge the notion that syntax is not sufficient for semantics. They note that it was once believed that compression waves in the air could not produce sound and that oscillating electromagnetic forces could not produce light.[70] Both of these positions are now discredited.[71] Someday we may realize, the argument goes, that a sufficiently complex syntactical system can indeed produce meaning.[72] If you wave a bar magnet in a dark room you do not get any visible light, just as a person leafing slowly through what would be an extraordinarily large rule book does not appear to obtain any visible understanding.[73] In both cases the situation would appear quite different as our understanding of the processes involved increased.[74] And there are other responses to Searle as well.[75]

This is not the place to evaluate the strength of Searle's argument. The crucial point from our perspective is that Searle has attracted popular attention because he seems to oppose those who would explain away human uniqueness. Thus the *New York Times,* after discussing the Chinese room, concluded that Searle questions "the premise of Western science: that the world we live in and the world inside our heads can be understood by the human mind."[76] Meanwhile, a law professor asserts that Searle has shown that "consciousness and intentionality . . . constitute human thought."[77] When computers start beating grandmasters at chess, it is time to find a new discontinuity between man and machine. The subjective experience of human self-awareness has emerged as a likely candidate.

The irony here is that Searle himself, as he has continually emphasized, is hardly the man to defend the notion that there is some unknowable corner of the human mind or that humans somehow are fundamentally different from machines. Searle's argument applies only to the notion that binary computation alone can give rise to consciousness. He does not maintain that no machine can think, indeed, he has written:

[W]e are all machines. We can construe the stuff inside our heads as a meat machine. And of course, we can all think. So, in one sense of "machine," namely that sense in which a machine is just a physical system which is capable of performing certain kinds of operations, in that sense, we are all machines, and we can think.[78]

Nor has Searle argued that only biologically based systems can think.[79] He has written explicitly that "[r]ight now [biologically based systems] are the only systems we know for a fact can think, but we might find other systems in the universe that can produce conscious thoughts, and we might even come to be able to create thinking systems artificially."[80] His point is that binary manipulation alone is not sufficient to create conscious thought. Indeed Searle, far from believing in some immaterial corner of the human mind, takes precisely the opposite position on the mind-body problem. An ardent opponent of dualism, he regards all mental phenomena, including consciousness, as being caused by processes going on in the brain.[81] To Searle, brains cause consciousness in the same way that stomachs cause digestion.[82] Searle accuses proponents of strong artificial intelligence as being victims of "a residual dualism."[83] No one would believe that a computer simulation of a stomach can actually digest anything, but people want to believe that a simulation of a brain can actually think. This is only possible, Searle asserts, if one believes the mind is independent of the physical brain, a classic dualist position.[84] We must, Searle concludes, "escape the clutches of two thousand years of dualism" and recognize that "consciousness is a biological phenomenon like any other."[85]

Regardless of whether proponents of artificial intelligence are dualists or whether dualism is as bankrupt as Searle argues, the point is simply that the Chinese room offers no refuge for those who seek a special place for humanity. Viewing humans as "meat machines" and consciousness as a "biological phenomenon" is hardly the approach for those who would retain a discontinuity between men and machines.

A similar irony is present in the public reaction to *The Emperor's New Mind* by noted mathematician Roger Penrose.[86] Penrose's work is a lengthy, complex treatment of a variety of topics in modern physics and mathematics. It is nonetheless a bestseller, a tribute in part to its underlying theme that digital computers are not the same as human minds.[87] As one commentator put it, people do not like "to see themselves as digital computers. . . . To be told by someone with impeccable scientific credentials that they are nothing of the kind can only be pleasing."[88] One popular magazine puts the matter bluntly: "Those Computers Are Dummies" reads the headline, and the text asserts that "Penrose's central conclusion is that computers will never think."[89]

It is certainly correct that Penrose rejects the claim of strong artificial intelligence that digital computers can do and experience all that human brains can do and experience. But here, as with Searle, when we look more closely at his position we find little to comfort those who want a special status for humans.

Penrose criticizes strong artificial intelligence on different grounds than Searle does, although he starts in the same place. Penrose, like Searle, emphasizes that digital computers, no matter how complex, rely on step-by-step algorithms to solve problems.[90] Whereas that approach is adequate for an extraordinarily wide range of problems, Penrose maintains that the brain necessarily uses other approaches in certain of its activities.[91] Unlike Searle, Penrose places particular stress on Gödel's undecidability theorem, which, he believes, demonstrates that humans can intuit as true certain propositions that cannot be established in a series of algorithmic steps.[92] Finally, Penrose, unlike Searle, speculates that to fully understand how brains work and how consciousness arises, more will have to be learned about unresolved problems relating to quantum theory and other aspects of modern physics.[93]

Thus it is clear, as Penrose explicitly states, that he does "not believe the *strong*-AI contention that the mere enaction of an algorithm would evoke consciousness,"[94] and for this conclusion Penrose has been criticized in the artificial intelligence community.[95] It has been argued, for example, that the neurons in the brain are simply too large to be affected by the quantum behavior Penrose stresses.[96] But whether Penrose is right

or wrong, the crucial point from our perspective is that he is not someone who maintains that there is something discontinuous between human beings and the rest of the physical universe. On the contrary, he
seeks precisely the type of scientific unity typically sought by those who
build grand theories. And in the end, he can see only two possibilities
for understanding the conscious human mind. Either it grew out of "the
thousands of millions of years of *actual* evolution that lie behind us," [97]
or it results from physical qualities that we may ultimately understand,
thus enabling us "to construct such [conscious] objects for ourselves." [98]
In the latter case—the human-built brain—the consequences could be
dramatic:

> One could imagine that these objects could have a tremendous advantage over
> us, since they could be designed *specifically* for the task at hand, namely to
> *achieve consciousness*. They would not have to grow from a single cell. They
> would not have to carry around the "baggage" of their ancestry (the old and
> "useless" parts of the brain or body that survive in ourselves only because of the
> "accidents" of our remote ancestry). One might imagine that, in view of these
> advantages, such objects could succeed in *actually* superseding human beings,
> where (in the opinions of such as myself) the algorithmic computers are doomed
> to subservience.[99]

Thus the alternatives that Penrose sees are human minds as continuous with the animal kingdom through the mechanism of evolution or
human minds as replicable, even surpassable, by human-made machines.
Neither is a refuge for those who crave discontinuity.

Neurobiologist Gerald Edelman also challenges the notion of a thinking computer. His *Bright Air, Brilliant Fire* sets forth his view of the
origins of human consciousness and of the debate over machine consciousness.[100] Like Searle and Penrose, Edelman rejects the idea that the
human brain can be usefully likened to a digital computer. He argues,
in a complex and controversial theory called neural Darwinism, that
consciousness is an outgrowth of human evolution working at the level
of groups of neurons reacting to sensory inputs. Edelman distinguishes
between what he calls primary consciousness—an awareness of immediate surroundings without a sense of past or future—from higher order
consciousness, which involves a sense of self and of time. The former
may exist in some animals, such as dogs, whereas the latter is probably
limited, in Edelman's view, to humans.

Reactions to Edelman's book have emphasized the point that Edelman rejects the strong claims made by some in the artificial intelligence movement. Edelman, we are told by journalists, argues that "the brain is not like a computer," [101] that the "richness of human experience could not be fitted into a mechanical or computer theory of the nervous system." [102]

But, as with Searle and Penrose, Edelman is not, in fact, an unambiguous supporter of human uniqueness. He does emphasize that we come from a particular evolutionary background and are, in that sense, unlike other creatures. But, as an opponent of dualism, he sees the mind as a subject for scientific study in the ordinary sense. He believes that our higher order consciousness may have its origins in chimpanzees who have not just concepts, but some elements of self-concept. [103] Most strikingly, like Searle and Penrose, he sees no reason in principle why artifacts could not be constructed with high-order consciousness. [104] He thinks the day is far off, but concludes that "[m]y personal belief is that the construction of conscious artifacts will take place." [105]

Our discourse is so dominated by scientists that our hunger for an alternative to humans as machines is fed by antidualist philosophers, mathematicians, and evolutionary biologists. There are in fact still thoughtful people, religious and otherwise, who believe the mind is in a fundamental way different than the body, but their voices are not loud. [106] There is an echo of those lost voices in John Updike's *Rabbit at Rest*. When Rabbit Angstrom resists heart surgery, his friend asks "What's wrong with running your blood through a machine? What else you think you are, champ? " Rabbit responds to himself, "A God-made one-of-a-kind with an immortal soul breathed in. A vehicle of grace. A battlefield of good and evil." [107]

The scientific efforts to explain the mind should go on and they should be a vital part of public discourse. But there is room as well for discussions of the soul, and for nonscientific visions of the essence of humanity.

Consciousness and the Legal Definition of Death

The question of the uniqueness of human consciousness is of particular importance because it may play a role in one of the most vexing legal and social controversies of our time—the cessation of medical treatment and the definition of death. As Robert Veatch notes, any concept of the death of a person depends directly on those qualities thought to make humans unique.[108] By that standard the modern trend is clear—in the space of a few decades technology has pushed us from a world in which a beating heart symbolizes life to a world in which heartbeat, breathing, eating, and even responding to external stimuli are less important than human consciousness. The question raised by developments in computer science is what might happen if we no longer viewed consciousness as unique to humans.

In the first half of this century, the interdependence of breathing, blood circulation, and the brain made the determination of death relatively uncontroversial.[109] The absence of breath and a heartbeat signified death.[110] Beginning in the 1950s, however, artificial respirators and other life-support systems began to change the situation.[111] It became possible to keep the body alive when the brain had ceased functioning.[112] Indeed, it gradually became possible to replace virtually every part of the body except the brain with an artificial substitute.[113]

It may be difficult for us to recall, but these developments caused a tremor in mankind's sense of self. A government commission discussed "the problem of the 'man-machine symbiosis'—that is, the extent to which technological processes should be imposed upon, or substituted for, the natural processes of human beings."[114] The focus of controversy was on the artificial heart. As the government commission put it, "The heart has held pre-eminence in poetry and in common speech as the seat of bravery, love, joy, and generosity. Will its replacement by a mechanical pump and motor not merely place technology deep in man's bosom but place man more deeply in the bosom of technology?"[115]

But the development of the artificial heart and other mechanical life-support devices hardly forced mankind to admit equivalence with machines. The human thirst for uniqueness was easily satisfied by moving all important characteristics to the one irreplaceable organ, the brain. A focus on the heart was dismissed as "symbolism" and as "irrational."[116] As one ethicist put it in response to concerns over the artificial heart, "One can understand and psychologically become adjusted to the fact that the heart is a vital organic pump, and that it is not the inner core of the 'self.'"[117]

But the transfer of concern to the brain left difficult problems for medicine and law. When society was first confronted with comatose individuals whose breathing and heartbeat were sustained by machines, it was not clear how to proceed; on the one hand, no one wanted to end the existence of someone who was likely to regain brain functioning, but on the other hand, the sense of respect for human dignity, the cost of medical treatment, and the desire for organs that might be transplanted into others all counseled for ending life support in certain cases.[118] The result was a growing interest in "brain death," a concept that permitted death to be declared while the heart was still beating.[119]

In this country, the first major step toward defining death in terms of the brain was the report of an ad hoc committee at the Harvard Medical School in 1968.[120] The committee emphasized that with modern technology, respiration and a heart beat could be maintained "even when there is not the remotest possibility of an individual recovering consciousness following massive brain damage."[121] Accordingly, the committee proposed standards for determining when patients should be declared dead because their brain was permanently nonfunctioning.[122]

It immediately became apparent, however, that the word *brain* was arguably too broad for the purpose of defining death. The Harvard committee itself recognized the distinction between cortical and brain stem functioning.[123] Generally speaking, consciousness and cognition are carried on in the higher brain, that is, in the cerebrum, particularly the neocortex.[124] By contrast, vegetative functions such as breathing and blood pressure are carried out by the brain stem, a portion of the lower brain.[125] The distinction matters because in many heart attacks and accidents the disturbance of circulatory or respiratory functions is too brief to destroy the brain stem but sufficient to destroy the neocortex.[126] The result is an individual who is alive under a "whole brain" definition of death, because the lower part of the brain still works, but who would not be alive if a "higher brain" definition were used.[127] Such individuals are often in what is termed a persistent vegetative state.[128] They can be kept alive with intravenous feeding and antibiotics, but they are unlikely ever to recover further.[129] These individuals need no mechanical aid to breathe, maintain a heartbeat, react to light, or engage in other automatic functions, but they lack all awareness and thought.[130]

As early as 1971, an editorial in *Lancet* referred to studies of comatose individuals who breathe but have no cortical functioning.[131] The editorial concluded that because "death of a human being means death of his [her] brain—indeed of his [her] mind" an individual would not want his or her vegetative existence to be prolonged after his or her cortex was destroyed.[132]

An understanding of the legal regime that grew out of these developments requires that you keep in mind how rapidly things were changing. In the space of a few decades, the centuries-old identification of death with the cessation of the heartbeat and of breathing was giving way to a brain-centered definition. Fundamental moral issues were being addressed at the same time that new diagnostic techniques were being developed. As we shall see, the net result was that the legal definition of death moved to recognition that death of the whole brain meant death of the human being, even if the heart and lungs were still being artificially maintained.[133] At the same time, decisions on the cessation of treatment, including the cessation of mechanical feeding,[134] recognized that treatment could end not only when the whole brain was dead, but also when only the higher brain was destroyed.[135] It was, after all, the higher brain's ability to sustain consciousness that marked the uniquely human trait.

The legal definition of death moved quickly to reflect the considerations set forth in the report of the ad hoc Harvard committee. An influential step in this direction was the 1972 article by Capron and Kass proposing a model brain death statute.[136] Drawing in part on the Harvard committee's report, the authors proposed that if artificial means were keeping respiration and circulation going, a person would be considered dead if "he [she] has experienced an irreversible cessation of spontaneous brain functions."[137] The authors made clear that by "brain functions" they meant the whole brain, so that someone who had lost only higher brain functions would not be dead.[138] But the authors did not defend the proposition that lower brain functioning alone—a condition marked by spontaneous reflexes but no consciousness—constituted human life: on the contrary, they admitted that "the exclusion of patients without neocortical function from the category of death may appear somewhat arbitrary."[139] They defended the exclusion on the ground that they were taking a "modest" step to bring the definition of death in line with modern medicine, and they emphasized that modern medicine was not yet able routinely to diagnose irreversible higher brain death as clearly as whole brain death.[140] Moreover, they left the door open to the notion that individuals with higher brain death should be allowed to die by stressing that they were discussing the question "is he dead?," not the question "should he be allowed to die?"[141]

Two influential reports by the Presidents' Commission for the Study of Ethical Problems in Medicine and Biomedical and Behavioral Research took the same tack. The first, a 1981 report titled (in short) *Defining Death*, opted for a whole brain rather than a higher brain definition of death.[142] The second, a 1983 report titled *Deciding to Forego Life-Sustaining Treatment*, said that families could justifiably remove artificial feeding tubes from patients with no higher brain functions in order to cause the death of those patients.[143]

The law has generally followed these approaches. In virtually every jurisdiction, statute or common law provide that individuals are dead if their whole brain has ceased functioning, even if breathing and circulation are artificially maintained.[144] At the same time, prior to the *Cruzan* decision, "an unbroken stream of cases has authorized procedures for the cessation of treatment of patients in persistent vegetative states," that is, patients who have suffered higher brain death.[145] Many of these cases involve the removal of feeding tubes.[146] The courts have used various theories, ranging from an assessment of the patient's previously expressed wishes to an analysis of the benefits of continued treatment,[147] but the results have been the same. Even outside the realm of litigation, many physicians, despite the long standing medical presumption in favor of treatment,[148] have come to believe that withdrawal of food and water from permanently unconscious patients is appropriate.[149]

So in just the space of a few decades, a remarkable consensus has grown up that those who have permanently been deprived of self-awareness by cessation of higher brain functioning can be allowed to die. And the emphasis on the higher brain has clearly been driven by a concern for those qualities that make humans special. The cases upholding, on various theories, the withdrawal of diverse treatments from those in a persistent vegetative state are replete with references to this concern. In the first widely reported case of this type, that involving Karen Ann Quinlan, the court stressed medical testimony that Ms. Quinlan was "totally unaware," and she lacked those brain functions that are "uniquely human."[150] In its seminal 1986 *Brophy* decision, the Supreme Judicial Court of Massachusetts, in allowing removal of a tube providing food and water from an individual in a persistent vegetative state, argued that in such cases "the burden of maintaining the corporeal existence degrades the very humanity it was meant to serve."[151] In 1988, the court in *Gray v. Romeo,* presented with the same facts as *Brophy,* reached the same conclusion: "The facts in [this] case support the finding that [the patient] would consider that efforts now to sustain her life demean her humanity."[152]

At the same time, a wide variety of ethicists have also concluded that the absence of higher brain functions deprives individuals of their essential humanity.[153] Many of these writers would not only allow the withdrawal of treatment from such individuals, they would declare the individuals dead.[154] There is a remarkable agreement in these writings on the essential importance of human self-awareness. Moreover, this view grew up very quickly after modern developments in medical technology made it possible to support the body when the brain was dead. Recall that the ad hoc Harvard committee issued its initial cautious report on determining brain death in 1968. Veatch, himself a supporter of the higher brain definition of death,[155] reports that in 1970 when Henry Beecher was asked what was essential to the definition of human life, he replied simply, "Consciousness."[156] Since that time several philosophers discussing death have identified the essential human characteristic as the consciousness and self-awareness that resides in the higher brain. In 1975, William Charron argued for a "psychological definition of death" that focused on "irreversible loss of all consciousness."[157] Five years later, Michael Green and Daniel Wikler contended that because personal identity does not survive death of the conscious brain, such death constitutes death of the person.[158] In 1981, Allen Buchanan, relying on a "cognitivist" concept of life that turns in large measure on "self-awareness," concluded that a higher brain definition of death was "inescapable."[159] Finally, in 1986, a law professor, David Randolph Smith, argued that the legal definition of death should be "neocortical death" because of the "centrality of consciousness and cognition as the quintessential attributes of human life."[160]

Although Smith may have lost the legal battle, his views have won the war. As we have seen, an individual in a persistent vegetative state is not legally dead (because the whole brain is not dead), but treatment, including artificially introduced food and water, will almost inevitably be removed from that individual until legal death takes place.[161] Indeed, an outsider to our society would be justified in concluding that in practice, if not in our codes, we treat those with an irreversible loss of consciousness as dead. We do not immediately bury them, but immediate burial is not our practice in many cases. When a hospitalized individual on a respirator suffers a fatal heart attack we do not bury that person with the respirator running—we remove the respirator, we wait for relatives, we make arrangements.[162] In our culture there are moral constraints on our conduct toward those who are no longer living.[163] An outsider might conclude that when an individual is dead because of a permanent loss of consciousness, our customs require a solemn determination that the loss has taken place, a removal of feeding tubes, and then a burial.

The U.S. Supreme Court's much-publicized decision in *Cruzan v. Director, Missouri Department of Health*[164] did not end this trend. The Court, in *Cruzan,* allowed the state of Missouri to insist there be clear and convincing evidence of an individual's intent before food and water is terminated when someone is in a persistent vegetative state. This was seen by some as a setback for the "right to die" because it prevented for a time the termination of treatment for Nancy Cruzan. But only for a time. After the Supreme Court's decision, Cruzan's parents, presenting new evidence that Nancy would not have wanted treatment in her current state, petitioned the Missouri courts to remove her feeding tube on the ground that the evidence of her intent was now clear. Their petition was granted, the tube was removed, and Nancy Cruzan died.[165] Thus even under a demanding legal standard, our culture continually opts for the centrality of consciousness.

But what if a consensus developed in our society that computers are indeed self-aware in the same sense as humans? It is unlikely to happen in the foreseeable future, but such a consensus might arise someday concerning digital computers or it might accompany the development of other machines, such as those discussed by Searle, Penrose, or Edelman. Perhaps if that day ever comes we would finally cease trying to find distinctions between ourselves and our machines.[166]

Western history suggests, however, that we would not give in so easily.[167] More likely, we will react by seeking some new trait we do not share with conscious computers. If the artificial heart did not phase us for long, perhaps the artificial mind will not either. One candidate for a uniquely human characteristic beyond self-awareness is already available. Some ethicists have described the capacity for social interaction as an essential human trait that is very different from mere consciousness.[168] This capacity is central to one observer's view of why playing chess with the grandmaster program Deep Thought is not the same as playing with a human:

My father taught me chess when I was six or seven years old. We played often during winters when little work could be done at the farm. Comfortably encamped in front of the living-room stove, a large bowl of freshly popped corn nearby, we engaged in mortal combat as snow fell outside and cold winds howled.

I just cannot envision so relaxing and enjoyable a scene were Deep Thought's monitor substituted for my father.

More recently, on the evening I learned my grandparents were seriously ill, a friend invited me to play chess so I would not have to be alone just then, but also wouldn't be compelled to talk much if I didn't feel like it.

"Deep Thought" is incapable of a simple act of friendship and kindness such as that. Nor could the machine have given me the emotional support I needed at that difficult time.

Give me . . . mere mortals . . . with whom to play chess—for the simple pleasures by which they enrich my life—win, lose, or stalemate. Surely the machine has not been nor ever can be invented to improve upon that.[169]

Thus computers force us to see chess playing, once regarded as a remarkable intellectual feat focusing on introspection and intuition, as really an occasion for human interaction. Even if Deep Thought knows it is playing chess, it is not good at discussing how its human opponent feels about the game. At least until computers are built that can provide solace for humans, this step would give us some psychological distance from machines. But if we know anything from recent history, moving the essence of humanity in this direction could have profound implications for the legal definition of death. If computers push our sense of uniqueness away from self-awareness toward social interaction, the definition of death may eventually follow. The groundwork has already been laid—without reference to machine self-awareness, law review articles have already proposed that human interaction should supplant mere consciousness as the legal standard for life. Kevin Quinn suggests that the definition of life should be set at a "threshold . . . higher than minimal consciousness": the standard supported is "a minimum capacity for interpersonal relationships."[170] When that capacity is irretrievably lost, life-sustaining treatment may be removed.[171] Nancy Rhoden contends that when "analysis of the patient's capacities shows that she [he] is unable to enjoy the distinctly human pleasures of relating to her [his] environment and to others, then family discretion is warranted [on whether to end treatment]."[172] Rhoden states explicitly that such patients have capacities beyond those of an individual in a persistent vegetative state.[173]

The adoption of these views is much more likely to come about if a consensus grows that computers have self-awareness. Of course, such a consensus, if it developed at all, would grow slowly and would never be complete. Absolute proof that another human is self-aware, let alone a machine, is not available; consciousness is intrinsically a subjective phenomenon. But we treat other humans as though they were conscious and we may come to act that way toward certain machines. It would be a gradual process as we came to think of particular devices as not merely doing things but as knowing they were doing things. As we have seen, nothing that Searle, Penrose, or Edelman proposes suggests that machines generally must lack self-awareness. If consciousness is merely a product of a machine—indeed, if, as Searle himself says, consciousness is to brains as digestion is to stomachs[174]—consciousness will come to be viewed as no more special for the definition of life than breathing or circulating blood.

A diminished sense of the uniqueness of consciousness and a corresponding broadening of the category of those regarded as dead would also happen gradually, as change in the law generally does. Most likely, we would begin by continuing to call those who lack the capacity for social interaction alive, while we remove their means of existence, as we have done for those who lack consciousness.[175] But however gradually, the trend could move in this direction. There are after all, other pressures pushing toward the same end; many have long predicted or feared, for example, that social worth and economic considerations could force withdrawal of treatment from ill geriatric patients.[176] We now must recognize that the emergence of an increasingly rarified sense of what it is to be human could have the same impact. Indeed, this new pressure could prove to be the most important. One can argue rationally about the social justice issues involved in deciding which people are entitled to expensive treatment. But when one begins to view the subjects of treatment not as people, but as indistinguishable from machines, the outcome of the debate is likely to be foreordained.

A view of what this future would look like is provided by Quinn and Rhoden's analysis of the *Conroy* case.[177] In *Conroy*, the Supreme Court of New Jersey, the court that decided the *Quinlan* case, considered whether a feeding tube could be removed from an elderly brain-damaged woman who was hospitalized with a variety of serious permanent ailments and who had a limited life expectancy.[178] Ms. Conroy could not speak or interact with other people, but she appeared to retain consciousness—she would, for example, scratch herself, pull at her bandages, and smile when her hair was combed or when she received a "comforting rub."[179] The court explicitly noted that she was not in a persistent vegetative state.[180] The court concluded that the feeding tube could not be removed.[181] Ms. Conroy had not made clear that she would have wanted such a result, nor was the court satisfied that the burdens of her life outweighed the benefits or that the pain of her life rendered treatment inhumane.[182]

Quinn challenges this result on the ground that because an individual in Ms. Conroy's situation cannot engage in "interpersonal relationships" she has "no possibility of personal life" and thus there is no obligation to maintain "biological life."[183] Rhoden explains her support for removing Ms. Conroy's feeding tube in somewhat different terms.[184] Ms. Conroy, she suggests, is not "able to experience or enjoy life."[185] The court in *Conroy*, when it said feeding could not be terminated, "in essence reduced Ms. Conroy, or the person that she was, to an object that passively experienced physical sensations."[186] It is easy to see how this view would gain strength from the development of machines we regard as self-aware. Viewing Ms. Conroy, a conscious individual, as "an object" is a tendency that can only be strengthened when we have "objects," such as thinking machines, that we view as conscious.

Scientific developments, as we have seen, do not always lead in a direct and obvious way to practical applications.[187] When Einstein first developed the special theory of relativity he had no idea it would lead to nuclear power.[188] The impact of science on law is even more complex and uncertain. But it is no less real. Developments in artificial intelligence could change not only the machines we use, but our views of ourselves. And when those views change, our views of the proper legal standards for life and death could change as well.

The impact of artificial intelligence on legal doctrine is not as obvious as the impact of a medical innovation, such as the heart-lung machine. But it is not just medical devices that produce legal change. Darwin's theory of evolution had a dramatic impact on the development of the animal rights movement, a movement that seeks changes in the laws governing the treatment of animals.[189] In the early part of this century psychoanalysis shaped developments in the insanity defense and in the criminal law generally.[190] Given this history, artificial intelligence—the latest field to challenge humanity's sense of uniqueness—clearly has the potential to shape the legal standard for death.

There are, as we have noted, other factors pushing toward an enlarged definition of death. The enormous costs of medical treatment for the elderly and sick may, for example, move society in that direction.[191] In an issue arising at the beginning of life, it has been argued that anencephalic infants—those born with no higher brain, but with rudimentary brainstem activity—should be declared dead so that organ donation will become possible.[192] But multiple causation is hardly unusual in the law. The legal changes involving animal rights and those involving the insanity defense were not solely the result of Darwin and Freud.[193]

It is speculative at best to suppose that we will, in fact, see developments in artificial intelligence that will alter our view that human consciousness is unique, and even more speculation is necessary to suggest that these developments will alter our legal standard for human life. But this kind of speculation is useful to show where our public debate is going. At present our discussions of human consciousness are dominated on one side by artificial intelligence experts who see the possibility of consciousness in digital computers, and on the other by philosophers and scientists who believe different artifacts would be needed to achieve consciousness. Religious perspectives link human consciousness to a nonorganic mind and human uniqueness to an immortal soul,[194] but those perspectives are absent in this discourse. Moreover, if public attitudes change and consciousness is seen as nothing special, it will not be the fault of the artificial intelligence movement or of its secular opponents (such as Searle, Penrose, and Edelman) if this eventually leads to an expanded definition of death. Their arguments are focused on the scientific capabilities of machines. They are not discussing legal and moral human obligations. It is not their fault if public silence elsewhere allows science to carry weight far from its appropriate jurisdiction. Let this be an early warning—important values are at stake. The definition of death and the sanctity of human life should not turn on whether a digital computer or any other device appears to be conscious. But, farfetched as it may seem, that is a risk we currently run.

TEN

Conclusion

The relationship between law and science in America can now be summarized. Basic research flourishes under the control of basic researchers. This is not because science is "free of legal control," but because the legal system we have gives power to the scientific community. Without the protections in the Constitution and statutes, our peer review system scattered over scores of agencies and hundreds of universities would not exist. Under our laws, effective control of who receives research funding lies with scientists, not with elected officials or judges.

Moreover, our legal system shields science from religion, a traditional rival. Religious doctrine cannot prevent the teaching of science in the public schools. Our law's tolerance for religious diversity prevents the emergence of a dominant religious perspective even in the private sphere. Indeed, the favorable legal position of science has contributed to a situation in which science plays an unusually large role in public debate on values.

With technology, the tables are turned. Now the legal system stresses adversary-style settings in which diverse voices are heard. The lawyers' process norms dominate, and the progressive values of science are just one point of view, and a relatively weak one at that. The result is the regulatory gap. Ideas that were outstanding from a scientific point of view are not automatically ideal from a social perspective. The consequences range from a slight slowdown in areas like computer software to a dramatic halt in fields like nuclear fission. And the future promises more of the same. So long as our products are incubated in a setting in which scientific norms dominate and born into a world in which legal norms reign, smooth transitions will be the exception rather than the rule.

The main force working to narrow the regulatory gap is the science counselor. In recent years scientists have increasingly become aware that social consequences must be looked at more closely in the research world. As those consequences begin to shape their work, they become science counselors. Budgets are no longer the only important social reality for the scientist. For the science counselor, health, safety, environmental, and intellectual property concerns work their way ever earlier into the research process itself. It is a matter of self-defense: too many unhappy experiences with technology can lead to reduced public support for science or to something even worse—control by politicians and lawyers over the course of research. Science counselors need not be famous or even known to the public; as time goes by, more and more ordinary scientists become science counselors as they temper their belief in the progressive norms of science with the goal of producing socially acceptable technology. They infuse their scientific work with social concerns.

What can and should be changed in this picture? First of all, it is vital to note that our goal is primarily descriptive. For better or for worse, this is the way things are. Moreover, many of the realities we are describing are not easily changed. The legal status of science and technology is deeply embedded in our laws and customs. And no one would lightly change a system that does to a considerable extent provide freedom for research and an important measure of social control over technology. The process is often messy and inefficient but it has much to recommend it.

The two main areas where change appears possible and worthy of consideration concern the role of science in public debate over values and the role of the science counselor.

The powerful voice of science in matters of morality is something of an oddity. It can perhaps be best thought of as an unintended consequence of the framers' attitudes toward religion, science, and the state. Preventing the establishment of religion has never meant, either historically or in court, that religious perspectives cannot be expressed in public debates over morality. But those perspectives are heard less often than one would expect today, in part because of the astonishing diversity of religious beliefs in America, and in part because of an overgeneralization from judicial decisions limiting religious teachings in public schools.

At the same time, the philosophical implications of scientific discoveries receive a remarkable degree of attention. Science is virtually the last bastion of the optimistic, progressive part of the American ethos. And it is easy for everyone to slip carelessly from the descriptive power of science to prescriptions. Genetic engineering makes transformations in the human species theoretically possible but that does not mean those transformations ought to be made. Because a new energy source makes abundance theoretically possible does not mean that abundance should be an end in itself. Traditional religious and moral leaders have much to say about essential features of the human endeavor. There is no reason in law or logic that their voices should not be heard at least as loudly as the voices announcing the latest scientific breakthrough. Of course, anyone is free to argue, and some do, that science is all there is; that morality, if it exists, can only be discussed in evolutionary or biological terms. But if the free marketplace of ideas means anything, it means our national debate can include other perspectives as well.

But whereas science plays a surprisingly large role in discussions about our moral natures, the regulatory gap assures that the technology it spawns often does not live up to advance billing. Thus an increasing number of science counselors and an increasing role for those counselors in shaping research is a likely outcome of our current situation.

Are there alternatives for narrowing the regulatory gap? There are calls by government and industrial leaders for research that is more relevant, more goal directed. But there have always been such calls. At times, particularly in carefully targeted areas, they can be effective without endangering the research enterprise. But there is a limit to the effectiveness of this approach. The point of the regulatory gap is that on the science side, the scientific establishment has the bulk of the power. Outsiders, whether they are lawyers, politicians, business leaders, or former scientists working for others, cannot presently exercise effective control over the research process. And very few people, whether scientists or not, want to scrap the peer review, consensus-oriented approach run by the scientific community that now dominates the research landscape. It has simply been too successful in doing science, and there is simply too much of a chance that nonscientists would do worse from every perspective.

This is why the science counselors are so important. Because they are part of the research establishment, they might plausibly have an actual impact on scientific work. So we must look more closely at the impact they could have and whether that impact is desirable.

The first question is whether science counselors, with their interest in social considerations, could really change the nature of the scientific endeavor. In other words, can social considerations actually affect the ethos of science, or will they never be anything more than a set of outside constraints imposed on scientists and resisted accordingly?

Traditional scientists may well doubt that social issues can ever deflect serious scientists from the joy of their work. It is true that scientists have always grumbled about bureaucratic paper shuffling, administrative responsibilities, and budget meetings keeping them from the lab. But an increasing concern with broader social issues may be different. Not only is it important to the progress of science, it is an attractive activity. The challenge of balancing research progress with a heavier-than-usual dose of social implications can be seductive. Lawyers know their work in shaping social decisions is often fascinating. Science counselors discover the same thing.

It is hard to predict the impact of growing social consciousness on the doing of science. This is in part because we are not talking about an all-or-nothing situation. There has always been a continuum on which researchers have varied in the extent that their work reflects a concern for the outside world. But whereas the path from pure scientist to science counselor has been gradual, a great distance has been traversed. Vannevar Bush's classic 1945 report, *Science, The Endless Frontier*, which helped shape the modern research establishment, said the government should fund "the free play of free intellects, working on subjects of their own choice, in the manner dictated by their curiosity for exploration of the unknown."[1] That approach would now appear foolhardy to many researchers.

Let us highlight the potential impact of current trends by speculating about a future research environment utterly dominated by thoroughgoing science counselors. In such a world, the ethic of socially acceptable progress would permeate all research. In other words, basic research would no longer represent one of two cultures—law and science—vying for dominance in our society. No longer would science embody a belief in the progressive growth of knowledge that stands in sharp contrast with the law's process-oriented belief in the peaceful resolution of social disputes. The science counselor would represent one culture in which progress and process have merged into an ethic of social progress.

There are gains in this scenario—the regulatory gap would be narrowed in the short run, meaning that appropriate technology would be available more efficiently. But there are costs as well, because a complete triumph of the science counselor would not be consistent with productive science in the long run.

Traditional science marches forward, spurred by the goal of priority—the desire to be the first to add a particular bit of knowledge to the cumulative store. Even mission-oriented scientists have absorbed this ethic from the pure scientists. The science counselor, however, will be a mission-oriented scientist who absorbs the ethic of social progress, where priorities are unclear, knowledge is not always cumulative, and progress itself is an ill-defined term. Indeed science counselors, by engaging in socially directed research, may overlook some of the entirely unexpected developments that spur so much of science.

Science counselors grew in influence precisely because the scientific notion of progress does not perfectly match society's desires. On the other hand, society does not want to shut off the flow of science completely; it wants to pick and choose among scientific developments and use or shape those it likes. It is difficult to have it both ways. Because society's efforts to shape science are likely to be clumsy, scientists are forced to temper their own work. In so doing they gradually change the culture of science. As one leading commentator has put it, scientists, in order to forestall government intervention, must sometimes "do what most would consider a form of blasphemy: give up the research."[2] A scientific world utterly dominated by science counselors would take that step far too often.

Science counselors differ in degree, not in kind, from the budget or profit conscious scientists who work in government or private laboratories, but that is hardly reassuring. If scientists cared only about budgets and profits there would be little left of science. The same is true if scientists cared only about environmental, health, and safety issues.

In other words, it is not regulation that most directly threatens modern science. There is no army of litigators or environmentalists or pacifists at the laboratory door. Legal restraints today come primarily after research leaves the laboratory. Law does not threaten science through the legal control of basic research; it threatens science through the adoption of legal norms by basic researchers. Bridging the regulatory gap requires that science be shaped to social ends, and scientists are better able to do that than anyone. The science counselor seeks to avoid wasteful regulation by bringing science in line with reasonable social goals. In doing so, however, those who would save science, threaten it. The danger is that science will be loved to death, smothered in the embrace of social considerations.

But we have been speculating about a research world utterly dominated by science counselors. The lesson is that such a world is not desirable. The emergence of science counselors need not presage the extinction of traditional science. It is in the interests of the scientific community and the public at large that we always retain a prominent place for those pure scientists who care first and foremost about science's progress, not its implications. It may seem ironic that so soon after scientists were urged to embrace social concerns they are being warned not to go too far, but the warning is apt.

The influence of science counselors in the scientific community is likely to be far more pervasive than most scientists realize. Fortunately, there is no logical reason science counselors cannot coexist with traditional pure scientists, so long as there are enough of the latter in the scientific community. Given all of the pressures forcing science into a socially acceptable mold, it is worthwhile to assure that enough traditional pure science survives. It is, after all, in society's interest to spend at least some money and some tolerance on the unalloyed search for testable hypotheses. The path of scientific progress is sufficiently uncertain that society should take the chance on a surprisingly useful development. And knowledge for its own sake, although it should not be our only value, can nonetheless be treasured. Science counselors at their best will balance social and scientific values. If representatives of the latter fade away, science counselors may not be able to keep a meaningful scientific perspective of any kind. Accordingly, every once in a while, amidst the discussions of how scientific developments can serve the world, a word should be said about how scientific developments can serve science.

So in the end, our imperfect reality can only be improved in imperfect ways. A heavier dose of social concern is coming into the scientific world, and, if that dose remains a limited part of the research endeavor, it can perform a valuable service in narrowing the regulatory gap. There are no exact standards available here, but a clear understanding of law and science in American life makes steps in the right direction more likely.

Notes

Notes to Chapter 1

1. *See, e.g.,* DON K. PRICE, THE SCIENTIFIC ESTATE (1965).
2. *See., e.g.,* M. R. Smith, *Technology, Industrialization, and the Idea of Progress in America, in* RESPONSIBLE SCIENCE: THE IMPACT OF TECHNOLOGY ON SOCIETY 1 (Kevin B. Byrne, ed., 1986).
3. RALPH E. LAPP, THE NEW PRIESTHOOD (1965).
4. C. P. SNOW, THE TWO CULTURES AND THE SCIENTIFIC REVOLUTION (1959). Snow's book caused considerable discussion and debate. For a representative collection of articles, *see* DAVID K. CORNELIUS & EDWIN ST. VINCENT, CULTURES IN CONFLICT: PERSPECTIVES ON THE SNOW-LEAVIS CONTROVERSY (1964). For a more recent contribution to the controversy, *see* RICHARD OLSON, SCIENCE DEIFIED AND SCIENCE DEFIED 1–7 (1982). I have previously set forth the views that follow on Snow's work in Steven Goldberg, *The Central Dogmas of Law and Science,* 36 J. LEGAL EDUC. 37 (1986).
5. C. P. SNOW, THE TWO CULTURES AND THE SCIENTIFIC REVOLUTION 4 (1959).
6. C. P. SNOW, THE TWO CULTURES AND A SECOND LOOK 69 (1964).
7. GERALD GRAFF, LITERATURE AGAINST ITSELF: LITERARY IDEAS IN MODERN SOCIETY 7, 15 (1979). On the "vogue of indeterminism" that grew up in the 1930's, *see* MERLE CURTI, THE GROWTH OF AMERICAN THOUGHT 702–9 (3rd ed. 1982). For an argument that America has never had the sort of influential literary elite that marked Old-World culture, *see* DON PEMBER, MASS MEDIA IN AMERICA 39–43 (1974).
8. Peter H. Schuck, *Multi-Culturalism Redux: Science, Law and Politics,* 11 YALE L. & POL'Y REV. 1, 2 (1993).

9. GERTRUDE HIMMELFARB, MARRIAGE AND MORALS AMONG THE VICTORIANS 92 (1986).
10. ALEXIS DE TOCQUEVILLE, DEMOCRACY IN AMERICA 348–51 (New York, Sever & Francis, 1862) (1841).
11. EDMUND BURKE, SELECTED WRITINGS AND SPEECHES 161 (Peter J. Stanlis, ed., 1963).
12. *See, e.g.,* ALEXIS DE TOCQUEVILLE, DEMOCRACY IN AMERICA 352–55 (New York, Sever & Francis, 1862) (1841).

Notes to Chapter 2

1. An earlier version of portions of this chapter appears in Steven Goldberg, *The Reluctant Embrace: Law Science in America,* 75 GEO. L. J. 1341 (1987).
2. EDWARD N. DAC ANDRADE, SIR ISAAC NEWTON 11, 120 (1954).
3. *See* LOYD S. SWENSON, JR., GENESIS OF RELATIVITY: EINSTEIN IN CONTEXT 238 (1979); Robert K. Faulkner, *John Marshall in History, in* JOHN MARSHALL 170 (Stanley I. Kutler, ed., 1972).
4. The importance of priority in the scientific community is discussed in Robert K. Merton, *Priorities in Scientific Discovery: A Chapter in the Sociology of Science, in* THE SOCIOLOGY OF SCIENCE 447 (Bernard Barber & Walter Hirsh, eds., 1962). I have discussed those features of the scientific enterprise of central concern to lawyers in Steven Goldberg, *The Central Dogmas of Law and Science,* 36 J. LEGAL EDUC. 371, 376–79 (1986).
5. KARL POPPER, THE LOGIC OF SCIENTIFIC DISCOVERY 27 (1968).
6. Willard V. Quine & J. S. Ullian, *Hypothesis, in* WILLARD V. QUINE & J. S. ULLIAN, THE WEB OF BELIEF 64, 80 (1978).
7. Deconstructionist scholars who study science are discussed in SHEILA JASANOFF, THE FIFTH BRANCH: SCIENCE ADVISERS AS POLICYMAKERS 12–14 (1990).
8. THOMAS S. KUHN, THE STRUCTURE OF SCIENTIFIC REVOLUTIONS (1962).
9. *Id.* at 10.
10. *Id.* at 35–42.
11. *Id.* at 52.
12. THOMAS S. KUHN, THE STRUCTURE OF SCIENTIFIC REVOLUTIONS 84 (1962).
13. *Id.* at 93.
14. Willard. V. Quine & J. S. Ullian, *Hypothesis, in* WILLARD V. QUINE & J. S. ULLIAN, THE WEB OF BELIEF 64, 71 (1978).
15. Thomas S. Kuhn, *Objectivity, Value Judgment, and Theory Choice, in* THOMAS S. KUHN: THE ESSENTIAL TENSION 320 (1977).
16. *See* I. BERNARD COHEN, REVOLUTION IN SCIENCE 25–28, 389–404 (1985).

17. THOMAS S. KUHN, THE STRUCTURE OF SCIENTIFIC REVOLU-
    TIONS 165, 172 (1962).
18. *Id.* at 167.
19. *See, e.g.*, Robert Hollinger, *From Weber to Habermas*, in E. D. KLEMKE,
    ET. AL., INTRODUCTORY READINGS IN THE PHILOSOPHY OF SCI-
    ENCE (1988); BRUNO LATOUR & STEVE WOOLGAR, LABORATORY
    LIFE (1986); I. BERNARD COHEN, REVOLUTION IN SCIENCE 559–
    61 (1985).
20. SHEILA JASANOFF, THE FIFTH BRANCH: SCIENCE ADVISERS AS
    POLICYMAKERS 14 (1990).
21. An attack on creationism from the viewpoint of the scientific community is
    contained in NATIONAL ACADEMY OF SCIENCES, SCIENCE AND
    CREATIONISM (1984). Some of the science community's criticism of the
    alleged effectiveness of laetrile is summarized in United States v. Rutherford,
    442 U.S. 544, 557, n.15 (1979).
22. BANESH HOFFMAN, ALBERT EINSTEIN: CREATOR AND REBEL 80–
    82 (1972).
23. *See, e.g.*, DAVID P. BILLINGTON, THE TOWER AND THE BRIDGE 8–
    10 (1983).
24. ROBERT OPPENHEIMER: LETTERS AND RECOLLECTIONS 317 (Al-
    ice K. Smith & Charles Weiner, eds., 1980).
25. Peter H. Schuck, *Multi-Culturalism Redux: Science, Law, and Politics*, 11
    YALE L. & POL'Y REV. 1, 25 (1993).
26. Steven Goldberg, *On Legal and Mathematical Reasoning*, 22 JURIMET-
    RICS J. 83 (1981).
27. *See generally* CHAIM PERELMAN, JUSTICE, LAW, AND ARGUMENT
    120–24 (1980); Chaim Perelman, *Rhetoric and Politics*, 17 PHIL. &
    RHETORIC 129, 129–30 (1984).
28. Oliver W. Holmes, *Law in Science and Science in Law*, 12 HARV. L. REV.
    443, 459–60 (1899).
29. *See* Richard Stewart, *The Reformation of American Administrative Law*, 88
    HARV. L. REV. 1667, 1683–84 (1975).
30. David Bazelon, *Coping with Technology through the Legal Process*, 62
    CORNELL L. REV. 817, 825 (1977) (emphasis in original).
31. ROBERT OPPENHEIMER: LETTERS AND RECOLLECTIONS 317 (Al-
    ice K. Smith & Charles Weiner, eds., 1980).
32. McNabb v. United States, 318 U.S. 332, 347 (1943).
33. WERNER HEISENBERG, PHYSICS AND BEYOND: ENCOUNTERS
    AND CONVERSATIONS 69 (1971); *see* ON AESTHETICS IN SCIENCE
    (Judith Wechsler, ed., 1978) (relationship of science and beauty).
34. Ricketts v. Pennsylvania R.R. Co., 153 F.2d 757, 764 (2d Cir. 1946) (Frank,
    J., concurring). Frank believed that even physicists did not carry their desire
    for consistency to excess. *Id.* at 764 n.23.
35. Daubert v. Merrell Dow Pharmaceuticals, 113 S. Ct. 2786 (1993).

36. *Id.* at 2793. The "generally accepted" test came from Frye v. United States, 54 App. D.C. 46, 293 F. 1013 (1923). *Id.*
37. The Court cited some of these amicus briefs in its opinion. *See, e.g.,* Daubert v. Merrell Dow, 113 S. Ct. 2786, 2795 (1993).
38. Brief of Amici Curiae of Nicolaas Blembergen, et. al., at 4, Daubert v. Merrell Dow Pharmaceuticals, 113 S. Ct. 2786 (1993) (No. 92-102).
39. *Id.* at 11.
40. Brief of Amici Curiae of Physicians, Scientists, and Historians of Science in Support of Petitioners at 2, Daubert v. Merrell Dow Pharmaceuticals, 113 S. Ct. 2786 (1993) (No. 92-102).
41. Daubert v. Merrell Dow, 113 S. Ct. 2786, 2796–97 (1993).
42. *Id.*
43. *Id.* at 2798.
44. *Id.* at 2798.
45. *Id.* at 2799.
46. *Id.* at 2798–99.
47. SHEILA JASANOFF, THE FIFTH BRANCH: SCIENCE ADVISERS AS POLICYMAKERS 76 (1990).
48. Victor F. Weisskopf, *Why Pure Science?*, BULL. ATOM. SCIENTISTS, Apr. 1965, at 4, 8. *See also* Leon M. Lederman, *The Value of Fundamental Science*, SCI. AM., Nov. 1984, at 40, 45.

Notes to Chapter 3

1. An earlier version of portions of this chapter can be found in Steven Goldberg, *The Constitutional Status of American Science*, 1979 U. ILL. L. FOR. 1 (1979).
2. 2 PETER GAY, THE ENLIGHTENMENT: AN INTERPRETATION 126–66 (1969); ERNST CASSIRER, THE PHILOSOPHY OF THE ENLIGHTENMENT 43–45 (1960).
3. 2 PETER GAY, THE ENLIGHTENMENT: AN INTERPRETATION 127–87 (1969).
4. THE WORKS OF ALEXANDER POPE 390 (William J. Courthope, et. al., eds., 1967). *See also* 2 PETER GAY, THE ENLIGHTENMENT: AN INTERPRETATION 103 (1969); CARL BECKER, THE HEAVENLY CITY OF THE EIGHTEENTH-CENTURY PHILOSOPHERS 57–63 (1932).
5. ERNEST CASSARA, THE ENLIGHTENMENT IN AMERICA 31 (1975); HENRY F. MAY, THE ENLIGHTENMENT IN AMERICA 211–14 (1976); Frederick E. Brasch, *The Newtonian Epoch in the American Colonies*, 49 AM. ANTIQUARIAN SOC'Y PROC. 314 (1939); I. Bernard Cohen, *Science and the Growth of the American Republic*, 38 REV. POL. 359, 364–71 (1976); Richard Delgado & David R. Millen, *God, Galileo, and*

Government: Toward Constitutional Protection for Scientific Inquiry, 53 WASH. L. REV. 349, 354–61 (1978).

6. *See generally* BROOKE HINDLE, DAVID RITTENHOUSE (1964); EDWARD FORD, DAVID RITTENHOUSE (1946).

7. *See* DANIEL J. BOORSTIN, THE LOST WORLD OF THOMAS JEFFERSON 14–16 (1960); BROOKE HINDLE, THE PURSUIT OF SCIENCE IN REVOLUTIONARY AMERICA 1735–89, 239–40, 297–98 (1956).

8. *See* BROOKE HINDLE, THE PURSUIT OF SCIENCE IN REVOLUTIONARY AMERICA 320–23 (1956); Harry H. Clark, *The Influence of Science on American Ideas: From 1775 to 1809,* 35 TRANSACTIONS WIS. ACAD. 312 n.44 (1943); EDWIN T. MARTIN, THOMAS JEFFERSON: SCIENTIST (1952); DUMAS MALONE, JEFFERSON AND THE RIGHTS OF MAN 83–85 (1951).

9. EDWARD M. BURNS, JAMES MADISON: THE PHILOSOPHER OF THE CONSTITUTION 24–25 (1968); GAILLARD HUNT, THE LIFE OF JAMES MADISON 96–97 (1902).

10. JAMES T. FLEXNER, THE YOUNG HAMILTON: A BIOGRAPHY 47, 62 (1978); BROADUS MITCHELL, ALEXANDER HAMILTON: YOUTH TO MATURITY 54 (1957).

11. PETER GAY, THE ENLIGHTENMENT: A COMPREHENSIVE ANTHOLOGY 766 (1973); I. BERNARD COHEN, FRANKLIN AND NEWTON 36–37 (1966).

12. *See* DON K. PRICE, THE SCIENTIFIC ESTATE 85–89 (1965); DANIEL J. BOORSTIN, THE LOST WORLD OF THOMAS JEFFERSON 244 (1960); Robert K. Merton, *Science and the Social Order, in* THE SOCIOLOGY OF SCIENCE 254, 265 (Norman W. Storer, ed., 1973).

13. *See, e.g.,* Arnold Thackray, *The Industrial Revolution and the Image of Science, in* SCIENCE AND VALUES 3 (Arnold Thackray & Everett Mendelsohn, eds., 1974); WHITFIELD BELL, EARLY AMERICAN SCIENCE: NEEDS AND OPPORTUNITIES FOR STUDY 8 (1955).

14. 10 THE WRITINGS OF THOMAS JEFFERSON 141 (Andrew A. Lipscomb, et. al., eds., 1904).

15. *See* I. Bernard Cohen, *Science and the Growth of the American Republic,* 38 REV. POL. 359, 365 (1976). On the role of science in the creation of American institutions *see, e.g.,* Harry H. Clark, *The Influence of Science on American Ideas: From 1775 to 1809,* 35 TRANSACTIONS WIS. ACAD. 312 n.44 (1943); GARRY WILLS, INVENTING AMERICA (1978); DANIEL J. BOORSTIN, THE REPUBLIC OF TECHNOLOGY 57–60 (1978); GRANT GILMORE, THE AGES OF AMERICAN LAW 4–5 (1977); Douglass Adair, *"That Politics May Be Reduced to a Science": David Hume, James Madison, and the Tenth Federalist,* 20 HUNTINGTON LIB. Q. 343 (1957); Thomas I. Emerson, *Colonial Intentions and Current Realities of the First Amendment,* 125 U. PA. L. REV. 737, 741 (1977).

16. Philip M. Freneau & H. H. Brackenridge, *The Rising Glory of America, in*

POEMS OF FRENEAU 12–13 (Harry H. Clark, ed., 1929.) Freneau embodied the love of science and political engagement characteristic of his period. *See* MARY W. BOWDEN, PHILIP FRENEAU 9–10 (1976); FRANK L. MOTT, AMERICAN JOURNALISM 123–27 (3d ed. 1962).

17. POEMS OF FRENEAU 103 (Harry H. Clark, ed., 1929).
18. BROOKE HINDLE, THE PURSUIT OF SCIENCE IN REVOLUTIONARY AMERICA 249–53 (1956).
19. 7 THE WRITINGS OF THOMAS JEFFERSON 329 (Andrew A. Lipscomb et. al., eds., 1904).
20. 15 *id.* at 339; 16 *id.* at 182. On Jefferson's use of the word *science, see* 10 THE WRITINGS OF THOMAS JEFFERSON 141 (Andrew A. Lipscomb, et al., eds., 1904). Jefferson's statement, written in 1821, reflected his longstanding belief in the intimate relationship between freedom and science. *See* THOMAS JEFFERSON, ON SCIENCE AND FREEDOM: THE LETTER TO THE STUDENT WILLIAM G. MUNFORD (Julian P. Boyd, ed., 1964). *See also* Dr. Isaiah Bowman, *Jeffersonian "Freedom of Speech" from the Standpoint of Science,* 82 SCIENCE 529 (1935).
21. Levy has summarized his view of Jefferson's position on free speech as follows: "His threshold of tolerance for hateful political ideas was less than generous. Eloquently and felicitously he declared himself in favor of freedom of speech and press, but invariably either in favor of the liberty of his own political allies or merely in abstract propositions. . . . He cared deeply for the intellectual liberty of religious, scientific or philosophical heretics — unless political heresies of his own adherence were involved." Leonard W. Levy, *Jefferson as a Civil Libertarian, in* THOMAS JEFFERSON: THE MAN . . . HIS WORLD . . . HIS INFLUENCE 197 (Lally Weymouth, ed., 1973).
22. 1 JOURNALS OF THE CONTINENTAL CONGRESS 108 (1904). Although Levy contends that the sentiments in the letter were at times not practiced by Congress, he does not question congressional views on scientific freedom. *See* Leonard W. Levy, *Jefferson as a Civil Libertarian, in* THOMAS JEFFERSON: THE MAN . . . HIS WORLD . . . HIS INFLUENCE 188 (Lally Weymouth, ed., 1973).
23. L.R. 3 Q.B. 360 (1868). Use of the Hicklin test in American courts is discussed in Roth v. United States, 354 U.S. 476, 488–89 (1957).
24. 3 Q.B. at 366.
25. The history and relevant case law is discussed in Parmelle v. United States 113 F.2d 729, 734–36 (D.C. Cir. 1940). A particularly important early decision was United States v. Dennett, 39 F.2d 564 (2d Cir. 1930), which held a sex education manual not to be obscene.
26. 354 U.S. 476 (1957).
27. In the course of arguing that obscenity is not protected by the First Amendment, the government's brief presented a "comparative scale of value" by which it proposed First Amendment claims should be judged. Brief for the

United States at 28, Roth v. United States, 354 U.S. 476 (1957)(No. 582). Science fares well under this approach. The government suggested that different kinds of speech be ranked as follows: political speech, religious, economic, scientific, general news and information, social and historical commentary, literature, art, entertainment, music, humor, commercial advertisements, gossip, comic books, epithets, libel, obscenity, profanity, commercial pornography. *Id.* at 29. Those who oppose the two-tiered analysis adopted in Roth may take comfort in the Court's apparent rejection of this nineteen-tiered system. Had it been adopted, hard cases might have resulted from, for example, the decision to rank "humor" three steps above "comic books." Nonetheless, a more flexible ranking of the value of various kinds of speech may well be an important part of modern First Amendment jurisprudence. *See, e.g.,* F.C.C. v. Pacifica Foundation, 438 U.S. 726 (1978). The Pacifica plurality specifically retains a high status for scientific speech. *Id.* at 746.

28. 354 U.S. at 487. The Court cites United States v. Dennett, 39 F.2d 564 (2d Cir. 1930) for this proposition. Earlier in the Roth opinion, the Court relies on the 1774 letter of the Continental Congress to the Citizens of Quebec to delineate the proper scope of the First Amendment. 354 U.S. at 484; 1 JOURNALS OF THE CONTINENTAL CONGRESS 108 (1904).

29. United States v. 31 Photographs, 156 F. Supp. 350 (S.D.N.Y. 1957). *See also* Henley v. Wise, 303 F. Supp. 62, 67 (N.D. Ind. 1969).

30. 413 U.S. 15 (1973).

31. *Id.* at 34.

32. *Id.* at 26.

33. New York Times Co. v. United States, 403 U.S. 713 (1971); Near v. Minnesota, 283 U.S. 697 (1931).

34. Firestone v. First Dist. Dental Soc'y. 299 N.Y.S.2d 551, 554, 697 (1931).

35. Gertz v. Robert Welch, Inc., 418 U.S. 323, 340–41 (1974); New York Times Co. v. Sullivan, 376 U.S. 254, 279 (1971).

36. Demuth Dev. Corp. v. Merck and Co., Inc., 432 F. Supp. 990, 993 (E.D.N.Y. 1977) (citing Gertz v. Robert Welch, Inc., 418 U.S. 323, 340 [1974]).

37. Bates v. State Bar of Arizona, 433 U.S. 350 (1977); Virginia State Bd. of Pharmacy v. Virginia Citizens Consumer Council, Inc., 425 U.S. 748 (1976).

38. Metpath v. Imperato, 450 F. Supp. 115 (S.D.N.Y. 1978).

39. *See, e.g.,* Konigsberg v. State Bar of California, 366 U.S. 36, 49 (1961) ("[W]e reject the view that freedom of speech and association . . . are 'absolutes.'. . .").

40. *See, e.g., Developments in the Law: The National Security Interest and Civil Liberties,* 85 HARV. L. REV. 1130, 1190–1207 (1972). Under one executive order, information was classified as "top secret" it if contained, *inter alia,* "scientific or technological developments vital to national security."

Knopf v. Colby, 509 F.2d 1362, 1368 (4th Cir.), *cert. denied,* 421 U.S. 992 (1975).

41. *Developments in the Law: The National Security Interest and Civil Liberties,* 85 HARV. L. REV. 1130, 1195 (1972).

42. *See generally* WALTER GELLHORN, SECURITY, LOYALTY AND SCIENCE (1950); Wallace Parks, *Secrecy and the Public Interest in Military Affairs,* 26 GEO. WASH. L. REV. 23, 36–43 (1957).

43. Near v. Minnesota, 283 U.S. 697, 716 (1931).

44. United States v. The Progressive, Inc., 467 F. Supp. 990 (W.D. Wisc.). After this decision was handed down, another journal published the article in question. An appellate court then dismissed the case as moot. 610 F.2d 819 (7th Cir. 1979). It is widely accepted that the government properly kept the design of the atomic bomb secret during World War II; *see, e.g., Developments in the Law: The National Security Interest and Civil Liberties,* 85 HARV. L. REV. 1130, 1190–91, 1195 (1972); John T. Edsall, *Scientific Freedom and Responsibility: Report of the AAAS Committee on Scientific Freedom and Responsibility,* 188 SCIENCE 687, 689 (1975).

45. Stanley v. Georgia, 394 U.S. 557, 567 (1969).

46. *See* Brandenburg v. Ohio, 395 U.S. 444 (1969).

47. *See, e.g.,* Williams v. Rhodes, 393 U.S. 23, 32 (1968); Buckley v. Valeo, 424 U.S. 1, 39 (1976); ALEXANDER MEIKLEJOHN, POLITICAL FREEDOM 27 (1966).

48. *See, e.g.,* Alexander Meikeljohn, *The First Amendment Is an Absolute,* 1961 SUP. CT. REV. 245, 257 (1961); Harry Kalven, *The New York Times Case: "A Note of The Central Meaning of the First Amendment,"* 1964 SUP. CT. REV. 191, 221 (1964); Thomas I. Emerson, *Toward a General Theory of the First Amendment,* 72 YALE L. J. 877, 883 (1963). Robert H. Bork, *Neutral Principles and Some First Amendment Problems,* 47 IND. L. J. 1, 28 (1971).

49. *See, e.g.,* SILVIO A. BENDINI, THE LIFE OF BENJAMIN BANNEKER 103–36 (1972).

50. *See, e.g.,* A. HUNTER DUPREE, SCIENCE IN THE FEDERAL GOVERNMENT: A HISTORY OF POLICIES AND ACTIVITIES TO 1940 14, 15, 293, 294 (1957). Madison undoubtedly recalled that, when he and Pinckney moved at the Constitutional Convention to give Congress power to create a national university, Gouverneur Morris replied, "It is not necessary. The exclusive power at the seat of government, will reach the object." The proposal was then defeated six votes to four, with Connecticut divided. *See* MAX FARRAND, 2 RECORDS OF THE FEDERAL CONVENTION 616 (1911); JAMES MADISON, 2 JOURNALS OF THE FEDERAL CONVENTION 726–27 (Erastus H. Scott, ed., 1893). Although Jefferson initially appeared to believe a national university could be created under the Constitution, when he became president he favored a constitutional amendment for that purpose. A. HUNTER DUPREE, SCIENCE IN THE FEDERAL

GOVERNMENT: A HISTORY OF POLICIES AND ACTIVITIES TO 1940 14–15, 23–24 (1957). In other areas, particularly in relation to surveys, President Jefferson managed to aid science even when it required modifying some of his strict constructionist statements. *See id.* at 24–29.

51. A. HUNTER DUPREE, SCIENCE IN THE FEDERAL GOVERNMENT: A HISTORY OF POLICIES AND ACTIVITIES TO 1940 26 (1957); DON K. PRÍCE, GOVERNMENT AND SCIENCE 10–11 (1954); Gordon B. Baldwin, *Law in Support of Science: Legal Control of Basic Research Resources,* 54 GEO. L. J. 559, 575 (1966).

52. DON K. PRICE, GOVERNMENT AND SCIENCE 38 (1954).

53. *See, e.g.,* ROBERT K. MERTON, SCIENCE, TECHNOLOGY AND SOCIETY IN SEVENTEENTH CENTURY ENGLAND 185–98 (1970).

54. *Id.,* at xiii, 184–207.

55. *See* DANIEL J. BOORSTIN, THE LOST WORLD OF THOMAS JEFFERSON 13–14 (1960). For discussion of Rittenhouse's extensive contributions to the war effort, *see* JOHN F. KASSON, CIVILIZING THE MACHINE 13 (1976); BROOKE HINDLE, THE PURSUIT OF SCIENCE IN REVOLUTIONARY AMERICA 229–31 (1956).

56. I. Bernard Cohen, *Science and the Revolution,* 47 TECH. REV. 367, 368 (1945). Saltpeter is potassium nitrate, a vital gunpowder ingredient that America had not produced prior to the Revolutionary War. JOHN F. KASSON, CIVILIZING THE MACHINE 11 (1976).

57. BROOKE HINDLE, THE PURSUIT OF SCIENCE IN REVOLUTIONARY AMERICA 244–45 (1956).

58. *See generally* I. Bernard Cohen, *Science and the Revolution,* 47 TECH. REV. 367 (1945).

59. I. Bernard Cohen, *Science and the Revolution,* 47 TECH. REV. 374 (1945).

60. *Id.;* SALVIO A. BENDINI, THINKERS AND TINKERS 365 (1975).

61. A. HUNTER DUPREE, SCIENCE IN THE FEDERAL GOVERNMENT: A HISTORY OF POLICIES AND ACTIVITIES TO 1940 26–28 (1957). Jefferson also invoked the commerce power to convince Congress to appropriate money for the expedition. *See also* DON K. PRICE, GOVERNMENT AND SCIENCE 10–11 (1954); Gordon B. Baldwin, *Law in Support of Science: Legal Control of Basic Research Resources,* 54 GEO. L. J. 559, 575 (1966). In addition, in 1807, a coastal survey was funded in part for military purposes. The survey was directed by Ferdinand Hassler, a leading scientist, later appointed the first superintendent of weights and measures. *See* A. HUNTER DUPREE, SCIENCE IN THE FEDERAL GOVERNMENT: A HISTORY OF POLICIES AND ACTIVITIES TO 1940 29–30 (1957); REXMOND C. COCHRANE, MEASURES FOR PROGRESS 515–26 (1966).

62. Military needs were central to the development of such institutions as the Naval Observatory and the Public Health Service. A. HUNTER DUPREE, SCIENCE IN THE FEDERAL GOVERNMENT: A HISTORY OF POLI-

CIES AND ACTIVITIES TO 1940 184–87, 256–70 (1957). The World War II Manhattan Project, which developed the atomic bomb, was under military command. DANIEL S. GREENBERG, THE POLITICS OF PURE SCIENCE 88 (1967).

63. U.S. CONST. art. I, § 8, cl. 12.

64. *See* MAX FARRAND, 2 RECORDS OF THE FEDERAL CONVENTION 508–9 (1911); JAMES MADISON, 2 JOURNALS OF THE FEDERAL CONVENTION 660–62 (Erastus H. Scott, ed., 1893).

65. *See, e.g.,* THE FEDERALIST NO. 24, at 148 (Alexander Hamilton)(Modern Library ed. 1937)("[t]hat clause which forbids the appropriation of money for the support of the army for any period longer than two years a precaution which, upon a nearer view of it, will appear to be a great and real security against the keeping up of troops without evident necessity.") *See also id.* at 163.

66. *See, e.g.,* Albert C. Lazure, *Why Research and Development Contracts Are Distinctive, in* RESEARCH AND DEVELOPMENT PROCUREMENT LAW 255, 262 (Albert C. Lazure & Andrew P. Murphy, eds., 1957). Most military research and development is performed under contract with private industry and universities. The uncertainties involved in planning and executing such contracts require close collaboration between defense agencies and scientists in the private sector. *See, e.g.,* DON K. PRICE, GOVERNMENT AND SCIENCE 36–40 (1954).

67. 25 Op. Att'y Gen. 105 (1904); 40 Op. Att'y Gen. 555 (1948). After the latter opinion, Congress enacted legislation that authorized the military to enter into research and contracts lasting up to ten years. 10 U.S.C. § 2352 (1976).

68. The Constitution provides that Congress shall have the power "to coin money, regulate the value thereof . . . and fix the standard of weights and measures." U.S. CONST. art. I, § 8, cl. 5.

69. A. HUNTER DUPREE, SCIENCE IN THE FEDERAL GOVERNMENT: A HISTORY OF POLICIES AND ACTIVITIES TO 1940 17–18 (1957).

70. *Id.* The early years under Rittenhouse were particularly difficult due in part to a shortage of supplies. *See* FRANK H. STEWART, HISTORY OF THE FIRST UNITED STATES MINT 57, 62 (reprint of 1928 ed.) (1974).

71. A. HUNTER DUPREE, SCIENCE IN THE FEDERAL GOVERNMENT: A HISTORY OF POLICIES AND ACTIVITIES TO 1940 17–18 (1957).

72. REXMOND C. COCHRANE, MEASURES FOR PROGRESS 21–33 (1966).

73. *Id.* at 24–27.

74. 31 Stat. 1449 (1901) (current version at 15 U.S.C. § 271 [1977]).

75. *See, e.g.,* DANIEL J. KEVLES, THE PHYSICISTS 66–67 (1977).

76. REXMOND C. COCHRANE, MEASURES FOR PROGRESS 559, 631–48 (1966).

77. *Id.* at 624–30.

78. U.S. CONST. art. I, § 8, cl. 8.
79. *See, e.g.,* Karl B. Lutz, *Patents and Science,* 18 GEO. WASH. L. REV. 50 (1949).
80. *See, e.g.,* Edward S. Irons & Mary H. Sears, *The Constitutional Standard of Invention: The Touchstone for Patent Reform,* 1973 UTAH L. REV. 653, 653 n.1 (1973).
81. *See, e.g.,* BRUCE W. BUGBEE, GENESIS OF AMERICAN PATENT AND COPYRIGHT LAW (1967). P. J. Federico, *Colonial Monopolies and Patents,* 11 J. PAT. OFF. SOC'Y 358 (1929); Kark Fenning, *The Origin of the Patent and Copyright Clause of the Constitution,* 17 GEO. L. J. 109 (1929); Edward S. Irons & Mary H. Sears, *The Constitutional Standard of Invention: The Touchstone for Patent Reform,* 1973 UTAH L. REV. 653, 653 n.1 (1973).
82. Proposals submitted to the Committee of Detail at the Constitutional Convention, but never reported out, would have given Congress power "to encourage, by proper premiums and provisions, the advancement of useful knowledge and discoveries." MAX FARRAND, 2 RECORDS OF THE FEDERAL CONVENTION 321, 325 (1911); JAMES MADISON, 2 JOURNALS OF THE FEDERAL CONVENTION 550 (Erastus H. Scott, ed., 1893); Karl Fenning, *The Origin of the Patent and Copyright Clause of the Constitution,* 17 GEO. L. J. 109 (1929). The patent clause as enacted did require the government to evaluate proposed inventions for patentability and thus ultimately led to creation of the U.S. Patent Office. A. HUNTER DUPREE, SCIENCE IN THE FEDERAL GOVERNMENT: A HISTORY OF POLICIES AND ACTIVITIES TO 1940 12–14, 46–47 (1957).
83. *See, e.g.,* BRUCE W. BUGBEE, GENESIS OF AMERICAN PATENT AND COPYRIGHT LAW 14 (1967).
84. *See, e.g.,* Harry H. Clark, *To Promote the Progress of . . . Useful Arts,* 43 N.Y.U. L. REV. 88, 94 (1968); Edward S. Irons & Mary H. Sears, *The Constitutional Standard of Invention: The Touchstone for Patent Reform,* 1973 UTAH L. REV. 653, 653 n.1 (1973).; BRUCE W. BUGBEE, GENESIS OF AMERICAN PATENT AND COPYRIGHT LAW 61, 130–31 (1967); A. HUNTER DUPREE, SCIENCE IN THE FEDERAL GOVERNMENT: A HISTORY OF POLICIES AND ACTIVITIES TO 1940 5 (1957).
85. *See* Graham v. Deere, 383 U.S. 1 (1966).
86. *See, e.g.,* Parker v. Flook, 437 U.S. 584 (1978); Gottschalk v. Benson, 409 U.S. 63, 67 (1972).
87. 1 ANNALS OF CONGRESS 933–34 (1790). Washington's entire statement demonstrates his support for "new and useful inventions" as well as scientific knowledge generally. *Id. See* DON K. PRICE, THE SCIENTIFIC ESTATE 85–89 (1965); Robert K. Merton, *Science and the Social Order, in* THE SOCIOLOGY OF SCIENCE 254, 265 (Norman W. Storer, ed., 1973). *See also* John W. Oliver, *Science and the "Founding Fathers,"* 48 SCI. MONTHLY 256, 256 (1939).

88. Alexander Hamilton, *Report on the Subject of Manufacturers, in* 1 THE WORKS OF ALEXANDER HAMILTON 226–36 (New York, Williams & Whiting, 1810).
89. *Id.* at 230–231.
90. *See* United States v. Butler, 297 U.S. 1 (1936).
91. SALVIO A. BEDINI, THINKERS AND TINKERS 349–51 (1975).
92. 1 ANNALS OF CONGRESS 171 (1789).
93. IRVING BRANT, JAMES MADISON: FATHER OF THE CONSTITUTION 331–32 (1950). Dupree, without specific reference to the views of Madison, suggests that favorable congressional action on Churchman's petition would have been based on the patent clause. A. HUNTER DUPREE, SCIENCE IN THE FEDERAL GOVERNMENT: A HISTORY OF POLICIES AND ACTIVITIES TO 1940 9–11 (1957). Although the congressional debate does not resolve the matter, *see* 1 ANNALS OF CONGRESS 142–43, 170–73 (1789); 2 *id.* at 1845–46, 1885 (1791); 3 *id.* at 312–15, 431–32 (1792), this outcome seems unlikely. The wording of the patent clause, protecting discoveries by securing exclusive rights, makes the spending power a far more probable and persuasive basis for favorable congressional action on the petition.
94. SALVIO A BEDINI, THINKERS AND TINKERS 351 (1975).
95. *See, e.g.,* Howard S. Miller, *The Political Economy of Science, in* NINETEENTH CENTURY AMERICAN SCIENCE: A REAPPRAISAL 98–99 (George H. Daniels, ed., 1972); Nathan Reingold, *Introduction, in* 1 THE NEW AMERICAN STATE PAPERS IN SCIENCE AND TECHNOLOGY 11–12 (1973).
96. One early federal-related scientific enterprise, the Smithsonian Institution, overcame constitutional objections in part because it was funded by a bequest. A. HUNTER DUPREE, SCIENCE IN THE FEDERAL GOVERNMENT: A HISTORY OF POLICIES AND ACTIVITIES TO 1940 66–68, 76–90 (1957).
97. 12 Stat. 388 (1862) (current version at 7 U.S.C. § 2201 [1977]). See GEORGE H. DANIELS, SCIENCE IN AMERICAN SOCIETY 268–69 (1971); A. HUNTER DUPREE, SCIENCE IN THE FEDERAL GOVERNMENT: A HISTORY OF POLICIES AND ACTIVITIES TO 1940 151 (1957). Although the legislation creating the department is silent as to its constitutional basis, *see* 12 Stat. 387–88 (1862), the appropriations for the agency "would seem not to be justifiable except under a power to raise and spend money for 'the general welfare.'" Charles K. Burdick, *Federal Aid Legislation,* 8 CORNELL L. Q. 324, 329 (1923).
98. A. HUNTER DUPREE, SCIENCE IN THE FEDERAL GOVERNMENT: A HISTORY OF POLICIES AND ACTIVITIES TO 1940 150 (1957); GEORGE H. DANIELS, SCIENCE IN AMERICAN SOCIETY 268–69 (1971); Reynold M. Wik, *Science and American Agriculture, in* SCIENCE AND SOCIETY IN THE UNITED STATES 81, 94, 96–97 (David D. Van

Tassel & Michael G. Hall, eds., 1966). Because Congress created the colleges by donating public land to the states for that purpose, 12 Stat. 503–5 (1862), the constitutional basis for the program was Congress' power "to dispose of and make all needful rules and regulations respecting the territory or other property belonging to the United States." U.S. CONST. art. IV, § 3, cl. 2. *See* Charles K. Burdick, *Federal Aid Legislation,* 8 CORNELL L. Q. 324, 324–27 (1923); Gordon B. Baldwin, *Law in Support of Science: Legal Control of Basic Research Resources,* 54 GEO. L. J. 559, 575 (1966). The land grant colleges established an influential pattern of federal-state cooperation. *See, e.g.,* Don K. Price, *The Scientific Establishment,* 31 GEO. WASH. L. REV. 713, 719–20 (1963).

99. *See, e.g.,* Reynold M. Wik, *Science and American Agriculture, in* SCIENCE AND SOCIETY IN THE UNITED STATES 81,94, 96–97 (David D. Van Tassel & Michael G. Hall, eds., 1966); LUTHER G. TWEETEN, FOUNDATIONS OF FARM POLICY 118–209 (1970).

100. 297 U.S. 1 (1936).

101. *Id.* at 65–67.

102. *See* Alexander Hamilton, *Report on the Subject of Manufacturers, in* 1 THE WORKS OF ALEXANDER HAMILTON 226–36 (New York, Williams & Whiting, 1810) (Hamilton supported pecuniary rewards to encourage manufacturers, including rewards for "new inventions and discoveries . . . particularly those which relate to machinery."); 297 U.S. at 66–67. The Court also cited Justice Story's *Commentaries,* which rely in part on the Hamiltonian discussion of premiums. *Id.* at 66. 2 JOSEPH STORY, COMMENTARIES ON THE CONSTITUTION OF THE UNITED STATES 389 n.2 (Boston, Hilliard, Grayd & Co., 1833). Later decisions have treated *Butler* as settling the dispute over the spending power in Hamilton's favor. *See, e.g.,* Buckley v. Valeo, 424 U.S. 1, 90–91 (1976); Helvering v. Davis, 301 U.S. 619, 640 (1937).

103. Brief for the United States, United Sates v. Butler, at 135, 153, 157–59 (1936)(No. 401).

104. 297 U.S. at 65.

105. *See* IRVING BRANT, JAMES MADISON: FATHER OF THE CONSTITUTION 331–32 (1950); *see also* 1 ANNALS OF CONGRESS 171 (1789).

106. Moreover, the Supreme Court allows Congress considerable discretion in determining what programs serve the general welfare. *See, e.g.,* Buckley v. Valeo, 424 U.S. 1, 90–91 (1976); Helvering v. Davis, 301 U.S. 619, 640–41 (1937).

107. *See, e.g.,* Charles V. Kidd, *American Universities and Federal Research, in* THE SOCIOLOGY OF SCIENCE 394, 400 (Bernard Barber & Walter Hirsch, eds., 1962). The major state science activities in the nineteenth century, geological and geographic surveys, at times competed with the federal government for the services of leading scientists. A. HUNTER

DUPREE, SCIENCE IN THE FEDERAL GOVERNMENT: A HISTORY OF POLICIES AND ACTIVITIES TO 1940 92(1957); Howard S. Miller, *The Political Economy of Science, in* NINETEENTH CENTURY AMERICAN SCIENCE: A REAPPRAISAL 100 (George H. Daniels, ed., 1972); GEORGE H. DANIELS, AMERICAN SCIENCE IN THE AGE OF JACKSON 21 (1968). But even with the surveys, federal-state cooperation was underway by 1843. *See* DANIEL J. ELAZAR, THE AMERICAN PARTNERSHIP 255–59 (1962). In agriculture science, another leading area of state science, federal-state cooperation was a central feature of the land-grant college arrangement. *See, e.g.,* Don K. Price, *The Scientific Establishment,* 31 GEO. WASH. L. REV. 713, 719–20 (1963). *See also* A. HUNTER DUPREE, SCIENCE IN THE FEDERAL GOVERNMENT: A HISTORY OF POLICIES AND ACTIVITIES TO 1940 150 (1957); GEORGE H. DANIELS, SCIENCE IN AMERICAN SOCIETY, 268–69 (1971).

108. Robert V. Bruce, *A Statistical Profile of American Scientists 1846–1876, in* NINETEENTH CENTURY AMERICAN SCIENCE: A REAPPRAISAL 63, 94 (George H. Daniels, ed., 1972).

109. A survey of 1954 science spending in six state governments showed federal spending for science more substantial in both absolute and percentage terms. FREDERIC N. CLEAVELAND, SCIENCE AND STATE GOVERNMENT 24 (1959). A 1973 survey of all states showed that their combined spending for science accounted for no more than 6.5 percent of national research and development expenditures at a time when the federal government accounted for over 50 percent of those expenditures. NATIONAL SCIENCE FOUNDATION, RESEARCH AND DEVELOPMENT IN STATE GOVERNMENT AGENCIES viii (1975).

110. Basic themes in post-Civil War political and economic thought are summarized in David Donald, *Uniting the Republic, in* THE GREAT REPUBLIC 735–58 (Bernard Bailyn, et al., eds., 1977).

111. PAUL STUDENSKI & HERMAN T. KROOS, FINANCIAL HISTORY OF THE UNITED STATES 163 (2d ed. 1963).

112. The dispute basically concerned the somewhat overlapping functions of the government's various survey agencies. Senator W. B. Allison headed a joint congressional commission that rejected the idea of a single Department of Science. A. HUNTER DUPREE, SCIENCE IN THE FEDERAL GOVERNMENT: A HISTORY OF POLICIES AND ACTIVITIES TO 1940 215–31 (1957).

113. Estimates of government spending for research and development, particularly for the years before 1953 when the National Science Foundation began collecting data, are both approximate and somewhat arbitrary. See MICHAEL D. REAGAN, SCIENCE AND THE FEDERAL PATRON 15 (1969). Testimony before the Allison commission showed, in 1884, spending of about $300,000 by the Interior Department's Geological Survey,

about $600,000 by the Treasury's Coast and Geodetic Survey, and nearly $1 million by the Army Signal Service, which was in charge of meteorology. *Testimony, Before the Joint Commission to Consider the Present Organizations of the Signal Service, et al., Mis. Doc. No. 82,* 49th Cong., 1st Sess. 47, 61 n.22 (1886). In addition, 1884 agriculture science spending was over $100,000. *See* U.S. TREASURY, TREASURY DEP'T DOC. NO. 1111, ACCOUNT OF THE RECEIPTS AND EXPENDITURES OF THE UNITED STATES FOR THE FISCAL YEAR ENDING JUNE 30, 1885 41–42 (1888). Similar amounts were spent on programs as diverse as the conservation efforts of the Fish commission and public health research in the military. *See* A. HUNTER DUPREE, SCIENCE IN THE FEDERAL GOVERNMENT: A HISTORY OF POLICIES AND ACTIVITIES TO 1940 237, 256–70 (1957).

114. *See* A. HUNTER DUPREE, SCIENCE IN THE FEDERAL GOVERNMENT: A HISTORY OF POLICIES AND ACTIVITIES TO 1940 215–31 (1957).

115. LOUIS L. JAFFEE & NATHANIEL L. NATHANSON, ADMINISTRATIVE LAW 12 (1976) ("It is customary and appropriate to date the present era from the creation of the Interstate Commerce Commission in 1887. . . . The [commission] broke new ground in the federal establishment.")

116. DON K. PRICE, THE SCIENTIFIC ESTATE 35 (1965).

117. MICHAEL D. REAGAN, SCIENCE AND THE FEDERAL PATRON 15 (1969). Historians of science in America often have emphasized the relatively limited achievements, by European standards, of nineteenth-century American science. *See, e.g.,* I. Bernard Cohen, *Science and the Growth of the American Republic,* 38 REV. POL. 359, 370–84 (1976). Scientific progress depends on more than constitutional structures; historians have contended that nineteenth-century America was a young country that at times placed undue emphasis on practical as opposed to theoretical projects. *Id.* In recent years reassessments of nineteenth-century American science have begun to paint a somewhat different picture; in particular, increased recognition of the federal government's science activities has revealed continuity between the founding fathers' love of science and the present federal science establishment. *See, e.g.,* Nathan Reingold, *Introduction, in* THE NEW AMERICAN STATE PAPERS IN SCIENCE AND TECHNOLOGY 11–14 (1973); GEORGE H. DANIELS, SCIENCE IN AMERICAN SOCIETY 21–26 (1971); George H. Daniels, *Introduction, in* NINETEENTH CENTURY AMERICAN SCIENCE: A REAPPRAISAL vii (George H. Daniels, ed., 1972); Charles E. Rosenberg, *On Writing the History of American Science, in* THE STATE OF AMERICAN HISTORY 184–85 (Herbert J. Bass, ed., 1970).

118. EXECUTIVE OFFICE OF THE PRESIDENT OF THE UNITED STATES, BUDGET OF THE UNITED STATES GOVERNMENT: FISCAL YEAR 1994 43–44 (1993).

119. PRESIDENT'S COUNCIL OF ADVISORS ON SCIENCE AND TECH-
NOLOGY, RENEWING THE PROMISE: RESEARCH-INTENSIVE
UNIVERSITIES AND THE NATION 3 (1992).

120. Even those conservatives who would reduce the federal role in many other
fields generally support federal spending on basic scientific research. *See*
CHARLES E. BARFIELD, SCIENTIFIC POLICY FROM FORD TO
REAGAN: CHANGE AND CONTINUITY xi–xii, 132–39 (1982).

121. GORDON TULLOCK, PRIVATE WANTS, PUBLIC MEANS 224–32
(1970).

122. Dickson, *Towards a Democratic Strategy for Science*, SCI. FOR PEOPLE,
July/Aug. 1984, at 6.

123. Miller v. California, 413 U.S. 15, 34 (1973).

124. *See* People v. Doubleday & Co., 297 N.Y. 687, 77 N.E. 2d 6 (1947), *aff'd*
(by equally divided Court), 335 U.S. 848 (1948) (Wilson's *Memoirs of
Hectate County* obscene); Besig v. United States, 208 F.2d 142 (9th Cir.
1953) (Miller's *Tropic of Cancer* and *Tropic of Capricorn* obscene). *See
generally* William B. Lockhart & Robert C. McClure, *Literature, the Law
of Obscenity, and the Constitution*, 38 MINN. L. REV. 295, 343–48
(1954).

125. Total 1993 appropriations for the arts through the National Endow-
ment for the Arts were approximately $175 million, making it one of
the smallest federal agencies. Joseph Fitchett, *In U.S., the Economics of
Culture*, INT'L HERALD TRIB., Oct. 30, 1993. States also contribute
to arts funding, with New York currently providing roughly $25 million.
Id.

126. *See, e.g.,* W. H. Adams, *Public Aid for the Arts: A Change of Heart?*, *in*
CULTURAL POLICY AND ARTS ADMINISTRATION 3 (Stephen A.
Greyser, ed., 1973); Robert Brustein, *The Artist and the Citizen*, NEW
REPUBLIC, June 24, 1978, at 23.

127. D. NETZER, THE SUBSIDIZED MUSE 3 (1978). On the transition from
royal to parliamentary support of art in Great Britain in the nineteenth
and twentieth centuries, see JANET MINIHAN, THE NATIONALIZA-
TION OF CULTURE (1977).

128. On Nazi science *see* ALAN D. BEYERCHEN, SCIENTISTS UNDER HIT-
LER 40–50, 168–98 (1977); DANIEL S. GREENBERG, THE POLITICS
OF PURE SCIENCE 91–92 (1967). On the Soviet Union experience *see*
BERNARD BARBER, SCIENCE AND THE SOCIAL ORDER 82–83
(1952).

129. *See* Joshua Lederberg, *The Freedoms and Control of Science Notes from
an Ivory Tower*, 455 CAL. L. REV. 596–601 (1972).

130. Miller v. California, 413 U.S. 15, 34 (1973).

131. Buckley v. Valeo, 424 U.S. 1, 23–29 (1976).

132. *Id.* at 26–27.

133. *Id.* at 235, 246–52 (Burger, C. J., concurring in part and dissenting in

part); *id.* at 290–94 (Rehnquist, J., concurring in part and dissenting in part).

134. *Id.* at 248; *but see id.* at 93, n.127.

135. *Id.* at 97 n.131. *See also* Mountain States Legal Foundation v. Denver School Dist. #1, 459 F. Supp. 357 (C.D. Colo. 1978) (First Amendment prohibits school board from spending public funds in attempt to defeat proposed state constitutional amendment); Anderson v. Boston, 380 N.E. 2d 628, 639 (Mass. 1978), *appeal dismissed*, 439 U.S. 1059 (1979) ("Fairness and the appearance of fairness [in the election process] are assured by a prohibition against public tax revenues to advocate a position which certain taxpayers oppose."). *But see* Laurence H. Tribe, *Toward a Metatheory of Free Speech*, 10 S. CAL. L. REV. 237, 245 n.34 (1978).

136. Rust v. Sullivan, 500 U.S. 173, 111 S. Ct. 1759 (1991).

137. Board of Trustees of the Leland Stanford Junior University v. Sullivan, 773 F. Supp. 472 (D.D.C. 1991), *appeal dismissed as moot*, No. 91–5392 (D.C. Cir. 1992). The case became moot before the appellate court could decide it when the contract in question ended.

138. *Id.* at 477.

139. *Id.* at 476, n.13.

140. *Id.* at 477.

141. *Id.* at 477, 478.

142. *Id.* at 478.

Notes to Chapter 4

1. National Science Foundation Act of 1950, Pub. L. no. 81–507, 64 stat. 149 (codified as amended at 42 U.S.C. §§ 1861–84 [1982]). I presented an earlier version of portions of this chapter in Steven Goldberg, *The Reluctant Embrace: Law and Science in America*, 75 GEO. L. J. 1341 (1987).

2. 42 U.S.C. §§ 1862(a)(1); 1873 (1982).

3. Research-and-development authority for the Defense Department is set forth at 10 U.S.C. § 2358 (1982), and for the Department of Energy at 42 U.S.C. § 7112(5) (1982). The statutory framework for the research done by the various institutes (such as the National Cancer Institute) that are part of the National Institutes of Health is described in Grassetti v. Weinberger, 408 F. Supp. 142 (N.D. Cal. 1976).

4. Lincoln v. Vigil, 113 S. Ct. 2024 (1993).

5. *Id.* at 2031.

6. Lawrence Feinberg, *Colleges Bypass Agencies to Get Federal Funds*, WASH. POST, June 5, 1984, at A1, col. 1.

7. *Id.* The *Post* article focused on efforts by Georgetown and Catholic Universities to obtain money from Congress. For another example, see Daniel S. Greenberg, *Keyworth and Fuqua Volley on Pork-Barrel R&D*, SCI. & GOV'T REP., Oct. 1, 1984, at 5 (describing exchange of correspondence

wherein executive official alleged "narrowly based political considerations" used by Congress to determine location of federally funded computer center).

8. *See, e.g.,* JOSEPH P. MARTINO, SCIENCE FUNDING: POLITICS AND PORKBARREL (1992).

9. *Pork: It's Academic,* WASH. POST, July 3, 1993, at A22.

10. OFFICE OF TECHNOLOGY ASSESSMENT, U.S. CONGRESS, FEDER-ALLY FUNDED RESEARCH: DECISIONS FOR A DECADE 87–94 (1991).

11. *Id.* at 87.

12. *Id.* at 90.

13. *Pork: It's Academic,* WASH. POST, July 3, 1993, at A22.

14. PRESIDENT'S COUNCIL OF ADVISORS ON SCIENCE AND TECH-NOLOGY, RENEWING THE PROMISE: RESEARCH-INTENSIVE UNI-VERSITIES AND THE NATION 24 (1992).

15. JOSEPH P. MARTINO, SCIENCE FUNDING: POLITICS AND PORK-BARREL 385 (1992).

16. High end estimates by the *Chronicle of Education* put "earmarking" in 1993 at $763 million out of a research and development budget of $76 billion. *Cf. Pork: It's Academic,* WASH. POST, July 3, 1993, at A22, and EXECUTIVE OFFICE OF THE PRESIDENT, BUDGET OF THE UNITED STATES GOVERNMENT: FISCAL YEAR 1994 43 (1993).

17. JOSEPH P. MARTINO, SCIENCE FUNDING: POLITICS AND PORK-BARREL 385 (1992).

18. BERNARD SCHWARTZ, ADMINISTRATIVE LAW 41–52 (1991).

19. Industrial Union Dept., AFL-CIO v. American Petroleum Institute, 448 U.S. 607, 675 (198) (Rehnquist, J., concurring in the judgment).

20. The quotation from Jefferson comes from a letter he wrote to Hugh Wil-liamson. *See* THE WORKS OF THOMAS JEFFERSON 458–59 (Paul L. Ford, ed., Knickerbocker Press, 1904). The evolution of the patent office is described in A. HUNTER DUPREE, SCIENCE IN THE FEDERAL GOV-ERNMENT: A HISTORY OF POLICIES AND ACTIVITIES TO 1940 11–14, 46–47 (1957).

21. JUDITH AREEN, ET AL., LAW, SCIENCE AND MEDICINE 528 (1984).

22. DENNIS J. RILEY, 1 FEDERAL CONTRACTS, GRANTS, AND ASSIS-TANCE 207–211 (1983).

23. *See* John J. Grossbaum, *Federal Support of Research Projects Through Contracts and Grants: A Rationale,* 19 AM. U. L. REV. 423, 427 (1970) (attempts to distinguish between grants and contracts rest on characteriza-tions that "are not particularly meaningful"); Leroy Kahn, *The Lawyer and the Scientific Community: Procuring Basic Research,* 29 LAW & CONTEMP. PROBS. 631, 637 (1964) (terming Defense Department's man-ner of letting military research by contract and letting research for "peaceful purposes" via grants a "somewhat synthetic" distinction).

24. Kornhauser, for example, reports that a government scientist, speaking of a private firm with which he was working, said "their research people will try to get the production people to accept our ideas," WILLIAM KORN-HAUSER, SCIENTISTS IN INDUSTRY 184 (1962).

25. Steven Goldberg, *Controlling Basic Science: The Case of Nuclear Fusion,* 68 GEO. L. J. 683, 711 (1980).

26. Don K. Price, *Endless Frontier or Bureaucratic Morass?,* DAEDALUS, Spring 1978, at 87.

27. C. P. SNOW, THE TWO CULTURES AND A SECOND LOOK 17 (1963).

28. Steven Goldberg, *Controlling Basic Science: The Case of Nuclear Fusion,* 68 GEO. L. J. 683, 707 (1980).

29. BERNARD ROSHCO, NEWSMAKING 16, 18–19 (1975).

30. WALTER LIPPMAN, PUBLIC OPINION 341 (1950).

31. RICHARD A. RETTIG, CANCER CRUSADE 300–302, 317–25 (1977).

32. Military Procurement Authorization Act, Pub. L. No. 91–121, § 203, 83 Stat. 204, 206 (1969).

33. *Id.*

34. Military Procurement Authorization Act, Pub. L. No. 91–441, § 203(a), 84 Stat. 905, 906 (1970).

35. *See* Stanton A. Glantz & N. V. Albers, *Department of Defense R&D in the University,* 186 SCIENCE 706 (1974) (limited impact of the Mansfield Amendment).

36. *See, e.g.,* A. HUNTER DUPREE, SCIENCE IN THE FEDERAL GOVERN-MENT: A HISTORY OF POLICIES AND ACTIVITIES TO 1940 215–20 (1957).

37. Calvin Bellamy, *Item Veto: Shield against Deficits or Weapon of Presidential Power?* 22 VAL. U. L. REV. 557, 558 (1988). *See also* Steven Goldberg, *Science Spending and Seretonin, in* THE NEUROTRANSMITTER REVO-LUTION: SEROTONIN, SOCIAL BEHAVIOR AND THE LAW 222 (Rogers D. Masters and Michael T. McGuire, eds., 1994).

38. *See, e.g.,* Paul R. Q. Wolfson, *Is a Presidential Item Veto Constitutional?* 96 YALE L. J. 838 (1987).

39. Hutchinson v. Proxmire, 443 U.S. III at 116 (1979). *See also* Steven Gold-berg, *Controlling Basic Science: The Case of Nuclear Fusion,* 68 GEO. L. J. 683, 707 (1980).

40. *See generally* BERNARD SCHWARTZ, ADMINISTRATIVE LAW 585–668 (2d ed. 1984).

41. A major opinion enunciating the modern role of courts in reviewing agency action is Environmental Defense Fund v. Ruckelshaus, 439 F.2d 584 (D.C. Cir. 1971).

42. *See generally* SHEILA JASANOFF, THE FIFTH BRANCH: SCIENCE AD-VISERS AS POLICYMAKERS 61–79 (1990).

43. *Id.*

44. *Id. See also* Charles McCutchen, *Peer Review: Treacherous Servant, Disas-*

trous Master, in 94 TECH. REV. 28 (1991); Rosemary Chalk, *Impure Science: Fraud, Compromise, and Political Influence in Scientific Research,* 96 TECH. REV. 69 (1993).

45. BRUCE L. R. SMITH, AMERICAN SCIENCE POLICY SINCE WORLD WAR II 179–184 (1990).

46. Jennie Moehlmann & Julie Ann Miller, *OSTP's Gibbons A Favorite on Capitol Hill,* 43 BIOSCIENCE 394 (1993).

47. SHEILA JASANOFF, THE FIFTH BRANCH: SCIENCE ADVISERS AS POLICYMAKERS 61–83 (1990).

48. *Id.* at 62 (citing STEPHEN LOCK, A DIFFICULT BALANCE: EDITORIAL PEER REVIEW IN MEDICINE 4 [1985]).

49. *See, e.g.,* Daniel S. Greenberg, *Case against Gallo Faces Tough Appeals Process,* 23 SCI. & GOV'T REPT. 1, 3–5 (1993).

50. Kletschka v. Driver, 411 F.2d 436 (2d Cir. 1969).

51. *Id.* at 440–41.

52. *Id.* at 439.

53. 5 U.S.C. § 702 (1982) ("person suffering legal wrong because of agency action, or adversely affected or aggrieved by agency within the meaning of a relevant statute, is entitled to judicial review"). The *Kletschka* court observed, however, that this right to review does not apply " 'to the extent that . . . [the] action is committed to agency discretion by law.' " 411 F.2d at 442 (quoting 5 U.S.C. § 701[a] [1982]). For a later interpretation of this provision, *see* Heckler v. Chaney, 470 U.S. 821, 832–33 (1985) (agency decision not to undertake enforcement action presumptively unreviewable). This provision was also invoked to bar review of how an agency spends money from a lump-sum appropriation. *See* Lincoln v. Vigil, 113 S. Ct. 2024 (1993).

54. 411 F.2d at 443.

55. *Id.* at 444.

56. Apter v. Richardson, 361 F. Supp. 1070 (N.D. Ill. 1973), *rev'd,* 510 F.2d 351 (7th Cir. 1975).

57. *Id.* at 1071–72.

58. *Id.* at 1073.

59. Apter v. Richardson, 510 F.2d 351, 354–55 (7th Cir. 1975).

60. *Id.* at 355.

61. *Id.*

62. The opinion of the trial court dismissing the case after remand is unpublished.

63. Grassetti v. Weinberger, 408 F. Supp. 142 (N.D. Cal. 1976).

64. *Id.* at 147.

65. *Id.* at 150.

66. *Id.*

67. Grassetti v. Weinberger, 408 F. Supp. 142, 151 (N.D. Cal. 1976).

68. Marinoff v. HEW, 456 F. Supp. 1120 (S.D.N.Y. 1978), *aff'd mem.*, 595 F.2d 1208, *cert. denied*, 442 U.S. 913 (1979).
69. 456 F. Supp. at 1121.
70. *Id.*
71. *Id.* at 1122.
72. Ujvarosy v. Sullivan, No. C-92–4538–EFL, 1993 U.S. Dist. LEXIS 6330 (N.D. Cal. May 5, 1993).
73. *Id.* The court nonetheless offered the further opinion that the claim was "frivolous." *Id.*
74. Cass R. Sunstein, *Administrative Law After Chevron*, 90 COLUM. L. REV. 2071, 2072–73 (1990).
75. JOHN CIBINIC & RALPH C. NASH, GOVERNMENT CONTRACT CLAIMS 39, 263–66 (1981).
76. ANDREW K. GALLAGHER, THE LAW OF FEDERAL NEGOTIATED CONTRACT FORMATION 329, 342–77 (1981). In general, it is hard to get the courts to reverse agency contract awards. JOHN CIBINIC & RALPH C. NASH, GOVERNMENT CONTRACT CLAIMS 266 (1981).
77. JERRY L. MASHAW, BUREAUCRATIC JUSTICE 18, 57 n.6 (1983); *see* Charles H. Koch, Jr. & David A. Koplow, *The Fourth Bite at the Apple: A Study of the Operation and Utility of the Social Security Administration's Appeals Council*, 17 FLA. ST. U. L. REV. 199, 226 (1990) (Both the number of federal appeals and the reversal rate have been variable from year to year; for example, in 1982, thirteen thousand new federal appeals were filed, with a reversal rate of 20 percent, and in 1984, twenty-six thousand new appeals were filed, with a reversal rate was 57 percent).
78. Ber v. Celebrezze, 332 F.2d 293 (2d Cir. 1964).
79. Lashen v. Secretary of Health and Human Servs., No. 92–3936, 1993 U.S. App. LEXIS 23976 (6th Cir. Sept. 15, 1993).
80. *Id.*
81. For contrasting views on the merits of judicial review in the social security disability system, see JERRY L. MASHAW, BUREAUCRATIC JUSTICE 1 (1983), *and* Lance Liebman and Richard B. Stewart, *Bureaucratic Vision*, 96 HARV. L. REV. 1952 (1983).
82. BERNARD SCHWARTZ, ADMINISTRATIVE LAW 457–59 (2d ed. 1984).
83. For an earlier version of the following discussion of Kafka see Steven Goldberg, *The Central Dogmas of Law and Science*, 36 J. LEGAL EDUC. 378 (1986).
84. ERNST PAWEL, THE NIGHTMARE OF REASON: A LIFE OF FRANZ KAFKA 188 (1984).
85. See MICHAEL POLANYI, SCIENCE, FAITH AND SOCIETY 63–65 (1946).

86. Stephen Cole, et. al., *Chance and Consensus in Peer Review*, 214 SCIENCE 881 (1981).

Notes to Chapter 5

1. Bryan R. Wilson, *Reflections on a Many Sided Controversy, in* RELIGION AND MODERNIZATION 199–200 (Steve Bruce, ed., 1992).
2. *See, e.g.*, WALTER PARCHOMENKO, SOVIET IMAGES OF DISSIDENTS AND NONCONFORMISTS 82–83 (1986).
3. MARGARITA MATHIOPOULOS, HISTORY AND PROGRESS: IN SEARCH OF THE EUROPEAN AND AMERICAN MIND 151 (1989).
4. *Cf.* J. B. BURY, THE IDEA OF PROGRESS (1932); *and* ROBERT NISBET, HISTORY OF THE IDEA OF PROGRESS (1980).
5. DAVID H. HOPPER, TECHNOLOGY, THEOLOGY AND THE IDEA OF PROGRESS 36–37 (1991).
6. MARGARITA MATHIOPOULOS, HISTORY AND PROGRESS: IN SEARCH OF THE EUROPEAN AND AMERICAN MIND 111 (1989).
7. MARGARET MATHIOPOULOS, HISTORY AND PROGRESS: IN SEARCH OF THE EUROPEAN AND AMERICAN MIND 151 (1989) (citing RALF DAHRENDORF, DIE ANGEWANDTE AUFLAURUNG [1968]).
8. M. A. DE WOLFE HOWE, THE GARDEN AND THE WILDERNESS 6, 25–26 (1965).
9. Everson v. Board of Education, 330 U.S. 1 (1947); School District v. Schempp, 374 U.S. 203 (1963).
10. Everson v. Board of Education, 330 U.S. 1 (1947). The Court has held that the Fourteenth Amendment's due process clause, enacted after the Civil War, makes the First Amendment applicable to the states. *Id.*
11. An earlier version of some of the following portions of this chapter appeared in Steven Goldberg, *The Constitutional Status of American Science*, 1979 U. ILL. L. FOR. 1 (1979).
12. THOMAS PRINCE, EARTHQUAKES: THE WORKS OF GOD AND TOKENS OF HIS JUST DISPLEASURE 23 (Boston, D. Fowle & Z. Fowle, 1755). *See also* Eleanor M. Tilton, *Lightning-Rods and the Earthquake of 1755*, 13 NEW ENG. Q. 85 (1940). Prince essentially reprinted a sermon first published in 1727 and added an appendix. *Id.* at 85–86.
13. Eleanor M. Tilton, *Lightning-Rods and the Earthquake of 1755*, 13 NEW ENG. Q. 85, 86–89 (1940). *See also* BROOKE HINDLE, THE PURSUIT OF SCIENCE IN REVOLUTIONARY AMERICA 95 (1956); DANIEL J. BOORSTIN, THE AMERICANS: THE COLONIAL EXPERIENCE 258 (1958).
14. Eleanor M. Tilton, *Lightning-Rods and the Earthquake of 1755*, 13 NEW ENG. Q. 85, 94 (1940). JOHN WINTHROP, TWO LECTURES ON COMETS 21–44 (1759).

15. 1 PETER GAY, THE ENLIGHTENMENT: AN INTERPRETATION 18 (1969); ERNST CASSIRER, THE PHILOSOPHY OF THE ENLIGHTENMENT 161–62 (1960).

16. ERNEST CASSARA, THE ENLIGHTENMENT IN AMERICA 31–32 (1975). Caldwallader Colden, whose attacks on the clergy are cited by Cassara, made his greatest contributions to the field of botany. DANIEL J. BOORSTIN, THE AMERICANS: THE COLONIAL EXPERIENCE 163 (1958).

17. See, e.g., Harry H. Clark, *The Influence of Science on American Ideas: From 1775 to 1809*, 35 TRANSACTIONS WIS. ACAD. 307–14 (1943); 1 PETER GAY, THE ENLIGHTENMENT: AN INTERPRETATION 200 (1969).

18. The Remonstrance is reprinted as an appendix to Everson v. Board of Education, 330 U.S. 1, 63, 67 (1947).

19. THOMAS JEFFERSON, NOTES ON THE STATE OF VIRGINIA 159–60 (W. Peden, ed., 1955).

20. LEONARD W. LEVY, FREEDOM OF SPEECH AND PRESS IN EARLY AMERICAN HISTORY 100 (1960); GEORGE F. SENSEBAUGH, MILTON IN EARLY AMERICA viii (1964).

21. CHRISTOPHER HILL, MILTON AND THE ENGLISH REVOLUTION 53–54 (1977); 1 DAVID MASON, THE LIFE OF JOHN MILTON 788, 821 (Peter Smith, ed., 2d ed. 1946) (1877).

22. See, e.g., ZECHARIAH CHAFFEE, FREE SPEECH IN THE UNITED STATES 3, 29, 298, 325, 498 (1967); LEONARD W. LEVY, FREEDOM OF SPEECH AND PRESS IN EARLY AMERICAN HISTORY 95–97 (1960).

23. JOHN MILTON, AREOPAGITICA 40 (R. Jebb, ed., AMS Press, 1971) (1918).

24. U.S. CONST. amend. I.

25. To a certain extent colonial Puritanism was compatible with science, albeit not as fully as Deism. See, e.g., Harry H. Clark, *The Influence of Science on American Ideas: From 1775 to 1809*, 35 TRANSACTIONS WIS. ACAD. 307–14 (1943); DANIEL J. BOORSTIN, THE AMERICANS: THE COLONIAL EXPERIENCE 222 (1958); Frederick G. Kilgour, *The Rise of Scientific Activity in Colonial New England*, 22 YALE J. BIOLOGY & MED. 123 (1949); Leonard Tucker, *President Thomas Clap of Yale College: Another "Founding Father" of American Science*, in EARLY AMERICAN SCIENCE 99 (Brooke Hindle, ed., 1976); CHARLES S. ROSENBERG, NO OTHER GODS: ON SCIENCE AND AMERICAN SOCIAL THOUGHT 2–4 (1976); DIRK J. STRUIK, YANKEE SCIENCE IN THE MAKING 30 (1948).

26. See, e.g., Brooke Hindle, *The Quaker Background and Science in Colonial Philadelphia*, 46 ISIS 243 (1955); see also ALAN D. BEYERCHEN, SCIENTISTS UNDER HITLER 27–39 (1977).

27. This analogy has been noted by many, including Freud in 1917. *See* BRUCE MAZLISH, THE FOURTH DISCONTINUITY: THE CO-EVOLUTION OF HUMANS AND MACHINES (1993).

28. MASAO WATANABE, THE JAPANESE AND WESTERN SCIENCE 67 (1990).

29. Edwin O. Reischauer, *Foreword,* to MASAO WATANABE: THE JAPANESE AND WESTERN SCIENCE ix-x (1990).

30. Of course, many Christians today accept evolution while retaining their faith. *See, e.g.,* RAYMOND A. EVE & FRANCIS B. HARROLD, THE CREATIONIST MOVEMENT IN MODERN AMERICA 3–4 (1991).

31. Scopes v. State, 289 S.W. 363 (1927).

32. The nonestablishment clause was first applied to the states in Everson v. Board of Education, 330 U.S. 1 (1947).

33. Scopes v. State, 289 S.W. 363 (1927).

34. *See, e.g.,* Rollin L. Hartt, *What Lies Beyond Dayton,* NATION, July 22, 1925, at 111–12. *See generally* SHELDON NORMAN GREBSTEIN, MONKEY TRIAL: THE STATE OF TENNESSEE VS. JOHN THOMAS SCOPES (1960).

35. *See, e.g., Amateur Dramatics at Dayton,* CHRISTIAN CENTURY, July 30, 1925, at 969–70.

36. Scopes v. State, 289 S.W. 363, 367.

37. *Id.*

38. *Id.*

39. 393 U.S. 97 (1968).

40. The Arkansas statute was similar to the Tennessee statute involved in the Scopes case, Scopes v. State, 289 S.W. 363 (1927). *See* Harry A. Kalven, *A Commemorative Case Note: Scopes v. State,* 27 U. CHI. L. REV. 505, 510 n.14 (1960); Thomas I. Emerson & Herbert Haber, *The Scopes Case in Modern Dress,* 27 U. CHI. L. REV. 522 (1960); Malcolm P. Sharp, *Science, Religion, and the Scopes Case,* 27 U. CHI. L. REV. 529 (1960). *See also* Note, *Constitutional Law: Validity of the Tennessee Anti-Evolution Law,* 5 TENN. L. REV. 242 (1927).

41. Brief of the National Education Ass'n of the United States and the National Science Teachers Ass'n as Amici Curiae at 13a, Epperson v. Arkansas, 393 U.S. 97 (1968) (No. 7).

42. Brief for Appellants at 16, Epperson v. Arkansas, 393 U.S. 97 (1968) (No. 7).

43. Transcript of Oral Argument at 17, Epperson v. Arkansas, 393 U.S. 97 (1968)(No. 7). Counsel for Arkansas replied, "I would, first of all, hope that the Courts and the people would think that would be an unreasonable encroachment." *Id.*

44. *See* 393 U.S. at 102 nn.9 & 10.

45. *See, e.g.,* LAURENCE H. TRIBE, AMERICAN CONSTITUTIONAL LAW 229 n.10, 230, 592, 836–37, 867 (1978); Paul Brest, *Palmer v. Thompson:*

An Approach to the Problem of Unconstitutional Legislative Motive, 1971 SUP. CT. REV. 95, 120 n.125 (1971); John H. Ely, *Legislative and Administrative Motivation in Constitutional Law,* 79 YALE L. J. 1205, 1318 (1970); Frederic S. LeClercq, *The Monkey Laws and the Public Schools: A Second Consumption?,* 27 VAND. L. REV. 209, 217 (1974); Laurence H. Tribe, *The Supreme Court 1972 Term: Foreword: Toward a Model of Roles in the Due Process of Life and Law,* 87 HARV. L. REV. 1, 22 n.103 (1973).

46. 393 U.S. at 107–9.
47. In Board of Education v. Allen, 392 U.S. 236 (1968), for example, the legislature enacted a textbook loan program that included parochial schools. The Court's entire discussion of religious purpose consists of the following: "The express purpose of {701 was stated by the New York Legislature to be furtherance of the educational opportunities available to the young. Appellants have shown us nothing about the necessary effects of the statute that is contrary to its stated purpose." *Id.* at 243. In *Epperson,* however, the Court refused to accept the argument that the anti-evolution statute might have been motivated by a desire to keep a controversial subject out of the schools. 393 U.S. at 112–13 (Black, J., concurring).
48. 393 U.S. at 107.
49. 393 U.S. at 101, 102.
50. Smith v. State, 242 So. 2d 692 (Miss. 1970).
51. *See* Daniel v. Waters, 515 F.2d 485, 487, 489 (6th Cir. 1975).
52. *Id.* at 489–91. The court found that "the result of this legislation is a clearly defined preferential position for the biblical version of creation as opposed to any account of the development of man based on scientific research and reasoning." *Id.* at 489. In Steele v. Waters, 527 S.W. 2d 72 (Tenn. 1975), the Supreme Court of Tennessee, following the Sixth Circuit decision, agreed that the Tennessee statute violated the establishment clause.
53. Moore v. Gaston County Board of Education, 357 F. Supp. 1037, 1038 (W.D.N.C. 1973).
54. *Id.* at 1038–39.
55. *Id.* at 1043.
56. *Id.* at 1042–43.
57. For an early discussion of the creationist endeavor, *see* Wendell R. Bird, *Freedom of Religion and Science Instruction in Public Schools,* 87 YALE L. J. 515 (1978).
58. NATIONAL ACADEMY OF SCIENCES, SCIENCE AND CREATIONISM (1984).
59. Edwards v. Aguillard, 482 U.S. 578 (1987).
60. *Id.* at 581.
61. *Id.* at 596, n.18.
62. *Id.* at 593.
63. STEPHEN L. CARTER, THE CULTURE OF DISBELIEF: HOW AMERI-

CAN LAW AND POLITICS TRIVIALIZE RELIGIOUS DEVOTION 168–169 (1993).

64. *See Leviticus* 18:22 ("Thou shalt not lie with mankind as with womankind, it is a abomination".) *See also id.* 18:23, 20:13, 15, 16; *Romans* 1:27. For a discussion of the religious origins of the laws against homosexuality *see, e.g.,* Note, *Sexual Freedom for Consenting Adults: Why Not?,* 2 PAC. L. J. 206, 210–12 (1971); Note, *Sodomy Statutes: A Need for Change,* 13 S.D. L. REV. 384–85 (1968).

65. *See, e.g.,* MORRIS PLOSCOWE, SEX AND THE LAW 184 (1962); Note, *Sexual Freedom for Consenting Adults: Why Not?,* 2 PAC. L. J. 206, 210, 211 n.29 (1971); Note, *Sodomy Statutes: A Need for Change,* 13 S.D. L. REV. 385 (1968).

66. *See* McGowan v. Maryland, 366 U.S. 420, 431–37, 442 (1961).

67. *See, e.g.,* Note, *Deviate Sexual Behavior: The Desirability of Legislative Proscription,* 30 ALB. L. REV. 291, 293–94 (1966).

68. *See generally* Note, *Sexual Freedom for Consenting Adults: Why Not?,* 2 PAC. L.J. 206 (1971).

69. *See, e.g.,* Caster v. State, 500 S.W.2d 368, 371–72 (1973); Connor v. State, 490 S.W.2d 114, 115 (1973); State v. Rhinehart, 424 P.2d 906, 910 (1967).

70. Doe v. Commonwealth's Attorney, 403 F. Supp. 1199 (E.D. Va. 1975), *aff'd mem.,* 425 U.S. 901 (1976).

71. *Id.* at 1202, n.2. *See also* Farr v. Mancusi, 70 Misc. 2d 830, 832 (N.Y. County Ct. 1972); State v. Stokes, 163 S.E. 2d 770, 774 (1968).

72. Bowers v. Hardwick, 478 U.S. 186 (1986).

73. Webster v. New Lenox School District No. 122, 917 F.2d 1004 (7th Cir. 1990).

74. Peolza v. Capistrano Unified School District, 782 F. Supp. 1412 (1992).

75. *Id.* at 1414, n.1.

76. STEPHEN L. CARTER, THE CULTURE OF DISBELIEF: HOW AMERICAN LAW AND POLITICS TRIVIALIZE RELIGIOUS DEVOTION 161 (1993).

77. Mozert v. Hawkins County Board of Education, 827 F.2d 1058 (6th Cir. 1987). The plaintiffs in this case challenged much more than just the teaching of evolution. *See* Naomi M. Stolzenberg, *"He Drew a Circle That Shut Me Out": Assimilation, Indoctrination, and the Paradox of a Liberal Education,* 106 HARV. L. REV. 581 (1993).

78. *Id.* at 1065.

79. *Id.* at 1064.

80. Roger Finke, *An Unsecular America, in* RELIGION AND MODERNIZATION 148–49 (Steve Bruce, ed., 1992).

81. *Id.* at 153.

82. *Id.* at 152.

83. Peter L. Berger, *Religion in a Revolutionary Society, in* AMERICA'S CONTINUING REVOLUTION 150 (1975).

84. *Id.* at 145–146. *See also* ROBERT N. BELLAH, THE BROKEN COVE-
NANT: AMERICAN CIVIL RELIGION IN TIME OF TRIAL (2d ed.
1992).

85. Peter L. Berger, *Religion in a Revolutionary Society, in* AMERICA'S CON-
TINUING REVOLUTION 143 (1975). There is dispute about whether
Eisenhower actually made this statement. *See* Richard J. Neuhaus, *Who
Needs God,* NAT'L REV., Nov. 10, 1989, at 52.

86. Proclamation 6508—Thanksgiving Day, 1992, 28 WEEKLY COMP.
PRES. DOC. 2312, 2313 (Nov. 20, 1992).

87. JOHN T. NOONAN, JR., THE BELIEVERS AND THE POWERS THAT
ARE: CASES, HISTORY, AND OTHER DATA BEARING ON THE
RELATION OF RELIGION AND GOVERNMENT 411 (1987).

88. *Id.* at 410–11.

89. *Id.* at 411.

90. Church of the Lukumi Babalu Aye, Inc. v. City of Hialeah, 113 S. Ct.
2217 (1993).

91. *Id.* at 2231.

92. Lynch v. Donnelly, 465 U.S. 668 (1984).

93. County of Allegheny v. American Civil Liberties Union, 492 U.S. 573
(1989).

94. McGowan v. Maryland, 366 U.S. 420 (1961).

95. Bowers v. Hardwick, 468 U.S. 186 (1986).

96. JOHN RAWLS, POLITICAL LIBERALISM 145–149 (1993).

97. STEPHEN L. CARTER, THE CULTURE OF DISBELIEF: HOW AMERI-
CAN LAW AND POLITICS TRIVIALIZE RELIGIOUS DEVOTION
273–74 (1993).

98. *Id.* at 266.

99. *Id.* at 274.

100. DAVID H. HOPPER, TECHNOLOGY, THEOLOGY, AND THE IDEA
OF PROGRESS 60, 63, 75–76 (1991); CHRISTOPHER LASCH, THE
TRUE AND ONLY HEAVEN: PROGRESS AND ITS CRITICS 41
(1991); EDWARD A. PURCELL, JR., THE CRISIS OF DEMOCRATIC
THEORY: SCIENTIFIC NATURALISM AND THE PROBLEM OF
VALUE 61 (1973).

101. CHRISTOPHER LASCH, THE TRUE AND ONLY HEAVEN: PROG-
RESS AND ITS CRITICS 43 (1991).

102. DAVID H. HOPPER, TECHNOLOGY, THEOLOGY, AND THE IDEA
OF PROGRESS 114 (1991).

103. *See generally* DAVID H. HOPPER, TECHNOLOGY, THEOLOGY, AND
THE IDEA OF PROGRESS (1991).

104. *See, e.g.,* JEFFRIE G. MURPHY, EVOLUTION, MORALITY, AND THE
MEANING OF LIFE (1982).

105. Paul L. Holmer, *Evolution and Being Faithful,* 84 CHRISTIAN CEN-
TURY 1491, 1494 (1967).

Notes to Chapter 6

1. *See, e.g.,* Wickard v. Filburn, 317 U.S. 111 (1942).
2. The drug regulation case is United States v. Sullivan, 332 U.S. 689 (1948). Congress has long used the commerce power to regulate new technology. In the 1830's explosions in steamboat boilers led to federally funded research followed by creation of the Steamboat Inspection Service, one of the nation's first regulatory agencies. DON K. PRICE, GOVERNMENT AND SCIENCE 10–11 (1954).
3. South Dakota v. Dole, 483 U.S. 203 (1987).
4. *See, e.g.,* John A. Robertson, *The Law of Institutional Review Boards,* 26 U.C.L.A. L. REV. 484 (1979).
5. For a case concerning the legal tests that govern when state law is preempted by federal law, see Gade v. National Solid Waste Management Association, 112 S. Ct. 2374 (1992).
6. *See, e.g.,* John A. Robertson, *The Scientists' Right to Research: A Constitutional Analysis,* 515 CAL. L. REV. 1203, 1254–56 (1978); James R. Ferguson, *Scientific Inquiry and the First Amendment,* 64 CORNELL L. REV. 639, 655 (1979). For a more expansive view of the government's power to control experimentation, see Gary L. Francione, *Experimentation and the Marketplace Theory of the First Amendment,* 136 U. PA. L. REV. 417 (1987).
7. On the distinction between speech and action in First Amendment law, see United States v. O'Brien, 391 U.S. 367 (1968).
8. *See, e.g.,* 42 U.S.C. § 2061 (1) (1976) (an Atomic Energy Act provision prohibiting private research activity involving certain nuclear materials.)
9. *See, e.g.,* 42 U.S.C. § 289(a) (1991) (research involving human subjects); 42 U.S.C. § 289(g) (1993) (fetal tissue research); 42 U.S.C. §§ 283(d), 283(e) (1991) (animal research).
10. The flag burning cases are Texas v. Johnson, 491 U.S. 397 (1989), and United Sates v. Eichman, 496 U.S. 310 (1990).
11. Harvey Brooks, *The Scientific Advisor, in* SCIENTISTS AND NATIONAL POLICY-MAKING 76 (Robert Gilpin & Christopher Wright, eds., 1964).
12. On the contrast between Congress' decision to keep saccharin on the market while cyclamates remain off, see Nancy L. Bue, *Comment, in* LAW AND SCIENCE IN COLLABORATION 203–4, (J. Daniel Nyhart & Milton M. Carrow, eds., 1983). Congressional rejection of an American supersonic transport plane is chronicled in LAURENCE H. TRIBE, CHANNELING TECHNOLOGY THROUGH LAW 101–29 (1973).
13. Portions of the remainder of this chapter appeared in an earlier form in Steven Goldberg, *The Reluctant Embrace: Law and Science in America,* 75 GEO. L. J. 1341 (1987).
14. 15 U.S.C. § 2605 (1982).
15. *See generally* Richard B. Stewart, *The Reformation of American Adminis-*

trative Law, 88 HARV. L. REV. 1667 (1975); RICHARD J. PIERCE, JR., ET AL., ADMINISTRATIVE LAW AND PROCESS 23–38 (2d Ed. 1992).

16. These figures are based on phone conversations with agency personnel officers in October 1993, and on attorney files in the LEXIS, MARHUB library. The total number of employees at the Nuclear Regulatory Commission at that time was about 3,200, while the number at the National Science Foundation was about 1,300, but the Foundation uses more outside scientific consultants than the commission.

17. James Q. Wilson, *The Politics of Regulation, in* THE POLITICS OF REGULATION 379 (James Q. Wilson, ed., 1980).

18. SHEILA JASANOFF, THE FIFTH BRANCH: SCIENCE ADVISERS AS POLICYMAKERS 8 (1990).

19. BRUCE L. R. SMITH, THE ADVISERS: SCIENTISTS IN THE POLICY PROCESS 1 (1992).

20. SHEILA JASANOFF, THE FIFTH BRANCH: SCIENCE ADVISERS AS POLICYMAKERS 250 (1990).

21. *See generally,* JUDITH C. AREEN, ET AL., LAW, SCIENCE AND MEDICINE (1984).

22. At times, tough judicial scrutiny has been called the "hard look" doctrine, although in practice scrutiny is always tougher in regulatory than in funding cases. For the evolution of the "hard look" doctrine, primarily in cases involving environmental law, see William H. Rodgers, *A Hard Look at Vermont Yankee: Environmental Law Under Close Scrutiny,* 67 GEO. L. J. 699 (1979).

23. James Q. Wilson, *The Politics of Regulation, in* THE POLITICS OF REGULATION 390 (James Q. Wilson, ed., 1980).

24. JAMES D. WATSON, THE DOUBLE HELIX 222 (1968).

25. This contrast is set forth in JUDITH C. AREEN, ET AL., LAW, SCIENCE AND MEDICINE 6–7, 22 (1984). Various examples of legal doctrines and technological developments adjusting to each other are provided in DAVID LOTH & MORRIS L. ERNST, THE TAMING OF TECHNOLOGY (1972).

26. *See, e.g.,* LAURENCE H. TRIBE, CHANNELING TECHNOLOGY THROUGH LAW 1 (1973).

27. *See, e.g.,* Good Samaritan Hospital v. Shalala, 113 S. Ct. 2151 (1993).

28. *See, e.g.,* Rosenburg v. Planning Board, 236 A.2d 895, 897 (Conn. 1967); *see also* PATRICK J. ROHAN, ZONING AND LAND USE CONTROLS 33–173 to 33–188, 37–44 to 37–63 (1986).

29. Dwight D. Eisenhower, The Atom for Progress and Peace (Dec. 8, 1953).

30. *See, e.g.,* IRVIN C. BUPP & JEAN-CLAUDE DERIAN, LIGHT WATER: HOW THE NUCLEAR DREAM DISSOLVED (1978).

31. Pacific Gas and Elec. Co. v. State Energy Resources Conservation and Dev. Comm'n, 461 U.S. 190 (1983).

32. Silkwood v. Kerr-McGee Corp., 464 U.S. 238 (1984).

33. Lawrence M. Lidsky, *The Trouble with Fusion,* TECH. REV. (1983), at 44.
34. Lawrence M. Lidsky, *The Reactor of the Future,* TECH. REV. (1984), at 52.
35. IRVIN C. BUPP & JEAN-CLAUDE DERIAN, LIGHT WATER: HOW THE NUCLEAR DREAM DISSOLVED 31 (1978).
36. *Id.*
37. Robert S. Dudney, et. al., *The Legacies of World War II: The Nuclear Age,* U.S. NEWS & WORLD REP., Aug. 5, 1985, at 43.
38. *See, e.g.,* William Sweet, *Argonne Proposes "Proliferation-resistant" Breeder,* 37 PHYSICS TODAY 62 (1984).
39. On the relationship of the 1890 census and later government needs to the development of the computer, see HERMAN H. GOLDSTINE, THE COMPUTER FROM PASCAL TO VON NEWMANN 66–71; 121–251 (1972). *See also* CHRISTOPHER EVANS, THE MAKING OF THE MICRO: A HISTORY OF THE COMPUTER 47–54 (1981).
40. Gottschalk v. Benson, 409 U.S. 63 (1972).
41. Parker v. Flook, 437 U.S. 584 (1978).
42. *Id.* at 598.
43. Diamond v. Diehr, 450 U.S. 175 (1981).
44. *Id.*
45. *See., e.g.,* Nancy Rutter, *The Great Patent Plague,* 151 FORBES S58 (1993).
46. Pamela Samuelson, et al., *Developments on the Intellectual Property Front: Legally Speaking,* 35 COMM. ASS'N COMPUTING MACHINERY 33 (1992); Steve Gibson, *Someone Needs to Reinvent America's Outdated Patent System,* INFOWORLD, Aug. 24, 1992, at 32.
47. *See, e.g.,* Gary M. Hoffman & Geoffrey M. Karny, *Can Justice Keep Pace with Science?,* WASH. POST, Apr. 10, 1988, at B3.
48. Esther Schachter, *Intellectual Property Takes Center Stage,* 63 ELECTRONICS 108 (1990).
49. *Id.*
50. *The Academic Debate: Considered Opinion and Advocacy; the Question of Whether Software Can and Should Be Patented,* 35 COMM. ASS'N COMPUTING MACHINERY 125 (1992).
51. Steven Goldberg, *The Reluctant Embrace: Law and Science in America,* 75 GEO. L. J. 1341, 1379–88 (1987).
52. RAE GOODELL, THE VISIBLE SCIENTISTS (1977).
53. The most famous expression of this view was J. Robert Oppenheimer's statement that "[i]n some sort of crude sense, which no vulgarity, no humor, no overstatement can quite extinguish, the physicists have known sin." PETER GOODCHILD, J. ROBERT OPPENHEIMER: SHATTERER OF WORLDS 174 (1981).
54. SHEILA JASANOFF, THE FIFTH BRANCH: SCIENCE ADVISERS AS POLICYMAKERS 6, *et. seq.* (1990).
55. On Office of Management and Budget review of science research, see John

Walsh & Barbara Culliton, *Office of Management and Budget: Skeptical View of Scientific Advice, in* SCIENCE, TECHNOLOGY AND NATIONAL POLICY 274–94 (Thomas J. Kuehn & Alan K. Porter, eds., 1981). The tension between corporate and scientific goals in the private sector is discussed in SIMON MARCSON, THE SCIENTIST IN AMERICAN INDUSTRY 3–6, 145–51 (1960).

56. Steven Goldberg, *Controlling Basic Science: The Case of Nuclear Fusion,* 68 GEO. L. J. 683 (1980).

57. Daniel Yankelovich, *Science and the Public Process: Why the Gap Must Close,* 1 ISSUES SCI. & TECH. 6, 12 (1984).

58. For an earlier version of my discussion of superconductivity, see Steven Goldberg, *Narrowing the Regulatory Gap Between Law and Science: The Prospects for Superconductivity,* 1 CTS., HEALTH SCI. & LAW 163 (1990).

59. The history of superconductivity research is summarized in Michael D. Lemonick, *Superconductors: The Startling Breakthrough that Could Change Our World,* TIME, May 11, 1987, at 64–75. Doubts about the scientific prospects in this field are described in R. Pool, *Superconductivity: Is the Party Over?,* 244 SCI. 914 (1989).

60. *Superconductivity: Hearings Before the Subcomm. on Transp., Aviation and Materials of the House Comm. on Science, Space, and Technology,* 100th Cong., 1st Sess., 92–97 (1987).

61. Michael D. Lemonick, *Superconductors: The Startling Breakthrough that Could Change Our World,* TIME, May 11, 1987, at 64–75.

62. *See generally* DOROTHY NELKIN, SELLING SCIENCE: HOW THE PRESS COVERS SCIENCE AND TECHNOLOGY (1987).

63. Merklin v. United States, 788 F.2d 172 (3d Cir. 1986).

64. *Id.* at 178.

65. *See, e.g.,* ROBERT E. GOSSELIN, ET AL., CLINICAL TOXICOLOGY OF COMMERCIAL PRODUCTS III-379 (1984); R. J. Cave, *Pick Your Poison,* 362 NATURE 204–5 (Mar. 18, 1993).

66. D. K. Christen and J. R. Thompson, *Superconductivity:Current Problems at High T_c,* 364 NATURE 98 (July 8, 1993).

67. Philip J. Hilts, *A Cautious Eye on the Bottom Line,* WASH. POST, May 19, 1987, at A1.

68. *Superconductivity: Hearings on H.R. 2069 Before the House Committee on Science, Space, and Technology,* 100th Cong., 1st Sess., 161–208, 265–309 (1987).

69. R. J. Cave, *Pick Your Poison,* 362 NATURE 204–5 (Mar. 18, 1993).

70. *See* Philip J. Hilts, *U.S. Superconductor Consortium Formed,* WASH. POST, May 24, 1989, at A1.

71. COMMITTEE TO ADVISE THE PRESIDENT ON HIGH-TEMPERATURE SUPERCONDUCTIVITY, WHITE HOUSE SCIENCE COUNCIL, HIGH TEMPERATURE SUPERCONDUCTIVITY: PERSEVERANCE

AND COOPERATION ON THE ROAD TO COMMERCIALIZATION 35 (1989).

Notes to Chapter 7

1. Excellent descriptions of the development of modern genetics can be found in JERRY E. BISHOP & MICHAEL WALDHOLZ, GENOME: THE STORY OF THE MOST ASTONISHING SCIENTIFIC ADVENTURE OF OUR TIME: 22–27 (1990); OFFICE OF TECHNOLOGY ASSESSMENT, IMPACTS OF APPLIED GENETICS 29–35 (1981); ERNEST BOREK, THE CODE OF LIFE (1965). The account that follows is based on these sources.
2. *See* ERNEST BOREK, THE CODE OF LIFE 2 (1965) (quoting CHARLES DARWIN, ON THE ORIGIN OF THE SPECIES BY MEANS OF NATURAL SELECTION 75 [London, John Murray, 1859]). Although Darwin wrote this in 1859, prior to Mendel's 1866 research, the quote appeared in a later revised edition published in 1872 as well. Darwin's later works also demonstrate he remained unaware of Mendel's research. *See also* 1 CHARLES DARWIN, VARIATION OF ANIMALS AND PLANTS UNDER DOMESTICATION 5–6 (Paul H. Barrett & R. B. Freeman, eds., 1988) (1873).
3. Olmstead v. United States, 277 U.S. 438, 471 (1928) (Brandeis, J., dissenting).
4. Katz v. United States, 389 U.S. 347 (1967).
5. Olmstead v. United States, 277 U.S. 438, 478 (1928) (Brandeis, J., dissenting.)
6. *See, e.g.,* G. EDWARD WHITE, TORT LAW IN AMERICA: AN INTELLECTUAL HISTORY 173 (1980) (discussing Samuel D. Warren & Louis D. Brandeis, *The Right to Privacy,* 4 HARV. L. REV. 193 [1890]).
7. ALPHEUS T. MASON, BRANDEIS: A FREE MAN'S LIFE 70 (1946).
8. *See* Samuel D. Warren and Louis D. Brandeis, *The Right to Privacy,* 4 HARV. L. REV. 193, 195 n.4 (1890).
9. THOMAS M. COOLEY, A TREATISE ON THE LAW OF TORTS OR THE WRONGS WHICH ARISE INDEPENDENT OF CONTRACT 29 (2d ed. 1888).
10. CLYDE E. JACOBS, LAWWRITERS AND THE COURTS 27–32 (1954).
11. JAMES D. WATSON, THE DOUBLE HELIX 205 (1968).
12. *Id.* at 217.
13. The account that follows relies on Christopher G. Shank, Note, *DNA Evidence in Criminal Trials: Modifying the Law's Approach to Protect the Accused from Prejudicial Genetic Evidence,* 34 ARIZ. L. REV. 829 (1992). *See also* Elizabeth M. Bezak, Note, *DNA Profiling Evidence: The Need for a Uniform and Workable Evidentiary Standard of Admissibility,* 26 VAL. U. L. REV. 595 (1992).

14. Andrews v. State, 533 So. 2d 841 (Fla. Dist. Ct. App. 1988).
15. Christopher G. Shank, Note, *DNA Evidence in Criminal Trials: Modifying the Law's Approach to Protect the Accused from Prejudicial Genetic Evidence,* 34 ARIZ. L. REV. 829, 861–62 (1992).
16. *Id.* at 854–55. The case is People v. Castro, 545 N.Y.S.2d 985 (N.Y. Sup. Ct. 1989).
17. *Id.* .
18. The description of the basic science that follows is drawn from NAT'L RESEARCH COUNCIL, MAPPING AND SEQUENCING THE HUMAN GENOME 2–21 (1988); U.S. DEP'T OF HEALTH AND HUMAN SERV. & U.S. DEP'T OF ENERGY, UNDERSTANDING OUR GENETIC INHERITANCE: THE U.S. HUMAN GENOME PROJECT; THE FIRST FIVE YEARS FY 1991–1995 9–10, 85–89 (1990); BARRY R. FURROW, ET. AL., BIOETHICS: HEALTH CARE LAW AND ETHICS 167–169 (1991).
19. Susan Okie, *Redrawing Life's Family Tree: Genes Offer Insight on Evolution,* WASH. POST, May 6, 1990, at A1.
20. *Id. See also* NOBEL FOUNDATION, THE HIERARCHY OF LIFE: MOLECULES AND MORPHOLOGY IN PHYLOGENETIC ANALYSIS 410 (1988).
21. The description that follows is based on Robert M. Cook-Deegan, *The Human Genome Project: The Formation of Federal Policies in the United States, 1986–1990, in* BIOMEDICAL POLITICS 99–169 (Kathi E. Hanna, ed., 1991); OFFICE OF ENERGY RESEARCH & OFFICE OF HEALTH AND ENVIRONMENTAL RESEARCH, U.S. DEP'T OF ENERGY, HUMAN GENOME, 1991–1992 PROGRAM REPORT 1–4 (1992).
22. Robert M. Cook-Deegan, *The Human Genome Project: The Formation of Federal Policies in the United States, 1986–1990, in* BIOMEDICAL POLITICS 99, 152–54 (Kathi E. Hanna, ed., 1991).
23. BARRY R. FURROW, ET. AL., BIOETHICS: HEALTH CARE LAW AND ETHICS 168 (1991).
24. OFFICE OF TECHNOLOGY ASSESSMENT, MAPPING OUR GENES: THE GENOME PROJECTS: HOW BIG, HOW FAST? 13 (1988).
25. Frank Press, The Dilemma of the Golden Age, Address to Members of the National Academy of Sciences (Apr. 26, 1988).
26. D. J. DE SOLLA PRICE, LITTLE SCIENCE, BIG SCIENCE (1963).
27. Herbert Friedman, *Big Science vs. Little Science: The Controversy Mounts,* 1 COSMOS 8, 14 (1991); OFFICE OF TECHNOLOGY ASSESSMENT, FEDERALLY FUNDED RESEARCH: DECISIONS FOR A DECADE 146–60 (1991).
28. Robert M. Cook-Deegan, *The Human Genome Project: The Formation of Federal Policies in The United States, 1986–1990, in* BIOMEDICAL POLITICS 99, 140 (Kathi E. Hanna, ed., 1991).

29. OFFICE OF TECHNOLOGY ASSESSMENT, FEDERALLY FUNDED RESEARCH: DECISIONS FOR A DECADE 146–160 (1991).
30. Robert M. Cook-Degan, *The Human Genome Project: The Formation of Federal Policies in the United States, 1986–1990, in* BIOMEDICAL POLITICS 142 (Kathi E. Hanna, ed., 1991).
31. U.S. DEP'T OF HEALTH AND HUMAN SERV. & U.S. DEP'T OF ENERGY, UNDERSTANDING OUR GENETIC INHERITANCE: THE U.S. HUMAN GENOME PROJECT; THE FIRST FIVE YEARS FY 1991–1995 vii (1990).
32. Judith P. Swazey, et. al., *Risks and Benefits, Rights and Responsibilities: A History of the Recombinant DNA Research Controversy*, 51 S. CAL. L. REV. 1019, 1022 (1978).
33. *Id.* at 1025.
34. *Id.* at 1029.
35. Donald S. Fredrickson, *Asilomar and Recombinant DNA: The End of the Beginning, in* BIOMEDICAL POLITICS 258 (Kathi E. Hanna, ed., 1991).
36. *See, e.g.,* Joan O'C. Hamilton, *Why Biotech Stocks May Be Sick for a While,* BUSINESS WEEK, May 18, 1992, at 120.
37. U.S. DEP'T OF HEALTH AND HUMAN SERV. & U.S. DEP'T OF ENERGY, UNDERSTANDING OUR GENETIC INHERITANCE; THE U.S. HUMAN GENOME PROJECT: THE FIRST FIVE YEARS FY 1991–1995 at 20–21, 65–73 (1991).
38. As part of its study of the ethical, legal, and social implications of the Human Genome Initiative, the National Institutes of Health funded a project carried out by the Arizona State University Center for the Study of Law, Science, and Technology. This project, which included workshops held in 1991 and 1992, was designed to create a legal research agenda for the initiative. As a participant in the workshops, I benefitted greatly from this chance to take an early look at the social side of the initiative. The discussion that follows relies greatly on the report of the Arizona State project, a report that appears in Dennis S. Karjala, *A Legal Research Agenda for the Human Genome Initiative,* 32 JURIMETRICS J. 121 (1992).
39. *See, e.g.,* Leon Jaroff, *Happy Birthday, Double Helix: Forty Years After Their Discovery of DNA's Secret, Watson and Crick Celebrate Its Impact on the World,* TIME, Mar. 15, 1993, at 56.
40. The account that follows is based on W. French Anderson, *Human Gene Therapy,* 256 SCIENCE 808 (1992); Larry Thompson, *The First Kids with New Genes: The Inside Story of Two Young Pioneers Whose Courage Helped Launch a Medial Revolution,* TIME, June 7, 1993, at 50.
41. W. French Anderson, *Human Gene Therapy,* 256 SCIENCE 808, 813 (1992).
42. *Id.*
43. JERRY E. BISHOP & MICHAEL WALDHOLZ, GENOME: THE STORY

OF THE MOST ASTONISHING SCIENTIFIC ADVENTURE OF OUR TIME 31 (1990).

44. Dennis S. Karjala, *A Legal Research Agenda for the Human Genome Initiative*, 32 JURIMETRICS J. 121, 166 (1992).

45. *Id.*

46. DANIEL J. KEVLES, IN THE NAME OF EUGENICS: GENETICS AND THE USES OF HUMAN HEREDITY 298 (1985).

47. Leon Jaroff, *Seeking a Godlike Power: Genetic Science Promises to Deliver the Blueprint for Human Life*, TIME, Oct. 15, 1992, at 58.

48. *Id.*

49. J. Madeline Nash, *The Frontier Within: By Plumbing the Deep Secrets of the Human Mind, Scientists Will Open the Way to Cures, Wonders—And Voyeurism*, TIME, Oct. 15, 1992, at 81.

50. Paul R. Krugman, *Are You Ready for the Twenty-first Century?*, FORTUNE, Apr. 5, 1993, at 125.

51. The following account of the limits of the implications of mapping the human genome is based on Dennis S. Karjala, *A Legal Research Agenda for the Human Genome Initiative*, 32 JURIMETRICS J. 121, 146–47 (1992).

52. *See, e.g.*, Andrew Purvis, *DNA and the Desire to Drink: Researchers Discover a Gene at the Root of Alcoholism*, TIME, Apr. 30, 1990, at 88.

53. Dennis S. Karjala, *A Legal Research Agenda for the Human Genome Initiative*, 32 JURIMETRICS J. 121, 147 (1992).

54. *See generally* DANIEL J. KEVLES, IN THE NAME OF EUGENICS: GENETICS AND THE USES OF HUMAN HEREDITY (1985).

55. *Id.* at 296.

56. *See, e.g.*, Mortimor J. Adler, *Forward* to YVES R. SIMON, FREEDOM OF CHOICE i, vii (1969).

57. Robert Fearey, *The Concept of Responsibility*, 45 J. CRIM. L., CRIMINOLOGY & POL. SCI. 21, 24 (1954).

58. STUART HAMPSHIRE, FREEDOM OF THE INDIVIDUAL 142 (expanded ed. 1975).

59. EDGAR BODENHEIMER, PHILOSOPHY OF RESPONSIBILITY 7 (1980).

60. Michael S. Moore, *Causation and the Excuses*, 73 CAL. L. REV. 1091, 1133 (1985).

Notes to Chapter 8

1. Bill Peterson, *U.S. Makes Major Advance in Nuclear Fusion*, WASH. POST, Aug. 13, 1978, at A1.

2. John Pease, *Fusion Research Twenty-five Years after Zeta*, NEW SCIENTIST, Jan. 20, 1983, at 166–67.

3. *1992 Hearing Before the Subcomm. on Energy of the House of Representa-*

tives Comm. on Science, Space, and Technology, 102nd Cong., 2d Sess., 3 (1992) (statement of Chairman Brown).

4. *Id.* at 22 (statement of Dr. Conn).

5. *Id.* at 9 (statement of Mr. Happer).

6. An earlier version of portions of the remainder of this chapter appeared in Steven Goldberg, *Controlling Basic Science: The Case of Nuclear Fusion,* 68 GEO. L. J. 683 (1980).

7. Curt Suplee, *Fusion Power Experiment Is Successful: Energy Source Moves Closer to Practicality,* WASH. POST, Nov. 11, 1991 at A1; Boyce Rensenberger, *Princeton Lab Sets Another Fusion Record,* WASH POST, Dec. 10, 1993, at A3.

8. *Id.*

9. *Id.*

10. S. D. FREEMAN, ENERGY: THE NEW ERA 278 (1974).

11. PRINCETON UNIVERSITY PLASMA PHYSICS LABORATORY, INFORMATION BULLETIN: FUSION POWER 6 (1993).

12. *Id.*

13. *Id.*

14. Steven Goldberg, *Controlling Basic Science: The Case of Nuclear Fusion,* 68 GEO. L. J. 683, 688 (1980).

15. Telephone Interview with Eugene Nardella, Office of Fusion Energy (July 23, 1993).

16. *1992 Hearing Before the Subcomm. on Energy of the House of Representatives Comm. on Science, Space, and Technology,* 102d Cong., 2d Sess., 17 (1992).

17. *Id.* at 8, 15.

18. *Id.* at 9.

19. S. SCHURR, ET AL., ENERGY IN AMERICA'S FUTURE 300 (1979).

20. Curt Suplee, *Fusion-Power Experiment Is Successful: Energy Source Moves Closer to Practicality,* WASH. POST, Nov. 11, 1991, at A1.

21. Steven Goldberg, *Controlling Basic Science: The Case of Nuclear Fusion,* 68 GEO. L. J. 683, 696 (1980).

22. Phil Vettel, *As a Matter of Fact,* CHICAGO TRIBUNE, May 17, 1987, at C4.

23. *Id.* at 705, n.178.

24. Charles Seabrook, *Watkins Plays Down Tritium Spill at SRS,* ATLANTA JOURNAL, Jan. 8, 1992, at C1; Abraham Kwok and Pamela Manson, *Nuclear Waste Dump Opposed,* ARIZONA REPUBLIC, Jan. 18, 1993, at B1.

25. *See,e.g.,* John Horgan, *Fusion's Future: Will Fusion-Energy Reactors Be "Too Complex and Costly"?,* SCI. AM., Feb. 1989, at 25, 26.

26. *1992 Hearing Before the Subcomm. on Energy of the House of Representatives Comm. on Science, Space, and Technology,* 102d Cong., 2d Sess., 17 (1992).

27. Mark Crawford, *Hot Fusion: A Meltdown in Political Support,* 241 SCI-ENCE 1534 (1990).
28. John Horgan, *Fusion's Future: Will Fusion-Energy Reactors Be "Too Complex and Costly"?,* SCI. AM., Feb. 1989, at 25, 28.
29. 42 U.S.C. §4332 (2)(C) (1976).
30. Hanley v. Kleindienst, 471 F.2d 823 (2d Cir. 1972), *cert. denied,* 412 U.S. 908 (1973).
31. 42 U.S.C. §4332(c)(iii) (1976).
32. *Compare* Gustave Speth, *The Federal Role in Technology Assessment and Control, in* FEDERAL ENVIRONMENTAL LAW 433–43 (E. Dolgin & T. Builbert, eds., 1974), *with* Daniel A. Dreyfus & Helen M. Ingram, *The National Environmental Policy Act: A View of Intent and Practice,* 16 NAT. RESOURCES J. 243, 261 (1976). *See also* Comment, *The National Environmental Policy Act Applied to Policy-Level Decisionmaking,* 3 ECOLOGY L. Q. 799 (1973).
33. ENERGY RES. & DEV. ADMIN., ERDA NO. 1544, FINAL ENVIRONMENTAL IMPACT STATEMENT, TOKAMAK FUSION TEST REACTOR FACILITIES (July 1975). The Energy Research and Development Administration was a predecessor agency to the Department of Energy.
34. 481 F.2d 1079 (D.C. Cir. 1973).
35. *Id.* at 1093–94.
36. *Id.* at 1094.
37. 427 U.S. 390 (1976).
38. *Id.* at 405–06.
39. *Id.* at 412.
40. *See, e.g.,* Note, *Program Environmental Impact Statements: Review and Remedies,* 75 MICH. L. REV. 107, 117 (1976); Note, *Environmental Law,* 55 N.C. L. REV. 484, 496 (1977); Note, *The Scope of the Program EIS Requirement: The Need for a Coherent Judicial Approach,* 30 STAN. L. REV. 767, 791–92 (1978); Note, *Environmental Law,* 50 TEMP. L. Q. 410, 418 (1977).
41. 817 F.2d 882 (D.C.Cir. 1987).
42. Foundation on Economic Trends v. Heckler, 756 F.2d 143, 159 (D.C. Cir. 1985).
43. 442 U.S. 347 (1979).
44. W. D. Kay, *The Politics of Fusion Research,* ISSUES IN SCIENCE AND TECHNOLOGY, Winter 1991–92, at 41.
45. David P. Hamilton, *The Fusion Community Picks Up the Pieces,* 255 SCIENCE 1203 (1992).
46. W. D. Day, *The Politics of Fusion Research,* ISSUES IN SCIENCE AND TECHNOLOGY, Winter 1991–92, at 40.
47. JOAN L. BROMBERG, FUSION: SCIENCE, POLITICS, AND THE INVENTION OF A NEW ENERGY SOURCE 252 (1982).

48. *See, e.g.,* John R. Gilleland, et al., *Moving Ahead with Fusion,* ISSUES IN SCIENCE AND TECHNOLOGY, Summer 1990, at 62; Robert W. Conn, et al., *The International Thermonuclear Experimental Reactor,* SCI. AM., Apr. 1992, at 103.

49. Robert W. Conn, et. al., *The International Thermonuclear Experimental Reactor,* SCI. AM., Apr. 1992, at 103.

50. John Horgan, *Fusion's Future: Will Fusion-Energy Reactors Be "Too Complex and Costly"?,* SCI. AM., Feb. 1989, at 25, 26.

51. For background on the development of photovoltaics, see PAUL D. MAYCOCK & EDWARD N. STIREWALT, PHOTOVOLTAICS: SUNLIGHT TO ELECTRICITY IN ONE STEP 169–71 (1981).

52. CHRISTOPHER FLAVIN, ELECTRICITY FROM SUNLIGHT: THE FUTURE OF PHOTOVOLTAICS 10 (1982).

53. For an overview of current research and research needs, *see* SOLAR PHOTOVOLTAIC ENERGY CONVERSION (Henry Ehrenreich, ed., The American Physical Society, 1979).

54. President's Message to Congress, 1 PUB. PAPERS: JIMMY CARTER 1098 (June 20, 1979).

55. Address Before the General Assembly of the United Nations on Peaceful Uses of Atomic Energy, 1 PUB. PAPERS: DWIGHT D. EISENHOWER 820 (Dec. 8, 1953).

56. W. D. JOHNSTON, JR., SOLAR VOLTAIC CELLS 197 (1980).

57. *Id.* at 198.

58. *Id.* at 198–99. For further information on the risks of photovoltaic devices, *see* JUDITH AREEN, ET AL., LAW, SCIENCE AND MEDICINE 1393–95 (1984).

59. *See* W. D. JOHNSTON, JR., SOLAR VOLTAIC CELLS 186 (1980); *see also* Testimony of Mickey E. Alper, Hearings Before the Subcommittee on Energy Development and Applications of the Committee on Science and Technology, United States House of Representatives, 97th Cong., 2d Sess. 386, July 28, 1982.

60. Amory Lovins, *Energy Strategy: The Road Not Taken?,* 55 FOREIGN AFF. 55 (1976).

61. *Id.* at n.20.

62. Aden B. Meinel & Marjorie P. Meinel, *Soft Path Leads to a New Dark Age, in* THE ENERGY CONTROVERSY 225 (Henry Nash, ed., 1979).

63. *See, e.g.,* SANDY F. KRAEMER, SOLAR LAW 130–132 (1978); Lyden, *An Integrated Approach to Solar Access,* 34 CASE W. RES. L. REV. 367 (1983–84).

64. NATIONAL ACADEMY OF SCIENCES, ENERGY IN TRANSITION 1985–2010 47 (1979).

65. E. F. SCHUMACHER, SMALL IS BEAUTIFUL 147, 156–58 (1973).

Notes to Chapter 9

1. HANS MORAVEC, MIND CHILDREN 8 (1988).
2. GEORGE F. LUGER & WILLIAM A. SUBBLEFIELD, ARTIFICIAL IN-TELLIGENCE: STRUCTURES AND STRATEGIES FOR COMPLEX PROBLEM SOLVING 7 (1993).
3. Id.
4. M. MITCHELL WALDROP, MAN-MADE MINDS: THE PROMISE OF ARTIFICIAL INTELLIGENCE 16 (1987).
5. Id. at 11–12 (provides a good account of the Dartmouth Conference). See also PAMELA MCCORDUCK, MACHINES WHO THINK 93–114 (1979).
6. JIM JUBAK, IN THE IMAGE OF THE BRAIN 7–40 (1992).
7. Curt Suplee, Artificial Life: Improving on Creation — Move Over, Darwin: A New Set of Sciences Might Just Revolutionize Biology, WASH. POST, May 6, 1990, at B1.
8. STEVEN LEVY, ARTIFICIAL LIFE: THE QUEST FOR A NEW CRE-ATION 13–17 (1992).
9. Id. at 17–18.
10. Id. at 49–58.
11. Id. at 115.
12. Philip Elmer-Dewitt, In Search of Artificial Life, TIME, Aug. 6, 1990, at 64.
13. STEVEN LEVY, ARTIFICIAL LIFE: THE QUEST FOR A NEW CRE-ATION 113–14 (1992).
14. 6 ARTIFICIAL LIFE: THE PROCEEDINGS OF AN INTERDISCIPLIN-ARY WORKSHOP ON THE SYNTHESIS AND SIMULATION OF LIV-ING SYSTEMS HELD SEPTEMBER, 1987 IN LOS ALAMOS, NEW MEXICO xvi (Christopher Langton, ed., 1987).
15. STEVEN LEVY, ARTIFICIAL LIFE: THE QUEST FOR A NEW CRE-ATION 151 (1992).
16. M. MITCHELL WALDROP, MAN-MADE MINDS: THE PROMISE OF ARTIFICIAL INTELLIGENCE 63 (1987).
17. Andrew Pollack, Pentagon Wanted a Smart Truck: What It Got Was Some-thing Else, N. Y. TIMES, May 30, 1989, at A1.
18. Artificial Intelligence: Brain Teaser, THE ECONOMIST, Aug. 17, 1991, at 62.
19. John J. Sviokla, Putting Expert Systems to Work, HARV. BUS. REV., Mar./Apr. 1988, at 91.
20. An earlier version of the remainder of this chapter appeared in Steven Goldberg, The Changing Face of Death: Computers, Consciousness, and Nancy Cruzan, 43 STAN. L. REV. 659 (1991).
21. SIGMUND FREUD, A GENERAL INTRODUCTION TO PSYCHO-ANALYSIS (rev. ed. 1935) (Chapter 18) reprinted in 54 GREAT BOOKS OF THE WESTERN WORLD 562 (R. M. Hutchins, ed., 1952).

22. *Id.*
23. *Id.* For a thorough analysis of Freud's view that he stood in a line with Copernicus and Darwin *see* BRUCE MAZLISH, THE FOURTH DISCONTINUITY: THE CO-EVOLUTION OF HUMANS AND MACHINES 3–6 (1993). *See also* Lawrence Tribe, *Technology Assessment and the Fourth Discontinuity: The Limits of Instrumental Rationality*, 46 S. CAL. L. REV. 617 (1973).
24. *See, e.g.,* COMMITTEE ON SCIENCE AND CREATIONISM, NATIONAL ACADEMY OF SCIENCES, SCIENCE AND CREATIONISM (1984).
25. *See, e.g.,* EDWARD J. LARSON, TRIAL AND ERROR: THE AMERICAN CONTROVERSY OVER CREATION AND EVOLUTION (1985).
26. *See, e.g.,* RICHARD HOFSTADTER & WALTER P. METZGER, THE DEVELOPMENT OF ACADEMIC FREEDOM IN THE UNITED STATES 324 (1955).
27. PETER SINGER, ANIMAL LIBERATION viii (2d ed. 1990).
28. *Id.* at 7.
29. *Id.* at 9–15. As part of this argument, Singer explicitly distinguishes animals from machines. He notes that "the nervous systems of other animals were not artificially constructed—as a robot might be artificially constructed—to mimic the pain behavior of humans." *Id.* at 11. Indeed, he argues that even "a cleverly constructed robot, controlled by a brilliant scientists so as to give all the signs of feeling pain, [is] really no more sensitive than any other machine." *Id.* at 10. As we shall see, this effort to draw a line between machines and nonmachines is quite controversial.
30. *Id.* at 19.
31. *Id.* at 224.
32. Alison Jolly, *A New Science that Sees Animals as Conscious Beings*, 15 SMITHSONIAN 66 (1985). See also HANS MORAVEC, MIND CHILDREN 43–44 (1988). For a theoretical argument that certain animals may have evolved consciousness similar but not identical to our own, see RAY JACKENDOFF, CONSCIOUSNESS AND THE COMPUTATIONAL MIND 325–326 (1987).
33. BRUCE MAZLISH, THE FOURTH DISCONTINUITY: THE CO-EVOLUTION OF HUMANS AND MACHINES 3 (1993).
34. James P. Carse, *Of Death and Dying/Of Life and Living*, NEW CATHOLIC WORLD, Nov./Dec. 1987, at 249–50.
35. Robert Byrne, *Chess-Playing Computer Closing in on Champions*, N. Y. TIMES, Sept. 26, 1989, at C1, col. 6.
36. Joseph McLellan, *Kasparov Showing the Computer a Few Moves*, WASH. POST, Oct. 23, 1989, at B1.
37. Robert Byrne, *Chess-Playing Computer Closing in on Champions*, N.Y. TIMES, Sept. 26, 1989, at C1, col. 6.

38. *Id.*
39. John R. Searle, *"The Emperor's New Mind": An Exchange,* N. Y. REV. BOOKS, June 14, 1990, at 59.
40. *Id.*
41. Daniel C. Dennett, *Introduction* to THE MIND'S I 8 (D. R. Hofstadter & D. C. Dennett, eds., 1981). Dennett himself believes that a clearer conceptualization of the idea of consciousness can remove any paradoxes. *Id.*
42. Noam Cohen, *Meta-Musings: The Self-Reference Craze,* NEW REPUBLIC, Sept. 5, 1988, at 17.
43. *Id.*
44. *See, e.g., Girardeau A. Spann, Hyperspace,* 84 MICH. L. REV. 642, nn.28, 29 (1986); Pierre Schlag, *Missing Pieces: A Cognitive Approach to Law,* 67 TEX. L. REV. 1248, n.200, 1249, n.201 (1989).
45. D. R. Hofstadter, *Reflections,* in THE MIND'S I 382 (D. R. Hofstadter & D. C. Dennett, eds., 1981).
46. George Johnson, *New Mind, No Clothes,* SCIENCES, Jul./Aug. 1990, at 45. On the definition of "strong" artificial intelligence, *see* JOHN L. POLLOCK, HOW TO BUILD A PERSON: A PROLEGOMENON ix (1989); JOHN R. SEARLE, MINDS, BRAINS, AND SCIENCE 28 (1984).
47. JOHN L. POLLOCK, HOW TO BUILD A PERSON: A PROLEGOMENON ix, 30 (1989).
48. HANS MORAVEC, MIND CHILDREN 39 (1988).
49. Alan Turing, *Computing Machinery and Intelligence,* 59 MIND 236 (1950), *reprinted in* THE MIND'S I 53 (D. R. Hofstadter & D. C. Dennett, eds., 1981).
50. In Turing's original version, which he called the "imitation game," a man and a woman are questioned by an interrogator, with the man pretending to be a woman. The man is then replaced by a computer that also tries to fool the interrogator. *Id.* The description given in the text is the usual modern formulation of the Turing test. *See, e.g.,* ROGER PENROSE, THE EMPEROR'S NEW MIND 6–7 (1989).
51. ROGER PENROSE, THE EMPEROR'S NEW MIND 7–8 (1989).
52. *Id.* at 7.
53. *Id.* at 8.
54. John Markoff, *Can Machines Think? Humans Match Wits,* N. Y. TIMES, Nov. 9, 1991, at A1.
55. THE MIND'S I 469 (D. R. Hofstadter & D. C. Dennett, eds., 1981).
56. *Id.*
57. *See, e.g.,* FRANK ROSE, INTO THE HEART OF THE MIND: AN AMERICAN QUEST FOR ARTIFICIAL INTELLIGENCE 161–63 (1984).
58. *See, e.g.,* John R. Searle, *Is the Brain's Mind a Computer Program?,* SCI. AM., Jan. 1990; Paul M. Churchland and Patricia Smith Churchland, *Could a Machine Think?,* 262 SCI. AM., Jan. 1990.

59. *See, e.g.,* George Johnson, *"Can Machines Learn to Think?",* N.Y. TIMES, May 15, 1988, Sec. 4, at 7; Malcolm Gladwell, *"Thinking Like Humans,"* WASH. POST, Mar. 5, 1990, Sec. 1, at A3.

60. The account that follows is taken from JOHN R. SEARLE, MINDS, BRAINS AND SCIENCE 32 (1984).

61. *Id.* at 33, 39.

62. FRANK ROSE, INTO THE HEART OF THE MIND: AN AMERICAN QUEST FOR ARTIFICIAL INTELLIGENCE 162 (1984).

63. John R. Searle, *Is the Brain's Mind a Computer Program?,* 262 SCI. AM., Jan. 1990.

64. John R. Searle, *"The Emperor's New Mind": An Exchange,* N.Y. REV. BOOKS, June 14, 1990, at 58–59.

65. *Id.*

66. JOHN R. SEARLE, MINDS, BRAINS AND SCIENCE 29–30 (1984). *See also* Ned Block, *Troubles with Functionalism, in* PERCEPTION AND COGNITION: ISSUES IN THE FOUNDATION OF PSYCHOLOGY 261, 264–65, 279–81 (C. Savage, ed., 1978).

67. D. R. Hofstadter, *Reflections, in* THE MIND'S I 373–82 (D. R. Hofstadter & D. C. Dennett, eds., 1981).

68. *Id.*

69. John R. Searle, *Minds, Brains, and Programs, in* THE MIND'S I 353, 366 (D. R. Hofstadter & D. C. Dennett, eds., 1981). In his original paper, Turing gives a similar reply to the suggestion that a computer that passed his test would lack consciousness. Alan Turing, *Computing Machinery and Intelligence,* 59 MIND 236 (1950), *reprinted in* THE MIND'S I 59–61 D. R. Hofstadter & D. C. Dennett, eds., 1981).

70. Paul M. Churchland and Patricia Smith Churchland, *Could a Machine Think?,* SCI. AM., Jan. 1990.

71. *Id.*

72. *Id.*

73. *Id.*

74. *Id.*

75. John Pollack, for example, argues that the flaw in Searle's argument as well as in a related, earlier argument presented by Ned Block is that they replace a computer, which is governed by ordinary physical laws, with a person, who we have trouble thinking of as being so governed. JOHN L. POLLACK, HOW TO BUILD A PERSON: A PROLEGOMENON, 78–79 (1989).

76. George Johnson, *Can Machines Learn to Think?,* N.Y. TIMES, May 15, 1988, Sec. 4, at 7, col. 4.

77. Nancy K. Rhoden, *Litigating Life and Death,* 102 HARV. L. REV. 375, 407, n.140 (1988).

78. JOHN R. SEARLE, MINDS, BRAINS AND SCIENCE 35 (1984).

79. John R. Searle, *Is the Brain's Mind a Computer Program?*, SCI. AM, Jan. 1990.
80. *Id.*
81. John R. Searle, *"The Emperor's New Mind": An Exchange*, N.Y. REV. BOOKS, June 14, 1990, at 58. See also RAY JACKENDOFF, CONSCIOUSNESS AND THE COMPUTATIONAL MIND, 10–11 (1987).
82. John R. Searle, *Is the Brain's Mind a Computer Program?*, SCI. AM., Jan. 1990.
83. John R. Searle, *"The Emperor's New Mind": An Exchange*, N.Y. REV. BOOKS, June 14, 1990, at 59.
84. *Id.*
85. *Id.*
86. ROGER PENROSE, THE EMPEROR'S NEW MIND (1989).
87. *See, e.g.,* the bestseller list in which Penrose's book is described as "[f]inding both computer theory and physics as yet incapable of explaining human intelligence. . . ." N.Y. TIMES, Nov. 26, 1989, Sec. 7, at 32, col. 2. *See also* Edwin McDowell, *A Rash of Thoughtful Best Sellers Has Made Publishers Think, Too*, N.Y. TIMES, Feb. 11, 1990, Sec. 4, at 6, col. 1.
88. John M. Smith, *What Can't the Computer Do?*, N.Y. REV. BOOKS, Mar. 15, 1990, at 25.
89. Michael D. Lemonick, *Those Computers Are Dummies*, TIME, June 25, 1990, at 74.
90. ROGER PENROSE, THE EMPEROR'S NEW MIND 30–70 (1989).
91. *Id.* at 111.
92. *Id.* at 110–11. Penrose is not the first to discuss the relevance of Gödel's theorem to artificial intelligence. *See, e.g.,* John R. Lucas, *The Godelian Argument*, 2 TRUTH 64 (1988).
93. ROGER PENROSE, THE EMPEROR'S NEW MIND 445–47 (1989).
94. *Id.* at 407.
95. *See, e.g.,* George Johnson, *New Mind, No Clothes*, THE SCIENCES, Jul./Aug. 1990, at 45, 48–49.
96. *Id.*
97. ROGER PENROSE, THE EMPEROR'S NEW MIND 416 (1989).
98. *Id.*
99. *Id.*
100. GERALD M. EDELMAN, BRIGHT AIR, BRILLIANT FIRE (1992).
101. *Books for Vacation Reading*, N.Y. TIMES, May 31, 1992, at 19.
102. *Nigel Hawkes, Darwin Theory 'only Way to Explain Richness of the Brain'*, TIMES [London], Sept. 8, 1992, Home News Sec.
103. GERALD M. EDELMAN, BRIGHT AIR, BRILLIANT FIRE 125 (1992).
104. *Id.* at 194–195.
105. *Id.* at 195.
106. Thomas Nagel, *The Mind Wins!*, N.Y. REV. BOOKS, Mar. 4, 1993, at 37.

107. JOHN UPDIKE, RABBIT AT REST 237 (1990).
108. ROBERT M. VEATCH, DEATH, DYING AND THE BIOLOGICAL REVOLUTION: OUR LAST QUEST FOR RESPONSIBILITY 19 (1989).
109. PRESIDENT'S COMMISSION FOR THE STUDY OF ETHICAL PROBLEMS IN MEDICINE AND BIOMEDICAL AND BEHAVIORAL RESEARCH, DEFINING DEATH: A REPORT ON THE MEDICAL, LEGAL AND ETHICAL ISSUES IN THE DETERMINATION OF DEATH 14–15 (1981).
110. *Id.*
111. *Id.* at 15, 21.
112. *Id.* at 16.
113. *See, e.g.,* George Alexander, *Science "Body Shop" Offers Spare Parts,* L.A. TIMES, Aug. 19, 1973, Sec. 1, at 1, col. 1.
114. ARTIFICIAL HEART ASSESSMENT PANEL, NATIONAL HEART AND LUNG INSTITUTE, THE TOTALLY IMPLANTABLE ARTIFICIAL HEART 5–11 (1973), *reprinted in* GEORGE J. ANNAS, ET. AL., AMERICAN HEALTH LAW 912 (1990).
115. *Id.*
116. *Id.*
117. ANDREW C. VARGA, THE MAIN ISSUES IN BIOETHICS 161 (1980.)
118. *Id.* at 21–24.
119. *Id.* at 22–30.
120. Ad Hoc Committee of the Harvard Medical School, *A Definition of Irreversible Coma,* 205 J.A.M.A. 337 (1968).
121. *Id.* at 339.
122. *Id.* at 337–340.
123. *Id.* at 340.
124. David R. Smith, *Legal Recognition of Neocortical Death,* 71 CORNELL L. REV. 850, 857–58 (1986).
125. *Id.* at 857.
126. *Id.* at 857.
127. PRESIDENT'S COMMISSION FOR THE STUDY OF ETHICAL PROBLEMS IN MEDICINE AND BIOMEDICAL AND BEHAVIORAL RESEARCH, DEFINING DEATH: A REPORT ON THE MEDICAL, LEGAL AND ETHICAL ISSUES IN THE DETERMINATION OF DEATH 38 (1981).
128. David R. Smith, *Legal Recognition of Neocortical Death,* 71 CORNELL L. REV. 850, 851, 857 (1986).
129. *Id.* at 857–58.
130. *Id.* at 858.
131. *Editorial, Death of a Human Being,* 2 LANCET 590 (1971).
132. *Id.* at 590, 591.
133. *See* text accompanying note 67, *infra.*
134. On the question of whether the provision of artificial feeding is in fact

treatment, *see* ROBERT M. VEATCH, DEATH, DYING AND THE BIO-LOGICAL REVOLUTION: OUR LAST QUEST FOR RESPONSIBILITY 83–85 (1989).

135. *See* text accompanying notes 68–69, *infra*.

136. Alexander M. Capron and Leonard Kass, *A Statutory Definition of the Standards for Determining Human Death: An Appraisal and a Proposal*, 121 U. PA. L. REV. 87 (1972).

137. *Id.* at 89–91, 111.

138. *Id.* at 114–15.

139. *Id.* at 115, n.97.

140. *Id.*

141. *Id.*

142. PRESIDENT'S COMMISSION FOR THE STUDY OF ETHICAL PROB-LEMS IN MEDICINE AND BIOMEDICAL AND BEHAVIORAL RE-SEARCH, DEFINING DEATH: A REPORT ON THE MEDICAL, LE-GAL AND ETHICAL ISSUES IN THE DETERMINATION OF DEATH 2 (1981).

143. PRESIDENT'S COMMISSION FOR THE STUDY OF ETHICAL PROB-LEMS IN MEDICINE AND BIOMEDICAL AND BEHAVIORAL RE-SEARCH, DECIDING TO FOREGO LIFE-SUSTAINING TREATMENT 190 (1983).

144. David R. Smith, *Legal Recognition of Neocortical Death*, 71 CORN. L. REV. 850, 853–55 (1986).

145. Cruzan v. Director, Missouri Department of Health, 58 U.S. L. W. 4916, 4939 (Stevens, J., dissenting).

146. *Id.* at n.21.

147. For a discussion and a critique of the numerous theories under which courts have determined whether to allow the cessation of treatment in a variety of settings see Nancy K. Rhoden, *Litigating Life and Death*, 102 HARV. L. REV. 375 (1988). Courts have, for example, used the "subjec-tive" approach under which the question is whether patients, through a living will or otherwise, have made their wishes clear prior to incapacita-tion, as well as the "objective" approach under which the question is whether the benefits of the patients' life outweighs the costs. *Id. See also* Rebecca Dresser, *Life, Death, and Incompetent Patients: Conceptual In-firmities and Hidden Values in the Law*, 28 ARIZ. L. REV. 373 (1986).

148. Nancy K. Rhoden, *Litigating Life and Death*, 102 HARV. L. REV. 375, 420 (1988).

149. Sidney Wanzer, et. al., *The Physician's Responsibility Toward Hopelessly Ill Patients: A Second Look*, 320 NEW ENG. J. MED. 844 (1989).

150. In the Matter of Karen Quinlan, 355 A.2d 647, 654 (1976), *cert. denied*, 429 U.S. 922 (1976). The Quinlan court approved removal of a respirator. *Id.* As it developed, Ms. Quinlan, like many in a persistent vegetative state, was able to breathe on her own, and thus, because no effort was made to

remove her feeding tube, she survived for nine years after the respirator was removed. Cruzan v. Harmon, 760 S.W.2d 408, 409 nn.6,7 (Mo. 1988)(en banc).

151. Brophy v. New England Sinai Hospital, Inc., 497 N.E.2d 626, 635 (Mass. 1986).

152. Gray v. Romeo, 697 F. Supp. 580, 588 (D. R.I. 1988).

153. David R. Smith, *Legal Recognition of Neocortical Death,* 71 CORN. L. REV. 850, 858 (1986).

154. *Id.*

155. ROBERT M. VEATCH, DEATH, DYING AND THE BIOLOGICAL REVOLUTION: OUR LAST QUEST FOR RESPONSIBILITY 27 (1989).

156. *Id.* at 25.

157. William C. Charron, *Death: A Philosophical Perspective on The Legal Definitions,* 1975 WASH. U. L. Q. 979, 1002 (1975).

158. Michael B. Green and Daniel Wikler, *Brain Death and Personal Identity,* 9 PHIL. & PUB. AFF. 105, 126 (1980). For a general discussion of philosophical issues relating to the persistence of personal identity, see ROBERT NOZICK, PHILOSOPHICAL EXPLANATIONS 29–114 (1981).

159. Allen E. Buchanan, *The Limits of Proxy Decisionmaking for Incompetents,* 29 UCLA L. REV. 386, 404 n.52, 408 (1981).

160. David R. Smith, *Legal Recognition of Neocortical Death,* 71 CORN. L. REV. 850, 859 (1986). A similar approach for the beginning of life, with implications for abortion, is presented in Gary Gertler, Note, *Brain Birth: A Proposal for Defining When a Fetus Is Entitled to Human Life Status,* 59 S. CAL. L. REV. 1061 (1986).

161. *See* text accompanying notes 67–69, *supra.*

162. ROBERT M. VEATCH, DEATH, DYING AND THE BIOLOGICAL REVOLUTION: OUR LAST QUEST FOR RESPONSIBILITY 31 (1989).

163. Allen E. Buchanan, *The Limits of Proxy Decisionmaking for Incompetents,* 29 UCLA L. REV. 386, 404 (1981).

164. 497 U.S. 261 (1990).

165. Tamar Lewin, *Nancy Cruzan Dies, Outlived by a Debate Over the Right to Die,* N.Y. TIMES, Dec. 27, 1990, at A1, col. 5.

166. That step might bring to the foreground the debate over whether computers should have rights. *See, e.g.,* Phil McNally & Sohail Inayatullah, *The Rights of Robots,* 20 FUTURES 119 (1988); JUDITH AREEN ET AL., LAW, SCIENCE AND MEDICINE 395 (Supp. 1989). Of course, that debate might also raise the question of whether people should have rights. FRANK ROSE, INTO THE HEART OF THE MIND 124 (1984). For an extensive discussion of the legal status of "unconventional entities generally—not merely lakes and mountains, but robots and embryos, tribes and species, future generations and artifacts", see Christopher Stone,

Should Trees Have Standing? Revisited: How Far Will Law And Morals Reach? A Pluralist Perspective, 59 S. CAL. L. REV. 1, 8 (1985).

167. One commentator has suggested that what makes humans unique is our desire to prove we are unique. Paul Chance, *Apart from the Animals: There Must Be Something about Us that Makes Us Unique*, PSYCHOL. TODAY, Jan. 1988, at 18–19.

168. ROBERT M. VEATCH, DEATH, DYING AND THE BIOLOGICAL REVOLUTION: OUR LAST QUEST FOR RESPONSIBILITY 28–29 (1989). Veatch suggests that distinguishing between the capacity for social interaction and consciousness may not be relevant to the definition of death. *Id.* at 29; *but see* Kevin P. Quinn, *The Best Interests of Incompetent Patients: The Capacity for Interpersonal Relationships as a Standard for Decisionmaking*, 76 CAL. L. REV. 897 (1988) and Nancy K. Rhoden, *Litigating Life and Death*, 102 HARV. L. REV. 375, 442 (1988). For others who support "the capacity to . . . interact" as crucial, *see* Rebecca Dresser, *Life, Death, and Incompetent Patients: Conceptual Infirmities and Hidden Values in the Law*, 28 ARIZ. L. REV. 373, 401 n.163 (1986); *see also* Allen E. Buchanan, *The Limits of Proxy Decisionmaking for Incompetents*, 29 UCLA L. REV. 386, 404 n.52 (1981).

169. Joe Patrick Bean, *Chess By Computer: Is This Progress?*, CHRISTIAN SCI. MONITOR, Oct. 16, 1989, at 18, col. 1.

170. Kevin P. Quinn, *The Best Interests of Incompetent Patients: The Capacity for Interpersonal Relationships as a Standard for Decisionmaking*, 76 CAL. L. REV. 897, 932 (1988).

171. *Id.* at 935. *See also* Rebecca Dresser, *Life, Death, and Incompetent Patients: Conceptual Infirmities and Hidden Values in the Law*, 28 ARIZ. L. REV. 373, 401, n.163 (1986).

172. Nancy K. Rhoden, *Litigating Life and Death*, 102 HARV. L. REV. 375, 442 (1988).

173. *Id.* Rhoden also discusses the impact of pain on treatment issues, *id.*, an issue beyond the scope of this volume.

174. *See note 150, supra.*

175. *See text accompanying notes 68–69, supra.*

176. Rebecca Dresser, *Life, Death and Incompetent Patients: Conceptual Infirmities and Hidden Values in the Law*, 28 ARIZ. L. REV. 373, 402 (1986).

177. *In re* Conroy, 486 A.2d 1209 (N.J. 1985).

178. *Id.* Ms. Conroy had died by the time the Supreme Court of New Jersey decided the case, but the court reached the merits on the ground that this was a matter capable of repetition that could evade review. *Id.* at 1219.

179. *Id.* at 1217.

180. *Id.*

181. *Id.* at 1242–43.

182. The inquiry into Ms. Conroy's intent was described as the "subjective"

test. *Id.* at 1229, 1242, 1243. The weighing of benefits and burdens, which comes into play when there is some evidence that the patient wanted treatment terminated, was called the "limited-objective" test. *Id.* at 1232, 1243. The inquiry into the possibly inhumane treatment that prolongs a painful existence was termed the "pure-objective" test. *Id.* at 1232, 1243.

183. Kevin P. Quinn, *The Best Interests of Incompetent Patients: The Capacity for Interpersonal Relationships as a Standard for Decisionmaking,* 76 CAL. L. REV. 897, 936 (1988). Quinn is discussing a hypothetical Mr. Q who is based in part on Ms. Conroy. *Id.* at 897 n.1. He concludes that if Mr. Q lacks the capacity for social interaction—which Ms. Conroy lacks—prolongation of life is inappropriate. *Id.* at 936.

184. Nancy K. Rhoden, *Litigating Life and Death,* 102 HARV. L. REV. 375, 376–378, 403–10, 442 (1988).

185. *Id.* at 442.

186. *Id.* at 409.

187. *See, e.g.,* Steven Goldberg, *The Reluctant Embrace: Law and Science in America,* 75 GEO. L. J. 1341, 1344 (1987).

188. *Id.*

189. *See* PETER SINGER, ANIMAL LIBERATION 79–80, 206–7 (2d ed. 1990).

190. ABRAHAM S. GOLDSTEIN, THE INSANITY DEFENSE 211–12 (1967).

191. *See Notes and Questions on Medical Care at the End of Life, in* CLARK C. HAVIGHURST, HEALTH CARE LAW AND POLICY 1255–57 (1988)("Courts are likely to be highly vigilant against any sign that the elderly and sick are being written off. Economic considerations are of course rarely even alluded to in these cases. [Will it always be so?]")

192. Jay A. Friedman, *Taking the Camel by the Nose: The Anencephalic as a Source for Pediatric Organ Transplants,* 90 COLUM. L. REV. 917 (1990).

193. *See* PETER SINGER, ANIMAL LIBERATION 72 (2d ed. 1990) and ABRAHAM S. GOLDSTEIN, THE INSANITY DEFENSE 211–12 (1967).

194. ROBERT M. VEATCH, DEATH, DYING AND THE BIOLOGICAL REVOLUTION: OUR LAST QUEST FOR RESPONSIBILITY 20–21, 22 (1989).

Notes to Chapter 10

1. VANNEVAR BUSH, SCIENCE: THE ENDLESS FRONTIER 12 (1960).

2. Stephen G. Carter, *The Bellman, the Snark, and the Biohazard Debate,* 3 Yale L. & Pol'y Rev. 358, 393 (1985).

Bibliography

Adair, Douglass, *"That Politics May Be Reduced to a Science": David Hume, James Madison, and the Tenth Federalist,* 20 HUNTINGTON LIB. Q. 343 (1957).

Adams, W. H., *Public Aid for the Arts: A Change of Heart?, in* CULTURAL POLICY AND ARTS ADMINISTRATION (Stephen A. Greyser, ed., 1973).

Alexander, George, *Science "Body Shop" Offers Spare Parts,* L.A. TIMES, Aug. 19, 1973.

Anderson, W. French, *Human Gene Therapy,* 256 SCIENCE 808 (1992).

AREEN, JUDITH, ET AL., LAW, SCIENCE AND MEDICINE (1984).

Baldwin, Gordon B., *Law in Support of Science: Legal Control of Basic Research Resources,* 54 GEO. L. J. 559 (1966).

BARBER, BERNARD, SCIENCE AND THE SOCIAL ORDER (1952).

BARFIELD, CHARLES E., SCIENTIFIC POLICY FROM FORD TO REAGAN: CHANGE AND CONTINUITY (1982).

Bazelon, David, *Coping with Technology through the Legal Process,* 62 CORNELL L. REV. 817 (1977).

Bean, Joe Patrick, *Chess by Computer: Is This Progress?,* CHRISTIAN SCI. MONITOR, Oct. 16, 1989.

BECKER, CARL, THE HEAVENLY CITY OF THE EIGHTEENTH-CENTURY PHILOSOPHERS (1932).

BELL, WHITFIELD, EARLY AMERICAN SCIENCE: NEEDS AND OPPORTUNITIES FOR STUDY (1955).

BELLAH, ROBERT N., THE BROKEN COVENANT: AMERICAN CIVIL RELIGION IN TIME OF TRIAL (2d ed. 1992).

Bellamy, Calvin, *Item Veto: Shield against Deficits or Weapon of Presidential Power?* 22 VAL. U. L. REV. 557 (1988).

BENDINI, SALVIO A., THE LIFE OF BENJAMIN BANNEKER (1972).

BENDINI, SALVIO A., THINKERS AND TINKERS (1975).

Berger, Peter L., *Religion in a Revolutionary Society, in* AMERICA'S CONTIN-UING REVOLUTION (1975).

BEYERCHEN, ALAN D., SCIENTISTS UNDER HITLER (1977).

Bezak, Elizabeth M., Note, *DNA Profiling Evidence: The Need for a Uniform and Workable Evidentiary Standard of Admissibility,* 26 VAL. U. L. REV. 595 (1992).

BILLINGTON, DAVID P., THE TOWER AND THE BRIDGE (1983).

Bird, Wendell R., *Freedom of Religion and Science Instruction in Public Schools,* 87 YALE L. J. 515 (1978).

BISHOP, JERRY E. & WALDHOLZ, MICHAEL, GENOME: THE STORY OF THE MOST ASTONISHING SCIENTIFIC ADVENTURE OF OUR TIME (1990).

Block, Ned, *Troubles with Functionalism, in* PERCEPTION AND COGNI-TION: ISSUES IN THE FOUNDATION OF PSYCHOLOGY (C. Savage, ed., 1978).

BODENHEIMER, EDGAR, PHILOSOPHY OF RESPONSIBILITY (1980).

BOORSTIN, DANIEL J., THE AMERICANS: THE COLONIAL EXPERI-ENCE (1958).

BOORSTIN, DANIEL J., THE LOST WORLD OF THOMAS JEFFERSON (1960).

BOORSTIN, DANIEL J., THE REPUBLIC OF TECHNOLOGY (1978).

BOREK, ERNEST, THE CODE OF LIFE (1965).

Bork, Robert H., *Neutral Principles and Some First Amendment Problems,* 47 IND. L. J. 1 (1971).

BOWDEN, MARY W., PHILIP FRENEAU (1976).

Bowman, Isaiah, *Jeffersonian "Freedom of Speech" from the Standpoint of Science,* 82 SCIENCE 529 (1935).

BRANT, IRVING, JAMES MADISON: FATHER OF THE CONSTITUTION (1950).

Brasch, Frederick E., *The Newtonian Epoch in the American Colonies,* 49 AM. ANTIQUARIAN SOC'Y PROC. 314 (1939).

Brest, Paul, *Palmer v. Thompson: An Approach to the Problem of Unconstitu-tional Legislative Motive,* 1971 SUP. CT. REV. 95 (1971).

BROMBERG, JOAN L., FUSION: SCIENCE, POLITICS, AND THE INVEN-TION OF A NEW ENERGY SOURCE (1982).

Brooks, Harvey, *The Scientific Advisor, in* SCIENTISTS AND NATIONAL POLICY-MAKING (Robert Gilpin & Christopher Wright, eds., 1964).

Bruce, Robert V., *A Statistical Profile of American Scientists 1846–1876, in* NINETEENTH CENTURY AMERICAN SCIENCE: A REAPPRAISAL (George H. Daniels, ed., 1972).

Brustein, Robert, *The Artist and the Citizen,* NEW REPUBLIC, June 24, 1978.

Buchanan, Allen E., *The Limits of Proxy Decisionmaking for Incompetents,* 29 U.C.L.A. L. REV. 386 (1981).

Bue, Nancy L., *Comment, in* LAW AND SCIENCE IN COLLABORATION (J. Daniel Nyhart & Milton M. Carrow, eds., 1983).

BUGBEE, BRUCE W., GENESIS OF AMERICAN PATENT AND COPYRIGHT LAW (1967).

BUPP, IRVIN C. & DERIAN, JEAN-CLAUDE, LIGHT WATER: HOW THE NUCLEAR DREAM DISSOLVED (1978).

Burdick, Charles K., *Federal Aid Legislation*, 8 CORNELL L. Q. 324 (1923).

BURKE, EDMUND, SELECTED WRITINGS AND SPEECHES (Peter J. Stanlis ed., 1963).

BURNS, EDWARD M., JAMES MADISON: THE PHILOSOPHER OF THE CONSTITUTION (1968).

BURY, J. B., THE IDEA OF PROGRESS (1932).

BUSH, VANNEVAR, SCIENCE: THE ENDLESS FRONTIER (1960).

Byrne, Robert, *Chess-Playing Computer Closing in on Champions*, N. Y. TIMES, Sept. 26, 1989.

Capron, Alexander M. & Kass, Leonard, *A Statutory Definition of the Standards for Determining Human Death: An Appraisal and a Proposal*, 121 U. PA. L. REV. 87 (1972).

Carse, James P., *Of Death and Dying/Of Life and Living*, NEW CATHOLIC WORLD, Nov./Dec. 1987.

Carter, Stephen L., *The Bellman, the Snark, and the Biohazard Debate*, 3 YALE L. & POL'Y REV. 358 (1985).

CARTER, STEPHEN L., THE CULTURE OF DISBELIEF: HOW AMERICAN LAW AND POLITICS TRIVIALIZE RELIGIOUS DEVOTION (1993).

CASSARA, ERNEST, THE ENLIGHTENMENT IN AMERICA (1975).

CASSIRER, ERNST, THE PHILOSOPHY OF THE ENLIGHTENMENT (1960).

Cave, R.J., *Pick Your Poison*, 362 NATURE 204 (Mar. 18, 1993).

CHAFFEE, ZECHARIAH, FREE SPEECH IN THE UNITED STATES (1967).

Chalk, Rosemary, *Impure Science: Fraud, Compromise, and Political Influence in Scientific Research*, 96 TECH. REV. 69 (1993).

Chance, Paul, *Apart from the Animals: There Must Be Something About Us that Makes Us Unique*, PSYCHOL. TODAY, Jan. 1988.

Charron, William C., *Death: A Philosophical Perspective on the Legal Definitions*, 1975 WASH. U. L. Q. 979 (1975).

Christen, D. K. & Thompson, J. R., *Superconductivity: Current Problems at High T_c*, 364 NATURE 98 (July 8, 1993).

Churchland, Paul M. & Churchland, Patricia Smith, *Could a Machine Think?*, SCI. AM., Jan. 1990.

CIBINIC, JOHN & NASH, RALPH C., GOVERNMENT CONTRACT CLAIMS (1981).

Clark, Harry H., *The Influence of Science on American Ideas: From 1775 to 1809*, 35 TRANSACTIONS WIS. ACAD. 312 (1943).

Clark, Harry H., *To Promote the Progress of . . . Useful Arts*, 43 N.Y.U. L. REV. 88 (1968).

CLEAVELAND, FREDERIC N., SCIENCE AND STATE GOVERNMENT (1959).

COCHRANE, REXMOND C., MEASURES FOR PROGRESS (1966).

COHEN, I. BERNARD, FRANKLIN AND NEWTON (1966).

COHEN, I. BERNARD, REVOLUTION IN SCIENCE (1985).

Cohen, I. Bernard, *Science and the Growth of the American Republic*, 38 REV. POL. 359 (1976).

Cohen, I. Bernard, *Science and the Revolution*, 47 TECH. REV. 367 (1945).

Cohen, Noam, *Meta-Musings: The Self-Reference Craze*, NEW REPUBLIC, Sept. 5, 1988.

Cole, Stephen, et al., *Chance and Consensus in Peer Review*, 214 SCIENCE 881 (1981).

Conn, Robert W., et al., *The International Thermonuclear Experimental Reactor*, SCI. AM., Apr. 1992.

Cook-Deegan, Robert M., *The Human Genome Project: The Formation of Federal Policies in the United States, 1986–1990, in* BIOMEDICAL POLITICS (Kathi E. Hanna, ed., 1991).

COOLEY, THOMAS M., A TREATISE ON THE LAW OF TORTS OR THE WRONGS WHICH ARISE INDEPENDENT OF CONTRACT (2d ed. 1888).

CORNELIUS, DAVID K. & ST. VINCENT, EDWIN, CULTURES IN CONFLICT: PERSPECTIVES ON THE SNOW-LEAVIS CONTROVERSY (1964).

Crawford, Mark, *Hot Fusion: A Meltdown in Political Support*, 241 SCIENCE 1534 (1990).

CURTI, MERLE, THE GROWTH OF AMERICAN THOUGHT (3rd ed. 1982).

DAC ANDRADE, EDWARD N., SIR ISAAC NEWTON (1954).

DAHRENDORF, RALF, DIE ANGEWANDTE AUFLAURUNG (1968).

DANIELS, GEORGE H., AMERICAN SCIENCE IN THE AGE OF JACKSON (1968).

Daniels, George H., *Introduction, in* NINETEENTH CENTURY AMERICAN SCIENCE: A REAPPRAISAL (George H. Daniels, ed., 1972).

DANIELS, GEORGE H., SCIENCE IN AMERICAN SOCIETY (1971).

DARWIN, CHARLES, VARIATION OF ANIMALS AND PLANTS UNDER DOMESTICATION (Paul H. Barrett & R. B. Freeman, eds., 1988) (1873).

Delgado, Richard & Millen, David R., *God, Galileo, and Government: Toward Constitutional Protection for Scientific Inquiry*, 53 WASH. L. REV. 349 (1978).

Dennett, Daniel C., *Introduction* to THE MIND'S I (D. R. Hofstadter & D. C. Dennett, eds., 1981).

DE TOCQUEVILLE, ALEXIS, DEMOCRACY IN AMERICA (New York, Sever & Francis, 1862) (1841).

Dickson, John, *Towards a Democratic Strategy for Science*, SCI. FOR PEOPLE, July/Aug. 1984.

Donald, David, *Uniting the Republic, in* THE GREAT REPUBLIC 735–58 (Bernard Bailyn, et al., eds., 1977).

Dresser, Rebecca, *Life, Death, and Incompetent Patients: Conceptual Infirmities and Hidden Values in the Law*, 28 ARIZ. L. REV. 373 (1986).

Dreyfus, Daniel A. & Ingram, Helen M., *The National Environmental Policy Act: A View of Intent and Practice*, 16 NAT. RESOURCES J. 243 (1976).

Dudney, Robert S., et al., *The Legacies of World War II: The Nuclear Age*, U.S. NEWS & WORLD REP., Aug. 5, 1985.

DUPREE, A. HUNTER, SCIENCE IN THE FEDERAL GOVERNMENT: A HISTORY OF POLICIES AND ACTIVITIES TO 1940 (1957).

EDELMAN, GERALD M., BRIGHT AIR, BRILLIANT FIRE (1992).

Editorial, Death of a Human Being, 2 LANCET 590 (1971).

Edsall, John T., *Scientific Freedom and Responsibility: Report of the AAAS Committee on Scientific Freedom and Responsibility*, 188 SCIENCE 687 (1975).

EISENHOWER, DWIGHT D., THE ATOM FOR PROGRESS AND PEACE (Dec. 8, 1953).

ELAZAR, DANIEL J., THE AMERICAN PARTNERSHIP (1962).

Elmer-Dewitt, Philip, *In Search of Artificial Life*, TIME, Aug. 6, 1990.

Ely, John H., *Legislative and Administrative Motivation in Constitutional Law*, 79 YALE L. J. 1205 (1970).

Emerson, Thomas I., *Colonial Intentions and Current Realities of the First Amendment*, 125 U. PA. L. REV. 737 (1977).

Emerson, Thomas I., *Toward a General Theory of the First Amendment*, 72 YALE L. J. 877 (1963).

Emerson, Thomas I. & Haber, Herbert, *The Scopes Case in Modern Dress*, 27 U. CHI. L. REV. 522 (1960).

EVANS, CHRISTOPHER, THE MAKING OF THE MICRO: A HISTORY OF THE COMPUTER (1981).

EVE, RAYMOND A. & HARROLD, FRANCIS B., THE CREATIONIST MOVEMENT IN MODERN AMERICA (1991).

FARRAND, MAX, RECORDS OF THE FEDERAL CONVENTION (1911).

Faulkner, Robert K., *John Marshall in History, in* JOHN MARSHALL (Stanley I. Kutler, ed., 1972).

Fearey, Robert, *The Concept of Responsibility*, 45 J. CRIM. L., CRIMINOL-OGY & POL. SCI. 21 (1954).

Federico, P. J., *Colonial Monopolies and Patents*, 11 J. PAT. OFF. SOC'Y 358 (1929).

Feinberg, Lawrence, *Colleges Bypass Agencies to Get Federal Funds*, WASH. POST, June 5, 1984.

Fenning, Karl, *The Origin of the Patent and Copyright Clause of the Constitution*, 17 GEO. L. J. 109 (1929).

Ferguson, James R., *Scientific Inquiry and the First Amendment*, 64 CORNELL L. REV. 639 (1979).

Finke, Roger, *An Unsecular America, in* RELIGION AND MODERNIZATION 148–49 (Steve Bruce, ed., 1992).

Fitchett, Joseph, *In U.S., the Economics of Culture*, INT'L HERALD TRIB., Oct. 30, 1993.

FLAVIN, CHRISTOPHER, ELECTRICITY FROM SUNLIGHT: THE FUTURE OF PHOTOVOLTAICS (1982).

FLEXNER, JAMES T., THE YOUNG HAMILTON: A BIOGRAPHY 47 (1978).

Francione, Gary L., *Experimentation and the Marketplace Theory of the First Amendment*, 136 U. PA. L. REV. 417 (1987).

Fredrickson, Donald S., *Asilomar and Recombinant DNA: The End of the Beginning, in* BIOMEDICAL POLITICS (Kathi E. Hanna, ed., 1991).

FREEMAN, S. D., ENERGY: THE NEW ERA (1974).

Freneau, Philip M. & Brackenridge, H. H., *The Rising Glory of America, in* POEMS OF FRENEAU (Harry H. Clark, ed., 1929).

FREUD, SIGMUND, A GENERAL INTRODUCTION TO PSYCHO-ANALYSIS (rev. ed. 1935) *reprinted in* GREAT BOOKS OF THE WESTERN WORLD (R. M. Hutchins, ed., 1952).

Friedman, Herbert, *Big Science vs. Little Science: The Controversy Mounts*, 1 COSMOS 8 (1991).

Friedman, Jay A., *Taking the Camel by the Nose: The Anencephalic as a Source for Pediatric Organ Transplants*, 90 COLUM. L. REV. 917 (1990).

Furrow, Barry R., et al., BIOETHICS: HEALTH CARE LAW AND ETHICS (1991).

GALLAGHER, ANDREW K., THE LAW OF FEDERAL NEGOTIATED CONTRACT FORMATION (1981).

GAY, PETER, THE ENLIGHTENMENT: A COMPREHENSIVE ANTHOLOGY (1973).

GAY, PETER, THE ENLIGHTENMENT: AN INTERPRETATION (1969).

GELLHORN, WALTER, SECURITY, LOYALTY AND SCIENCE (1950).

Gertler, Gary, Note, *Brain Birth: A Proposal for Defining When a Fetus Is Entitled to Human Life Status*, 59 S. CAL. L. REV. 1061 (1986).

Gibson, Steve, *Someone Needs to Reinvent America's Outdated Patent System*, INFOWORLD, Aug. 24, 1992.

Gilleland, John R., et al., *Moving Ahead with Fusion*, ISSUES IN SCIENCE AND TECHNOLOGY, Summer 1990.

GILMORE, GRANT, THE AGES OF AMERICAN LAW (1977).

Gladwell, Malcolm, *Thinking Like Humans*, WASH. POST, Mar. 5, 1990.

Glantz, Stanton A. & Albers, N. V., *Department of Defense R&D in the University*, 186 SCIENCE 706 (1974).

Goldberg, Steven, *The Central Dogmas of Law and Science*, 36 J. LEGAL EDUC. 37 (1986).

Goldberg, Steven, *The Changing Face of Death: Computers, Consciousness, and Nancy Cruzan*, 43 STAN. L. REV. 659 (1991).

Goldberg, Steven, *The Constitutional Status of American Science*, 1979 U. ILL. L. FOR. 1 (1979).

Goldberg, Steven, *Controlling Basic Science: The Case of Nuclear Fusion*, 68 GEO. L. J. 707 (1980).

Goldberg, Steven, *Narrowing the Regulatory Gap Between Law and Science: The Prospects for Superconductivity*, 1 CTS., HEALTH SCI. & LAW 163 (1990).

Goldberg, Steven, *On Legal and Mathematical Reasoning*, 22 JURIMETRICS J. 83 (1981).

Goldberg, Steven, *The Reluctant Embrace: Law and Science in America*, 75 GEO. L. J. 1341 (1987).

GOLDSTEIN, ABRAHAM S., THE INSANITY DEFENSE (1967).

GOLDSTINE, HERMAN H., THE COMPUTER FROM PASCAL TO VON NEWMANN (1972).

GOODCHILD, PETER, J. ROBERT OPPENHEIMER: SHATTERER OF WORLDS (1981).

GOODELL, RAE, THE VISIBLE SCIENTISTS (1977).

GOSSELIN, ROBERT E., ET AL., CLINICAL TOXICOLOGY OF COMMERCIAL PRODUCTS (1984).

GRAFF, GERALD, LITERATURE AGAINST ITSELF: LITERARY IDEAS IN MODERN SOCIETY (1979).

GREBSTEIN, SHELDON NORMAN, MONKEY TRIAL: THE STATE OF TENNESSEE VS. JOHN THOMAS SCOPES (1960).

Green, Michael B. & Wikler, Daniel, *Brain Death and Personal Identity*, 9 PHIL. & PUB. AFF. 105 (1980).

Greenberg, Daniel S., *Case against Gallo Faces Tough Appeals Process*, 23 SCI. & GOV'T REPT. 1 (1993).

Greenberg, Daniel S., *Keyworth and Fuqua Volley on Pork-Barrel R&D*, 14 SCI. & GOV'T REP. 5 (1984).

GREENBERG, DANIEL S., THE POLITICS OF PURE SCIENCE (1967).

Grossbaum, John J., *Federal Support of Research Projects through Contracts and Grants: A Rationale*, 19 AM. U. L. REV. 423 (1970).

Hamilton, Alexander, *Report on the Subject of Manufacturers*, in THE WORKS OF ALEXANDER HAMILTON (New York, Williams & Whiting, 1810).

Hamilton, David P., *The Fusion Community Picks Up the Pieces*, 255 SCIENCE 1203 (1992).

HAMPSHIRE, STUART, FREEDOM OF THE INDIVIDUAL (expanded ed. 1975).

Hartt, Rollin L., *What Lies Beyond Dayton*, NATION, July 22, 1925.

Hawkes, Nigel, *Darwin Theory "Only Way to Explain Richness of the Brain,"* TIMES [London], Sept. 8, 1992.

HEISENBERG, WERNER, PHYSICS AND BEYOND: ENCOUNTERS AND CONVERSATIONS (1971).

Hilts, Philip J., *U.S. Superconductor Consortium Formed,* WASH. POST, May 24, 1989.

HILL, CHRISTOPHER, MILTON AND THE ENGLISH REVOLUTION (1977).

Hilts, Philip J., *A Cautious Eye on the Bottom Line,* WASH. POST, May 19, 1987.

HIMMELFARB, GERTRUDE, MARRIAGE AND MORALS AMONG THE VICTORIANS (1986).

HINDLE, BROOKE, THE PURSUIT OF SCIENCE IN REVOLUTIONARY AMERICA (1956).

Hindle, Brooke, *The Quaker Background and Science in Colonial Philadelphia,* 46 ISIS 243 (1955).

HOFFMAN, BANESH, ALBERT EINSTEIN: CREATOR AND REBEL (1972).

Hoffman, Gary M. & Karney, Geoffrey M., *Can Justice Keep Pace with Science?,* WASH. POST, Apr. 10, 1988.

Hofstadter, D. R., *Reflections,* in THE MIND'S I (D. R. Hofstadter & D. C. Dennett, eds., 1981).

HOFSTADTER, RICHARD & METZGER, WALTER P., THE DEVELOPMENT OF ACADEMIC FREEDOM IN THE UNITED STATES (1955).

Hollinger, Robert, *From Weber to Habermas,* in E. D. KLEMKE, ET AL., INTRODUCTORY READINGS IN THE PHILOSOPHY OF SCIENCE (1988).

Holmer, Paul L., *Evolution and Being Faithful,* 84 CHRISTIAN CENTURY 1491 (1967).

Holmes, Oliver W., *Law in Science and Science in Law,* 12 HARV. L. REV. 443 (1899).

HOPPER, DAVID H., TECHNOLOGY, THEOLOGY AND THE IDEA OF PROGRESS (1991).

Horgan, John, *Fusion's Future: Will Fusion-Energy Reactors Be "Too Complex and Costly"?,* SCI. AM., Feb. 1989.

HOWE, M. A. DE WOLFE, THE GARDEN AND THE WILDERNESS (1965).

HUNT, GAILLARD, THE LIFE OF JAMES MADISON (1902).

Irons, Edward S. & Sears, Mary H., *The Constitutional Standard of Invention: The Touchstone for Patent Reform,* 1973 UTAH L. REV. 653 (1973).

JACKENDOFF, RAY, CONSCIOUSNESS AND THE COMPUTATIONAL MIND (1987).

JACOBS, CLYDE E., LAWWRITERS AND THE COURTS (1954).

JAFFEE, LOUIS L. & NATHANSON, NATHANIEL L., ADMINISTRATIVE LAW (1976).

Jaroff, Leon, *Happy Birthday, Double Helix: Forty Years After Their Discovery of DNA's Secret, Watson and Crick Celebrate Its Impact on the World,* TIME, Mar. 15, 1993.

Jaroff, Leon, *Seeking a Godlike Power: Genetic Science Promises to Deliver the Blueprint for Human Life,* TIME, Oct. 15, 1992.

JASANOFF, SHEILA, THE FIFTH BRANCH: SCIENCE ADVISERS AS POLICYMAKERS (1990).

JEFFERSON, THOMAS, NOTES ON THE STATE OF VIRGINIA (W. Peden, ED., 1955).

JEFFERSON, THOMAS, ON SCIENCE AND FREEDOM: THE LETTER TO THE STUDENT WILLIAM G. MUNFORD (Julian P. Boyd, ed., 1964).

Johnson, George, *Can Machines Learn to Think?,* N.Y. TIMES, May 15, 1988.

Johnson, George, *New Mind, No Clothes,* SCIENCES, Jul./Aug. 1990.

JOHNSTON, W. D., JR., SOLAR VOLTAIC CELLS (1980).

Jolly, Allison, *A New Science that Sees Animals as Conscious Beings,* 15 SMITHSONIAN 66 (1985).

JUBAK, JIM, IN THE IMAGE OF THE BRAIN (1992).

Kahn, Leroy, *The Lawyer and the Scientific Community: Procuring Basic Research,* 29 LAW & CONTEMP. PROBS. 631 (1964)

Kalven, Harry A., *A Commemorative Case Note: Scopes v. State,* 27 U. CHI. L. REV. 505 (1960).

Kalven, Harry A., *The New York Times Case: "A Note of The Central Meaning of the First Amendment,"* 1964 SUP. CT. REV. 191 (1964).

Karjala, Dennis S., *A Legal Research Agenda for the Human Genome Initiative,* 32 JURIMETRICS J. 121 (1992).

KASSON, JOHN F., CIVILIZING THE MACHINE (1976).

Kay, W. D., *The Politics of Fusion Research,* ISSUES IN SCIENCE AND TECHNOLOGY, Winter 1991–92.

KEVLES, DANIEL J., IN THE NAME OF EUGENICS: GENETICS AND THE USES OF HUMAN HEREDITY (1985).

KEVLES, DANIEL J., THE PHYSICISTS (1977).

Kidd, Charles V., *American Universities and Federal Research, in* THE SOCIOLOGY OF SCIENCE (Bernard Barber & Walter Hirsch, eds., 1962).

Kilgour, Frederick G., *The Rise of Scientific Activity in Colonial New England,* 22 YALE J. BIOLOGY & MED. 123 (1949).

Koch, Charles H., Jr. & Koplow, David A., *The Fourth Bite at the Apple: A Study of the Operation and Utility of the Social Security Administration's Appeals Council,* 17 FLA. ST. U. L. REV. 199 (1990).

KORNHAUSER, WILLIAM, SCIENTISTS IN INDUSTRY (1962).

KRAEMER, SANDY F., SOLAR LAW (1978).

Krugman, Paul R., *Are You Ready for the Twenty-first Century?,* FORTUNE, Apr. 5, 1993.

Kuhn, Thomas S., *Objectivity, Value Judgment, and Theory Choice, in* THOMAS S. KUHN: THE ESSENTIAL TENSION (1977).

KUHN, THOMAS S., THE STRUCTURE OF SCIENTIFIC REVOLUTIONS (1962).

Kwok, Abraham & Manson, Pamela, *Nuclear Waste Dump Opposed,* ARIZONA REPUBLIC, Jan. 18, 1993.

LAPP, RALPH E., THE NEW PRIESTHOOD (1965).

LARSON, EDWARD J., TRIAL AND ERROR: THE AMERICAN CONTROVERSY OVER CREATION AND EVOLUTION (1985).

LASCH, CHRISTOPHER, THE TRUE AND ONLY HEAVEN: PROGRESS AND ITS CRITICS (1991).

LATOUR, BRUNO & WOOLGAR, STEVE, LABORATORY LIFE (1986).

Lazure, Albert C., *Why Research and Development Contracts Are Distinctive,* *in* RESEARCH AND DEVELOPMENT PROCUREMENT LAW 255 (Albert C. Lazure & Andrew P. Murphy, eds., 1957).

LeClercq, Frederic S., *The Monkey Laws and the Public Schools: A Second Consumption?,* 27 VAND. L. REV. 209 (1974).

Lederberg, Joshua, *The Freedoms and Control of Science Notes from an Ivory Tower,* 455 CAL. L. REV. 596 (1972).

Lederman, Leon M., *The Value of Fundamental Science,* SCI. AM., Nov. 1984.

Lemonick, Michael D., *Superconductors: The Startling Breakthrough that Could Change Our World,* TIME, May 11, 1987.

Lemonick, Michael D., *Those Computers Are Dummies,* TIME, June 25, 1990.

LEVY, LEONARD W., FREEDOM OF SPEECH AND PRESS IN EARLY AMERICAN HISTORY (1960).

Levy, Leonard W., *Jefferson as a Civil Libertarian, in* THOMAS JEFFERSON: THE MAN . . . HIS WORLD . . . HIS INFLUENCE (Lally Weymouth, ed., 1973).

LEVY, STEVEN, ARTIFICIAL LIFE: THE QUEST FOR A NEW CREATION (1992).

Lewin, Tamar, *Nancy Cruzan Dies, Outlived by a Debate Over the Right to Die,* N.Y. TIMES, Dec. 27, 1990.

Lidsky, Lawrence M., *The Reactor of the Future,* TECH. REV. (1984).

Lidsky, Lawrence M., *The Trouble with Fusion,* TECH. REV., (1983).

Liebman, Lance & Stewart, Richard B., *Bureaucratic Vision,* 96 HARV. L. REV. 1952 (1983).

LIPPMAN, WALTER, PUBLIC OPINION (1950).

LOCK, STEPHEN, A DIFFICULT BALANCE: EDITORIAL PEER REVIEW IN MEDICINE (1985).

Lockhart, William B. & McClure, Robert C., *Literature, the Law of Obscenity, and the Constitution,* 38 MINN. L. REV. 295 (1954).

LOTH, DAVID & ERNST, MORRIS L., THE TAMING OF TECHNOLOGY (1972).

Lovins, Amory, *Energy Strategy: The Road Not Taken?,* 55 FOREIGN AFF. 55 (1976).

Lucas, John R., *The Godelian Argument,* 2 TRUTH 64 (1988).

LUGER, GEORGE F. & SUBBLEFIELD, WILLIAM A., ARTIFICIAL INTELLI-
GENCE: STRUCTURES AND STRATEGIES FOR COMPLEX PROBLEM
SOLVING (1993).

Lutz, Karl B., *Patents and Science*, 18 GEO. WASH. L. REV. 50 (1949).

Lyden, *An Integrated Approach to Solar Access*, 34 CASE W. RES. L. REV. 367
(1983–84).

MADISON, JAMES, JOURNALS OF THE FEDERAL CONVENTION (Erastus
H. Scott Ed., 1893)

MALONE, DUMAS, JEFFERSON AND THE RIGHTS OF MAN (1951).

MARCSON, SIMON, THE SCIENTIST IN AMERICAN INDUSTRY (1960).

Markoff, John, *Can Machines Think? Humans Match Wits*, N. Y. TIMES, Nov.
9, 1991.

MARTIN, EDWIN T., THOMAS JEFFERSON: SCIENTIST (1952).

MARTINO, JOSEPH P., SCIENCE FUNDING: POLITICS AND PORKBAR-
REL (1992).

MASHAW, JERRY L., BUREAUCRATIC JUSTICE (1983).

MASON, ALPHEUS T., BRANDEIS: A FREE MAN'S LIFE (1946).

MASON, DAVID, THE LIFE OF JOHN MILTON (Peter Smith, ed., 2d ed.
1946) (1877).

MATHIOPOULOS, MARGARITA, HISTORY AND PROGRESS: IN SEARCH
OF THE EUROPEAN AND AMERICAN MIND (1989).

MAY, HENRY F., THE ENLIGHTENMENT IN AMERICA (1976).

MAYCOCK, PAUL D. & STIREWALT, EDWARD N., PHOTOVOLTAICS:
SUNLIGHT TO ELECTRICITY IN ONE STEP (1981).

MAZLISH, BRUCE, THE FOURTH DISCONTINUITY: THE CO-EVOLU-
TION OF HUMANS AND MACHINES (1993).

MCCORDUCK, PAMELA, MACHINES WHO THINK (1979).

McCutchen, Charles, *Peer Review: Treacherous Servant, Disastrous Master*, 94
TECH. REV. 28 (1991).

McDowell, Edwin, *A Rash of Thoughtful Best Sellers Has Made Publishers
Think, Too*, N.Y. TIMES, Feb. 11, 1990.

McLellan, Joseph, *Kasparov Showing the Computer a Few Moves*, WASH.
POST, Oct. 23, 1989.

McNally, Phil & Inayatullah, Sohail, *The Rights of Robots*, 20 FUTURES
119 (1988).

Meiklejohn, Alexander, *The First Amendment Is an Absolute*, 1961 SUP. CT.
REV. 245 (1961).

Meinel, Aden B. & Meinel, Marjorie P., *Soft Path Leads to a New Dark Age, in*
THE ENERGY CONTROVERSY 225 (Henry Nash, ed., 1979).

Merton, Robert K., *Priorities in Scientific Discovery: A Chapter in the Sociology
of Science, in* THE SOCIOLOGY OF SCIENCE (Bernard Barber & Walter
Hirsh, eds., 1962).

Merton, Robert K., *Science and the Social Order, in* THE SOCIOLOGY OF
SCIENCE (Norman W. Storer, ed., 1973).

MERTON, ROBERT K., SCIENCE, TECHNOLOGY AND SOCIETY IN SEVENTEENTH CENTURY ENGLAND (1970).

Miller, Howard S., *The Political Economy of Science, in* NINETEENTH CENTURY AMERICAN SCIENCE: A REAPPRAISAL (George H. Daniels, ed., 1972)

MILTON, JOHN, AREOPAGITICA (R. Jebb, Ed., AMS Press, 1971) (1918).

MINIHAN, JANET, THE NATIONALIZATION OF CULTURE (1977).

MITCHELL, BROADUS, ALEXANDER HAMILTON: YOUTH TO MATURITY (1957).

Moehlmann, Jennie & Miller, Julie Ann, *OSTP's Gibbons: A Favorite on Capitol Hill,* 43 BIOSCIENCE 394 (1993).

Moore, Michael S., *Causation and the Excuses,* 73 CAL. L. REV. 1091 (1985).

MORAVEC, HANS, MIND CHILDREN (1988).

MOTT, FRANK L., AMERICAN JOURNALISM (3d Ed. 1962).

MURPHY, JEFFRIE G., EVOLUTION, MORALITY, AND THE MEANING OF LIFE (1982).

Nagel, Thomas, *The Mind Wins!,* N.Y. REV. BOOKS, Mar. 4, 1993.

Nash, J. Madeline, *The Frontier Within: By Plumbing the Deep Secrets of the Human Mind, Scientists Will Open the Way to Cures, Wonders—And Voyeurism,* TIME, Oct. 15, 1992.

NATIONAL SCIENCE FOUNDATION, RESEARCH AND DEVELOPMENT IN STATE GOVERNMENT AGENCIES (1975).

NELKIN, DOROTHY, SELLING SCIENCE: HOW THE PRESS COVERS SCIENCE AND TECHNOLOGY (1987).

NETZER, D., THE SUBSIDIZED MUSE (1978).

Neuhaus, Richard J., *Who Needs God,* NAT'L REV., Nov. 10, 1989.

NISBET, ROBERT, HISTORY OF THE IDEA OF PROGRESS (1980).

NOBEL FOUNDATION, THE HIERARCHY OF LIFE: MOLECULES AND MORPHOLOGY IN PHYLOGENETIC ANALYSIS (1988).

NOONAN, JOHN T., JR., THE BELIEVERS AND THE POWERS THAT ARE: CASES, HISTORY, AND OTHER DATA BEARING ON THE RELATION OF RELIGION AND GOVERNMENT (1987).

Note, *Constitutional Law: Validity of the Tennessee Anti-Evolution Law,* 5 TENN. L. REV. 242 (1927).

Note, *Deviate Sexual Behavior: The Desirability of Legislative Proscription,* 30 ALB. L. REV. 291 (1966).

Note, *Environmental Law,* 55 N.C. L. REV. 484 (1977).

Note, *Environmental Law,* 50 TEMP. L. Q. 410 (1977).

Note, *Program Environmental Impact Statements: Review and Remedies,* 75 MICH. L. REV. 107 (1976).

Note, *The Scope of the Program EIS Requirement: The Need for a Coherent Judicial Approach,* 30 STAN. L. REV. 767 (1978).

Note, *Sexual Freedom for Consenting Adults: Why Not?,* 2 PAC. L. J. 206 (1971).

Note, *Sodomy Statutes: A Need for Change*, 13 S.D. L. REV. 384 (1968).
Notes and Questions on Medical Care at the End of Life, in CLARK C. HAVIG-HURST, HEALTH CARE LAW AND POLICY (1988).
NOZICK, ROBERT, PHILOSOPHICAL EXPLANATIONS (1981).
OFFICE OF TECHNOLOGY ASSESSMENT, MAPPING OUR GENES: THE GENOME PROJECTS: HOW BIG, HOW FAST? (1988).
Okie, Susan, *Redrawing Life's Family Tree: Genes Offer Insight on Evolution*, WASH. POST, May 6, 1990.
Oliver, John W., *Science and the "Founding Fathers,"* 48 SCI. MONTHLY 256 (1939).
OLSON, RICHARD, SCIENCE DEIFIED AND SCIENCE DEFIED (1982).
PARCHOMENKO, WALTER, SOVIET IMAGES OF DISSIDENTS AND NONCONFORMISTS (1986).
Parks, Wallace, *Secrecy and the Public Interest in Military Affairs*, 26 GEO. WASH. L. REV. 23 (1957).
PAWEL, ERNST, THE NIGHTMARE OF REASON: A LIFE OF FRANZ KAFKA (1984).
Pease, John, *Fusion Research Twenty-five Years after Zeta*, NEW SCIENTIST, Jan. 20, 1983.
PEMBER, DON, MASS MEDIA IN AMERICA (1974).
PENROSE, ROGER, THE EMPEROR'S NEW MIND (1989).
PERELMAN, CHAIM, JUSTICE, LAW, AND ARGUMENT (1980)
Perelman, Chaim, *Rhetoric and Politics*, 17 PHIL. & RHETORIC 129 (1984).
Peterson, Bill, *U.S. Makes Major Advance in Nuclear Fusion*, WASH. POST, Aug. 13, 1978.
PIERCE, RICHARD J., JR., ET AL., ADMINISTRATIVE LAW AND PROCESS (2d ED. 1992).
PLOSCOWE, MORRIS, SEX AND THE LAW (1962).
POLANYI, MICHAEL, SCIENCE, FAITH AND SOCIETY (1946).
Pollack, Andrew, *Pentagon Wanted a Smart Truck: What It Got Was Something Else*, N. Y. TIMES, May 30, 1989.
POLLACK, JOHN L., HOW TO BUILD A PERSON: A PROLEGOMENON (1989).
Pool, R., *Superconductivity: Is the Party Over?*, 244 SCIENCE 914 (1989).
POPPER, KARL, THE LOGIC OF SCIENTIFIC DISCOVERY (1968).
Press, Frank, The Dilemma of the Golden Age, Address to Members of the National Academy of Sciences (Apr. 26, 1988).
PRICE, D. J. DE SOLLA, LITTLE SCIENCE, BIG SCIENCE (1963).
Price, Don K., *Endless Frontier or Bureaucratic Morass?*, DAEDALUS, Spring 1978.
PRICE, DON K., GOVERNMENT AND SCIENCE (1954).
Price, Don K., *The Scientific Establishment*, 31 GEO. WASH. L. REV. 713 (1963).
PRICE, DON K., THE SCIENTIFIC ESTATE (1965).

PRINCE, THOMAS, EARTHQUAKES THE WORKS OF GOD AND TOKENS OF HIS JUST DISPLEASURE (Boston, D. Fowle & Z. Fowle, 1755).

PRINCETON UNIVERSITY PLASMA PHYSICS LABORATORY, INFORMATION BULLETIN: FUSION POWER (1993).

PURCELL, EDWARD A., JR., THE CRISIS OF DEMOCRATIC THEORY: SCIENTIFIC NATURALISM AND THE PROBLEM OF VALUE (1973).

Purvis, Andrew, *DNA and the Desire to Drink: Researchers Discover a Gene at the Root of Alcoholism,* TIME, Apr. 30, 1990.

Quine, Willard V. & Ullian, J. S., *Hypothesis, in* WILLARD V. QUINE & J. S. ULLIAN, THE WEB OF BELIEF (1978).

Quinn, Kevin P., *The Best Interests of Incompetent Patients: The Capacity for Interpersonal Relationships as a Standard for Decisionmaking,* 76 CAL. L. REV. 897 (1988).

RAWLS, JOHN, POLITICAL LIBERALISM (1993).

REAGAN, MICHAEL D., SCIENCE AND THE FEDERAL PATRON (1969).

Reingold, Nathan, *Introduction, in* THE NEW AMERICAN STATE PAPERS IN SCIENCE AND TECHNOLOGY (1973).

RETTIG, RICHARD A., CANCER CRUSADE (1977).

Rhoden, Nancy K., *Litigating Life and Death,* 102 HARV. L. REV. 375 (1988).

RILEY, DENNIS J., 1 FEDERAL CONTRACTS, GRANTS, AND ASSISTANCE (1983).

ROBERT OPPENHEIMER: LETTERS AND RECOLLECTIONS (Alice K. Smith & Charles Weiner, eds., 1980).

Robertson, John A., *The Law of Institutional Review Boards,* 26 U.C.L.A. L. REV. 484 (1979).

Robertson, John A., *The Scientists' Right to Research: A Constitutional Analysis,* 515 CAL. L. REV. 1203 (1978).

Rodgers, William H., *A Hard Look at Vermont Yankee: Environmental Law Under Close Scrutiny,* 67 GEO. L. J. 699 (1979).

ROHAN, PATRICK J., ZONING AND LAND USE CONTROLS (1986).

ROSE, FRANK, INTO THE HEART OF THE MIND: AN AMERICAN QUEST FOR ARTIFICIAL INTELLIGENCE (1984).

ROSENBERG, CHARLES S., NO OTHER GODS: ON SCIENCE AND AMERICAN SOCIAL THOUGHT (1976).

Rosenberg, Charles E., *On Writing the History of American Science, in* THE STATE OF AMERICAN HISTORY (Herbert J. Bass, ed., 1970).

ROSHCO, BERNARD, NEWSMAKING (1975).

Rutter, Nancy, *The Great Patent Plague,* 151 FORBES S58 (1993).

Samuelson, Pamela, et al., *Developments on the Intellectual Property Front: Legally Speaking,* 35 COMM. ASS'N COMPUTING MACHINERY 33 (1992).

Schachter, Esther, *Intellectual Property Takes Center Stage,* 63 ELECTRONICS 108 (1990).

Schlag, Pierre, *Missing Pieces: A Cognitive Approach to Law,* 67 TEX. L. REV. 1248 (1989).

Schuck, Peter H., *Multi-Culturalism Redux: Science, Law and Politics,* 11 YALE L. & POL'Y REV. 1 (1993).

SCHUMACHER, E. F., SMALL IS BEAUTIFUL (1973).

SCHURR, S., ET AL., ENERGY IN AMERICA'S FUTURE (1979).

Seabrook, Charles, *Watkins Plays Down Tritium Spill at SRS,* ATLANTA JOURNAL, Jan. 8, 1992.

Searle, John R., *"The Emperor's New Mind": An Exchange,* N. Y. REV. BOOKS, June 14, 1990.

Searle, John R., *Is the Brain's Mind a Computer Program?,* SCI. AM., Jan. 1990.

SEARLE, JOHN R., MINDS, BRAINS AND SCIENCE (1984).

SENSEBAUGH, GEORGE F., MILTON IN EARLY AMERICA (1964).

Shank, Christopher G., Note, *DNA Evidence in Criminal Trials: Modifying the Law's Approach to Protect the Accused from Prejudicial Genetic Evidence,* 34 ARIZ. L. REV. 829 (1992).

Sharp, Malcolm P., *Science, Religion, and the Scopes Case,* 27 U. CHI. L. REV. 529 (1960).

SIMON, YVES R., FREEDOM OF CHOICE (1969).

SINGER, PETER, ANIMAL LIBERATION (2d. Ed. 1990).

SMITH, BRUCE L. R., THE ADVISERS: SCIENTISTS IN THE POLICY PROCESS (1992).

SMITH, BRUCE L. R., AMERICAN SCIENCE POLICY SINCE WORLD WAR II (1990).

Smith, David R., *Legal Recognition of Neocortical Death,* 71 CORNELL L. REV. BOOKS 850 (1986).

Smith, John M., *What Can't the Computer Do?,* N.Y. REV., Mar. 15, 1990.

Smith, M. R., *Technology, Industrialization, and the Idea of Progress in America, in* RESPONSIBLE SCIENCE: THE IMPACT OF TECHNOLOGY ON SOCIETY (Kevin B. Byrne, ed., 1986).

SNOW, C. P., THE TWO CULTURES AND THE SCIENTIFIC REVOLUTION (1959).

SNOW, C. P., THE TWO CULTURES AND A SECOND LOOK (1963).

Spann, Girardeau A., *Hyperspace,* 84 MICH. L. REV. 642 (1986).

Speth, Gustave, *The Federal Role in Technology Assessment and Control, in* FEDERAL ENVIRONMENTAL LAW (E. Dolgin & T. Builbert, eds., 1974)

STEWART, FRANK H., HISTORY OF THE FIRST UNITED STATES MINT (reprint of 1928 ed.) (1974).

Stewart, Richard B., *The Reformation of American Administrative Law,* 88 HARV. L. REV. 1667 (1975).

Stolzenberg, Naomi M., *"He Drew a Circle That Shut Me Out": Assimilation, Indoctrination, and the Paradox of a Liberal Education,* 106 HARV. L. REV. 581 (1993).

Stone, Christopher, *Should Trees Have Standing? Revisited: How Far Will Law And Morals Reach? A Pluralist Perspective*, 59 S. CAL. L. REV. 1 (1985).

STORY, JOSEPH, COMMENTARIES ON THE CONSTITUTION OF THE UNITED STATES (Boston, Hilliard, Grayd & Co., 1833).

STRUIK, DIRK J., YANKEE SCIENCE IN THE MAKING (1948).

STUDENSKI, PAUL & KROOS, HERMAN T., FINANCIAL HISTORY OF THE UNITED STATES (2d ed. 1963).

Sunstein, Cass R., *Administrative Law After Chevron*, 90 COLUM. L. REV. 2071 (1990).

Suplee, Curt, *Artificial Life: Improving on Creation—Move Over, Darwin: A New Set of Sciences Might Just Revolutionize Biology*, WASH. POST, May 6, 1990.

Suplee, Curt, *Fusion Power Experiment Is Successful: Energy Source Moves Closer to Practicality*, WASH. POST, Nov. 11, 1991.

Swazey, Judith P., et al., *Risks and Benefits, Rights and Responsibilities: A History of the Recombinant DNA Research Controversy*, 51 S. CAL. L. REV. 1019 (1978).

Sweet, William, *Argonne Proposes "Proliferation-resistant" Breeder*, 37 PHYSICS TODAY 62 (1984).

SWENSON, LOYD S., JR., GENESIS OF RELATIVITY: EINSTEIN IN CONTEXT (1979).

Thackray, Arnold, *The Industrial Revolution and the Image of Science, in* SCIENCE AND VALUES (Arnold Thackray & Everett Mendelsohn, eds., 1974).

Thompson, Larry, *The First Kids with New Genes: The Inside Story of Two Young Pioneers Whose Courage Helped Launch a Medial Revolution*, TIME, June 7, 1993.

Tilton, Eleanor M., *Lightning-Rods and the Earthquake of 1755*, 13 NEW ENG. Q. 85 (1940).

TRIBE, LAURENCE H., AMERICAN CONSTITUTIONAL LAW (1978).

TRIBE, LAURENCE H., CHANNELING TECHNOLOGY THROUGH LAW (1973).

Tribe, Laurence H., *The Supreme Court 1972 Term: Foreword: Toward a Model of Roles in the Due Process of Life and Law*, 87 HARV. L. REV. 1 (1973).

Tribe, Laurence H., *Technology Assessment and the Fourth Discontinuity: The Limits of Instrumental Rationality*, 46 S. CAL. L. REV. 617 (1973).

Tribe, Laurence H., *Toward a Metatheory of Free Speech*, 10 S. CAL. L. REV. 237 (1978).

Tucker, Leonard, *President Thomas Clap of Yale College: Another "Founding Father" of American Science, in* EARLY AMERICAN SCIENCE (Brooke Hindle, ed., 1976).

TULLOCK, GORDON, PRIVATE WANTS, PUBLIC MEANS (1970).

Turing, Alan, *Computing Machinery and Intelligence*, 59 MIND 236 (1950).

TWEETEN, LUTHER G., FOUNDATIONS OF FARM POLICY (1970).

UPDIKE, JOHN, RABBIT AT REST (1990).

VARGA, ANDREW C., THE MAIN ISSUES IN BIOETHICS (1980).

VEATCH, ROBERT M., DEATH, DYING AND THE BIOLOGICAL REVO-LUTION: OUR LAST QUEST FOR RESPONSIBILITY (1989).

Vettel, Phil, *As a Matter of Fact,* CHICAGO TRIBUNE, May 17, 1987.

WALDROP, M. MITCHELL, MAN-MADE MINDS: THE PROMISE OF AR-TIFICIAL INTELLIGENCE (1987).

Walsh, John & Culliton, Barbara, *Office of Management and Budget: Skeptical View of Scientific Advice, in* SCIENCE, TECHNOLOGY AND NATIONAL POLICY (Thomas J. Kuehn & Alan K. Porter, eds., 1981).

Wanzer, Sidney, et al., *The Physician's Responsibility Toward Hopelessly Ill Patients: A Second Look,* 320 NEW ENG. J. MED. 844 (1989).

Warren, Samuel D. & Brandeis, Louis D., *The Right to Privacy.* 4 HARV. L. REV. 193 (1890).

WATANABE, MASAO, THE JAPANESE AND WESTERN SCIENCE (1990).

WATSON, JAMES D., THE DOUBLE HELIX (1968).

Wesskopf, Victor F., *Why Pure Science?,* BULL. ATOM. SCIENTISTS, Apr. 1965.

WHITE, G. EDWARD, TORT LAW IN AMERICA: AN INTELLECTUAL HISTORY (1980).

Wik, Reynold M., *Science and American Agriculture, in* SCIENCE AND SOCI-ETY IN THE UNITED STATES (David D. Van Tassel & Michael G. Hall, eds., 1966).

WILLS, GARRY, INVENTING AMERICA (1978).

Wilson, James Q., *The Politics of Regulation, in* THE POLITICS OF REGULA-TION (James Q. Wilson, ed., 1980).

Wilson, Bryan R., *Reflections on a Many Sided Controversy, in* RELIGION AND MODERNIZATION (Steve Bruce, ed., 1992).

WINTHROP, JOHN, TWO LECTURES ON COMETS (1759).

Wolfson, Paul R. Q., *Is a Presidential Item Veto Constitutional?* 96 YALE L. J. 838 (1987).

Yankelovich, Daniel, *Science and the Public Process: Why the Gap Must Close,* 1 ISSUES SCI. & TECH. 6 (1984).

Index

science, 50; oversight of Human Genome Initiative, 120; role in regulation of technology, 87; role in science funding, 44–47

United States v. Butler, 37

United States v. Eichman, 87 n. 10

United States v. O'Brien, 86 n. 7

United States v. Sullivan, 85 n. 2

United States v. The Progressive, Inc., 30 n. 44

Updike, John, 166

Values: role of religion in shaping, 80–83, 130, 149–50, 166, 176–77, 179–80;

role of science in shaping, 81–83, 128–30, 145–46, 149, 172–77, 179–80

Veatch, Robert, 166, 171

Von Neumann, John, 153

"War on cancer," 51

Warren, Samuel D., 115

Washington, George, 32

Watson, J. D., 93, 115–16, 124

Webster v. New Lenox School District No. 122, 78 n. 73

Weisskopf, Victor, 24

Wikler, Daniel, 171

Wilson, James Q., 92